Call and Consequences

Call and Consequences

A Womanist Reading of Mark

Raquel A. St. Clair

Fortress Press
MINNEAPOLIS

CALL AND CONSEQUENCES
A Womanist Reading of Mark

Biblical quotations, unless otherwise marked, are from the New Revised Standard Version Bible, copyright © 1989 by the Division of Christian Education of the National Council of Churches of Christ in the USA. Used by permission. All rights reserved.

Cover image: Christ on the Cross, The Doré Bible, © Dover Publications, Inc. Woman's image, © George Allen Penton / Shutterstock, Inc.
Cover design: THE DESIGNWORKSGROUP, CHARLES BROCK
Book design: Michelle L. N. Cook

Library of Congress Cataloging-in-Publication Data
St. Clair, Raquel Annette.
  Call and consequences: a womanist reading of Mark / Raquel A. St. Clair.
    p. cm.
  Includes bibliographical references (p. 197) and index.
  ISBN 978-0-8006-3902-0 (alk. paper)
  1. Bible. N.T. Mark—Black interpretations. 2. Womanist theology. I. Title.
BS2585.52.S73 2008
226.3'06082—dc22   2008017549

The paper used in this publication meets the minimum requirements of American National Standard for Information Sciences—Permanence of Paper for Printed Library Materials, ANSI Z329.48-1984.

Manufactured in the U.S.A.

12   11   10   09   08   1   2   3   4   5   6   7   8   9   10

In memory of Doretha V. St. Clair

Love never ends (1 Cor 13:8)

∞ contents

acknowledgments

 "You can do *anything* you set your mind to." These were the words my father, Barry L. St. Clair, spoke into my life when I was a preschooler. This was to be a repetitive theme for him, one of the pillars upon which he set the foundation for my life. In 1979, he linked it to McFadden and Whitehead's hit single "Ain't No Stoppin' Us Now" as we danced in the basement with my cousins. My father decided that this song was to be the St. Clair theme song, so we sealed his decision with our special "six finger rub." Throughout my childhood, "You can do *anything* you set your mind to" was reincarnated in phrases like "You always start what you finish," "Use your own mind," and "No one can tell you what you *can't* do." During the lowest point of this project, when giving up seemed to be the least painful option, these are the words that transcended his death and compelled me to fight on.

There are so many people I wish to thank for helping me get to this point. First and foremost, I thank *almighty* God. I have seen the faithfulness, provision, and grace of God manifested in my life in unmistakable and amazing ways. I share the testimony of my forebears: God is indeed a way maker, prayer answerer, problem solver, heavy-load lifter, and door opener!

I am deeply grateful to Brian K. Blount, who has been a mentor to me and an advocate for me for over a decade. I am the humble beneficiary of his scholarly insight and painstaking attention to detail. I am thankful for his generous spirit and commitment to this work as he read chapters during his sabbaticals as well as while traveling by plane and train. I am most appreciative of his helping me to find my own voice and creatively explore an area of biblical scholarship that is in its nascent stages. Mark Lewis Taylor has been an invaluable reader. His comments brought to light theological questions, considerations, and areas of reflection I would have overlooked.

I am also thankful for the people of God known as St. James African Methodist Episcopal Church, Newark, New Jersey, for journeying with me throughout this process. Their presence is a constant reminder to "keep it real" and pursue scholarship that benefits those who study God's Word in the pews as well as the classrooms and libraries. I am forever grateful to God for my pastor and boss, William D. Watley, for shepherding me through this process and engaging in endless discussions on Mark, womanist theology, and suffering. He has been a most understanding, flexible, and supportive employer.

Last, but certainly not least, I thank my family both blood and fictive. I am especially and eternally grateful for my grandmother, Doretha V. St. Clair, who was the only mother I have known. Although she had never heard the term *womanist*, she was outrageous, audacious, courageous, and *willful*; responsible, in charge, and *serious* before these characteristics were positive female attributes. She was always confident that God had not brought me this far to leave me and that I would finish "that book" I was working on. To her memory, I dedicate this book.

introduction

Discipleship and Suffering

I HAVE COME TO BELIEVE THAT THEOLOGIANS,
IN THEIR ATTEMPT TO TALK TO AND ABOUT
RELIGIOUS COMMUNITIES, OUGHT TO GIVE
READERS SOME SENSE OF THEIR AUTOBIOGRAPHIES.
THIS CAN HELP AN AUDIENCE DISCERN WHAT
LEADS THE THEOLOGIAN TO DO THE KIND OF
THEOLOGY SHE DOES.

—Delores Williams, *Sisters in the Wilderness*[1]

My assignment was youth ministry in an urban context. I was to serve as church-school teacher, preach a few sermons, take the children on several field trips, direct a youth choir, and mentor the young people. I interviewed with the pastor and accepted the placement. I then embarked on what was perhaps the most theologically difficult ministerial experience I have ever had.

The appointment was in a liberal Presbyterian church pastored by a white, liberal, feminist woman.[2] Although the congregation was equally, if not primarily, composed of people of African descent, the church leadership was overwhelmingly Euro-American. The pastor's stance toward me was as one *sister* to another in the struggle for freedom from oppression. She presumed knowledge of and a kinship with me because we shared the two isms of sexism and classism. The issue of racism, however, was never mentioned in public or private discussions. It was enough to focus on our commonalities and ignore our differences, or so we (I) naively thought. But I would soon come to see how our differences affected our theological perspectives.

One Sunday after the regular worship service, the pastor convened a church meeting. I don't recall whether it was a regular meeting or a special session, nor do I remember the purpose of the meeting. The only thing I remember was the pastor's answer to a random question that had nothing to do with any agenda item. The parishioner, an African American man, commented that several of the hymns he remembered from the church he attended when a youth were not in this church's hymnbook. He then mentioned a few of the missing hymns, among them, "The Old Rugged Cross." "Why don't we have those hymns?" he asked.

The pastor began her response by acknowledging that their hymnbook was simply a collection of hymns that she had photocopied and organized to create their songbook. Consequently, some hymns were not included because she was either unfamiliar with them or did not have access to them at the time the book was being compiled. Some hymns, however, she intentionally omitted. One of them was "The Old Rugged Cross." The pastor informed the parishioner and the entire congregation that she refused to incorporate any songs mentioning "blood" or "the cross" into the hymnal. These songs, she told him, glorified the suffering of Jesus. The congregation would never sing "Power in the Blood" or "The Old Rugged Cross" as long as she was pastor.

Although the rationale for this decision seemed self-evident to her, it was not as apparent to the members of the congregation. Her response raised more questions than it had answered, questions that were mumbled in the fellowship hall after the meeting was over. The fact that male and female, Euro-American and African American parishioners continued to discuss the pastor's comments suggested that the pastor had touched on an issue that cut across gender and racial lines. The parishioner, although silent, sat with a questioning look on his face. He seemed unable to pose the questions needed to clarify his thoughts. I, too, sat in questioning silence. As I reflected on her comments, I came to realize that cross language was not a part of the music nor any of this congregation's liturgy. That meeting was the only time I recall hearing the cross mentioned during my nine-month tenure.

Yet I understood the pastor's decision. She ministered to people who suffered the shame of nonbeing in modern society—the poor, sick, incarcerated, uneducated, and addicted. She (and I) believed that the gospel affirmed their personhood and value as human beings created in the image of God. In spite of their present conditions, God had not sentenced them to a life of suffering from which they could not escape. She did not want her congregation to believe that God had preordained their current condition. That would lead them to the inevitable belief that their suffering was God's will.[3] Specifically, the pastor did not want to glorify the suffering of Jesus and thereby imply that his suffering should be emulated. For her, any suffering, even the redemptive suffering ascribed to Jesus, was problematic because it debilitated rather than empowered her congregation. Her view is not unique. Anthony Pinn writes, "Redemptive suffering and liberation are diametrically opposed ideas; they suggest ways of being in the world that, in effect, nullify each other."[4]

During my time at the church, I came to see that other concerns about suffering were just as critical for the pastor. She did not want the teenagers to connect, and thereby confuse, the innocent blood spilled by gangbanging and drive-by shootings with the blood Jesus shed on the cross. Perhaps they might think (incorrectly) that God could be working some good out of urban violence in the way that God had brought good out of Jesus' execution. She did not want them to conclude that poverty, addiction, poor education, and the violence often associated with them were crosses they were divinely commanded to bear.

The parishioner's question and the response of the pastor suggested, however, that the cross was not only a problematic symbol; it was also an enduring one. Removing the cross language from the hymnal, liturgy, and sermons did not remove the cross from the religious consciousness of the parishioner. The cross remained a powerful symbol. The removal of the cross songs demonstrated the pastor's recognition of the profound influence of this symbol. It was because she believed the cross to be such a powerfully negative symbol that she removed it.

Like the parishioner, I could not ignore the cross. In fact, I questioned whether one could remove the cross and still maintain the integrity of the gospel message. The issue for me was not whether but *how* we talk about, sing about, and preach about the cross. The cross is a key part of the biblical text. Although the pastor removed the cross songs from the hymnal, she could not remove cross language or the passion narratives from the Bible. In my opinion, she simply removed what instead needed to be reexamined and reinterpreted, especially in light of the congregation's sociocultural context filled with suffering, violence, and blood.

The parishioner's question provided an opportunity for the congregation to wrestle with the faith community's understanding of the cross and suffering as followers of Jesus. It was an opportunity to acknowledge the suffering of Jesus and thereby name and acknowledge the suffering they endured. Given the demographics of the congregation, it seemed to me that the pastor needed to explore, not ignore, the cross and the implications of Jesus' suffering with her parishioners.

I was immediately suspicious of the removal of the songs. My inability to articulate why I felt as I did suggested a level of connectedness to Jesus and the cross that I had not previously recognized. Karen Baker-Fletcher expresses this connection well:

> There is a visceral identity Black Americans have with the cross because of the hangings of thousands of our people on trees. For this reason, I believe African Americans will continue to feel a deep psychic and physical connection to the image of the crucifixion.[5]

The discussion about the cross songs only brought this unconscious link to the forefront of my mind. While the pastor removed a symbol she thought advocated suffering, she also removed a symbol that African Americans have traditionally understood to affirm God's presence with them during times of suffering.

One of the dominant African American understandings of Jesus is that he is the divine cosufferer.[6] African Americans conclude that because Jesus was a "man of sorrows, and acquainted with grief" (Isa 53:3 KJV), he "knows all about [their] struggles."[7] During slavery, the suffering of Jesus on the cross was a mirror of the reality of their lives.[8] African slaves' identification with Jesus' crucifixion was so profound that Negro spirituals often transcend the boundaries of space and time. The lyrics of the spirituals imply that the slaves were actually with Jesus during the crucifixion:

> Were you there when they crucified my Lord?
> Were you there when they crucified my Lord?
> Oh! Sometimes it causes me to tremble, tremble, tremble;
> Were you there when they crucified my Lord?[9]

In effect, the suffering of the slaves converged with the suffering of Jesus. The slaves became one with Jesus. Most important, they perceived Jesus to be one with them. Jesus' presence with them signified Jesus' willingness to work on their behalf. Jacqueline Grant claims that when African Americans affirm Jesus as their divine cosufferer, they also affirm that he "empowers them in situations of oppression."[10] Jesus is the one who delivers from bondage. Because Jesus rose from the dead, African slaves could affirm, "An' the Lord shall bear my spirit hom'."[11] Cone writes, "Herein lies the meaning of the resurrection. It means that the cross was not the end of God's drama of salvation."[12] It is clear, then, that the cross and the resurrection come together in African American religious consciousness. In other words, the cross not only symbolizes the suffering of Jesus but also confirms the resurrection. For African Americans, the cross and resurrection are intimately linked; there is no resurrection without the cross.

I suggest that African Americans will continue to feel this "psychic and physical connection" to the cross because they connect with Jesus' resurrection through his suffering.[13] The affirmation of Jesus as the divine cosufferer illumines this connection, for it is within the context of suffering that African Americans in general, and African American women in particular, have connected with Jesus. Because African American women carry a profound legacy of suffering, I maintain that it is important that we acknowledge Jesus' suffering as well as our own.

Our suffering includes bodies that were raped, beaten, and broken.[14] It includes minds imprisoned and impoverished through "miseducation" and the lack of education.[15] Our suffering includes spirits tortured by the calumnies of inferiority, inadequacy, and worthlessness, lies that said we were created more in the image of a gorilla than in the image of God. Because of this history, I contend that African American women want suffering—past and present—acknowledged so as not to be repeated.

This, I believe, was the sentiment expressed by the mother of Emmett Till. During the funeral services for her lynched teenage son, Mamie Till insisted that the casket remain open. She wanted the world to see what they did to her boy.[16] She wasn't glorifying her child's death. She wasn't making him out to be a martyr whose suffering and death ought to be emulated by scores of other young African American males. Instead, she wanted the world to see the manifestation of the injustice that plagued her people and had taken her son's life. She did not want the world to embrace the violence; she wanted them to see it. She wanted them to witness the violence in all its horrific realism so that they would set out to overturn it. It was her belief (and mine) that society would not muster the spiritual and physical resolve to stop the bloodshed unless it was first compelled to face it.

Mrs. Till's response to the viewing of her son's corpse illumined a subtle yet profound distinction between my perspective and that of the pastor during my tenure as youth minister. The pastor's and my own theological views on the cross and suffering were different because our sociocultural contexts were different. The pastor's history was interwoven with the threads of gender and class oppression. Her cultural and theological perspective considered only those two factors. My history, on the other hand, includes the tridimensional oppression of gender, *race*, and class.

African American women have historically suffered the dehumanizing effects of *racialized* sexism that results in classist oppression. Because persons of African descent were presumed to be a species higher than animals but lower than humans and women were presumed to be lower than men, women of African descent were relegated to the lowest rungs of society. At no point in this nation's history were women of European descent ever considered to be subhuman. Euro-American women have had to contend with sexism and its corresponding classism, which asserted they were less than men, but never with the presumption that they were less than human. Therefore, one cannot consider the sociocultural location of African American women without including racism among sexism and classism.

The pastor's decision suggested that she did not acknowledge the racial difference that played a critical role in the history of Euro-American and African American women, a role that made the former complicit in the oppression of the latter. She made a decision for her predominantly African American congregation using her experience as *the* experience for the community. In her efforts to counter their suffering, she exercised a paternalistic form of racism in which she made a decision in *their* best interest because she felt their best interest was identical to hers. My primary contention with her action is that she did not consider the sociocultural context of the majority of her congregation and how it informs their understanding of the cross, the suffering it symbolizes, and its implications for discipleship. Consequently, her solution stripped her congregants of a symbol that is intimately connected to their cultural identity. Moreover, she stripped them of a symbol that they may not have viewed in the completely negative ways she assumed.

I, for one, was not convinced that the symbol of the cross promoted only suffering or a form of suffering discipleship. African Americans' positive emphasis on the cross, which is given expression in the affirmation of Jesus as the divine cosufferer, reveals another perspective from which to explore this issue. Given the profound sociocultural connections between African American experience and the cross of Jesus, I maintain that the most fruitful course of action is not to remove or ignore the cross but to reexamine our understandings of the cross, suffering, and discipleship. Although the pastor's decision was based on some very real and valid concerns, I believe that a discussion that takes as its subject the cross, the suffering it symbolizes, and discipleship offers both problems *and* possibilities. What follows is my attempt to expose this issue and offer a biblical interpretation that shows some of the possibilities of a reexamination of the cross in our context. This reinterpretation necessitates reading the Bible from the perspective of African American women.

Chapter 1 establishes the sociocultural context for this project, its appeal to womanist theology. I begin with an overview of womanist theology and its historical development. This enables me to distinguish womanist theologians from African American women in general and to situate them among their immediate predecessors, black male and feminist theologians. Next, I survey womanist theologians' views on

Jesus, the cross, suffering, and discipleship. This exploration reveals three key issues that shape the sociocultural location of African American women—suffering, shame, and surrogacy—and helps to expose and clarify the ways in which African American women's affirmation of Jesus as the divine cosufferer promotes suffering. In addition, an exploration of womanist theology raises questions that require critical engagement with the biblical text. Specifically, Emilie Townes employs Audre Lorde's distinction between suffering and pain to nuance her discussion on suffering. Lorde defines suffering as "unscrutinized and unmetabolized pain," and pain as "an event, an experience that must be recognized, named and then used in some way in order for the experience to change, to be transformed into something else."[17] Based on these definitions, I am led to ask whether Jesus suffered or experienced pain. What implications does this have for discipleship? These questions not only necessitate an exploration of the biblical text but also highlight the need for a method that takes seriously the sociocultural context from which these questions arise.

Womanists agree that it is to the Synoptic Gospels that African American women need to turn in order to understand the ministry of Jesus Christ. I have therefore chosen the Gospel of Mark as the focus of my investigation. Frank J. Matera summarizes the occasion of Mark's Gospel: "The community has forgotten the centrality of the cross in the life of discipleship. Most importantly, then, Mark writes to remind them of the cross and the true meaning of discipleship."[18] Matera's comments suggest that Mark's community was in a similar situation as my field-education congregation—both communities had forgotten the cross. His comments also highlight that the cross and discipleship are integrally connected. Finally, Matera points to three important themes in the Gospel of Mark: discipleship, the cross, and, implicitly, the agony the cross symbolizes. These are the themes I wish to examine.

In chapter 2, I pose two questions to readers of Mark: (1) What is the relationship between the agony that the cross symbolizes and discipleship in Mark's Gospel? (2) Does the agony of the cross involve suffering or pain? Chapter 2 reveals that Mark 8:31, 34 contain all the critical elements of our discussion—the cross, agony, and discipleship. However, Markan scholars do not fully attend to the womanist concerns raised in chapter 1; my questions are not the questions that Markan scholars generally are asking. To continue my quest to read Mark's cross language through a womanist lens, I need a methodological approach that pushes beyond the boundaries of most Markan research.

Chapter 3 therefore draws on Brian K. Blount's cultural interpretation model, a sociolinguistic approach to biblical interpretation, as the framework for this project. Sociolinguistics aids biblical interpretation by not only emphasizing the examination of the internal structure of the language, as a linguist does, but also highlighting its social context. Blount expands the sociolinguistic program by considering both the context of the text and the context of the interpreter and/or interpretive community. His method allows me to integrate the sociocultural context of African American women and womanist perspectives into my inquiry, providing a womanist cultural lens through which readers can approach the text.

I do not wish to suggest that the womanist lens I am proposing is the only way of looking at the text from a consciously womanist perspective. I do assert, however, that this lens is true to womanist ideals and can, therefore, be called womanist. Because sociolinguistic theory affirms that a text is "language that is functional,"[19] this method allows me to consider how the language of the text functions in both the biblical context and the sociocultural context of African American women. In short, chapter 3 establishes the context of the interpreter. It discloses the presuppositions, derived from my engagement with womanist theology, that I bring to the text.

Chapter 4 constructs the second context for interpreting Mark's Gospel. Here I connect the issues of suffering, shame, and surrogacy and the negative effect they have on African American women addressed in chapter 1 with similar issues in the cultural background and story world of Mark's Gospel. Building on the work of others, I reconstruct the social context of Mark's Gospel using the cultural values of honor and shame.

Chapter 5 is a sociolinguistic interpretation of Mark 8:31-38 through a womanist cultural lens. Here I apply the questions raised in chapters 2 and 3 to examine the Markan text: (1) What is the relationship between the agony that the cross symbolizes and discipleship in Mark's Gospel? (2) Does the agony of the cross involve suffering or pain? I maintain that if we read Mark 8:31-38 through a womanist cultural lens, we can expose aspects of the text that Markan scholars have missed and attend to womanist concerns. Specifically, my reading of Mark 8:31-38 will show pain, rather than suffering, to be the agony of the cross and the consequence of discipleship. It will also provide a corrective to the traditional African American affirmation of Jesus as the divine cosufferer.

chapter one

The View through a Womanist Cultural Lens

WOMANIST THEOLOGY MUST DRAW FROM THE
MEANINGS THAT ALREADY EXIST IN BLACK
WOMEN'S LIVES. THE LIVED THEOLOGIES
OF INDIVIDUAL BLACK WOMEN CANNOT BE
DISMISSED AS THE EMPTY ACTIVITIES OF THE
IGNORANT. WOMANIST THEOLOGIANS RECOGNIZE
THE RICHNESS OF BLACK WOMEN'S COMMUNAL
EXPRESSIONS OF THEOLOGY. THESE LIVED
THEOLOGIES BECOME PART OF THE WOMANIST
THEOLOGICAL TEXT.

—Stephanie Y. Mitchem,
Introducing Womanist Theology[1]

ANY POSITION SHOULD SHOW HOW IT IS
ENTANGLED IN PARTICULAR SOCIAL LOCATIONS
AND INTELLECTUAL BIASES.

—Mark Kline Taylor, *Remembering Esperanza*[2]

Womanist theology, with its emphasis on the tridimensional oppression of African American women—with respect to gender, race and class—allows me to establish an African American female social context. First, by tracing the development of womanist theology, I distinguish womanists from African American women in general and situate them among their immediate predecessors—black male and feminist theologians. Next, I survey womanist theologians' views on Jesus, the cross, suffering, and discipleship. My goal is to expose and clarify the problems and possibilities associated with African American women's traditional understanding of Jesus as the divine cosufferer.

Womanist Theology

In 1983, Alice Walker prefaced her prose collection, *In Search of Our Mothers' Gardens*, with the definition of a word that would revolutionize the theological landscape: "womanist."

> 1. From *womanish*. (Opp. of "girlish," i.e., frivolous, irresponsible not serious.) A black feminist or feminist of color. From the black folk expression of mothers to female children, "You acting womanish," i.e., like a woman. Usually referring to outrageous, audacious, courageous or *willful* behavior. Wanting to know more and in greater depth than is considered "good" for one. Interested in grown-up doings. Acting grown up. Being grown up. Interchangeable with another black folk expression: "You trying to be grown." Responsible. In charge. *Serious*.
>
> 2. *Also:* A woman who loves other women, sexually and/or nonsexually. Appreciates and prefers women's culture, women's emotional flexibility (values tears as natural counterbalance of laughter), and women's strength. Sometimes loves individual men, sexually and/or nonsexually. Committed to the survival and wholeness of entire people, male *and* female. Not a separatist, except periodically, for health. Traditionally universalist, as in: "Mama, why are we brown, pink and yellow and our cousins are white, beige and black?" Ans.: "Well, you know, the colored race is just like a flower garden, with every color represented." Traditionally capable, as in: "Mama, I'm walking to Canada and I'm taking you and a bunch of other slaves with me." Reply: "It wouldn't be the first time."

3. Loves music. Loves dance. Loves the moon. *Loves* the Spirit. Loves love and food and roundness. Loves struggle. *Loves* the folk. Loves herself. *Regardless*.

4. Womanist is to feminist as purple is to lavender.[3]

Although the term bears no explicitly theological or Christian meaning[4] apart from "lov[ing] the Spirit," it aptly describes the reality of African American women. It is important to bear in mind, however, that even though Alice Walker's definition is the touchstone for womanist theology, its usage has not been without debate. In the formative years of womanist theology, Cheryl Sanders questioned whether or not Walker's term had been "misconstrued" to "suit our own [theological] purposes."[5] Despite Sanders's concerns, the nomenclature remained. Walker had constructed a label for and description of the unique social, cultural, historical, and theological experiences and understandings of African American women. The term *womanist* resonated with African American women because it gave them a way "to name themselves and their experiences without having to depend on either the sexist views of men (of all races) or the racist views of white women and white men."[6] *Womanism* provided an opportunity for African American women to "be and write out of who [they] are."[7]

Womanist theology, therefore, originates in the sociocultural spaces that African American women occupy. This becomes evident when one looks at its sources. One of the primary sources of womanist theology is the past and present experiences of African American women. For example, womanist theologians draw upon the nineteenth-century writings by and about African American women who had strong connections to the church and also affected society at large. Womanists acknowledge these women as their foremothers because their lives and writings embody the womanist ideals expressed in Walker's definition. The experiences of these women, as well as the everyday experiences of African American women in general, are sources for womanist theology regardless of whether these women describe themselves as womanists. Womanist theology, then, is consciously developed and articulated within the academies of theology, ethics, and biblical criticism. Their sources, however, can include the experiences of any African American woman.

The coining of the term *womanist* and the publication of full-length texts on womanist theology[8] proved to be a decisive moment in the development of African American women's self-understanding and theological perspective. Delores Williams identified three major turning points that led African American women to this juncture. First, she notes that womanist thought and theology reach as far back as the nineteenth century. The work of the 1980s was the result of a retrospective outlook in which African American women saw and embraced their connection to foremothers such as Anna Julia Cooper,[9] Maria Stewart,[10] and Ida B. Wells.[11] They saw in them the nascent characteristics of womanism only recently defined. They also saw the potential to work for the rights of women of all races and African Americans of both genders.[12] The second turning point was the civil rights movement of the 1950s and early 1960s. The hallmark of this movement was its communal focus on the racial issues that affected African American life. However, this "communal way of thinking obscured black women's oppression and black male sexism."[13] On the heels of the civil rights movement came the third turning point, the "second wave of feminism" in the late 1960s. Feminism made people aware of the oppression of women.[14] Although each of the above liberation movements included and benefited African American women, they had to deny a part of themselves to participate in them. The civil rights movement sought to liberate African Americans from the racial oppression experienced in a racist society. With the emphasis on race, gender issues were ignored. The liberation of women was not included in the agenda to liberate African Americans. This placed African American women in a "precarious situation" in that they "needed to maintain a partnership with black men in the struggle against white racism . . . [and] also realized . . . black men did not respect them as equals."[15]

The feminist movement, on the other hand, addressed sexism separately from racism, as its constituents were overwhelmingly white women. Although African American and white women were united in their struggle against sexism, racism divided them. White women in the feminist movement failed to see how they had universalized their experience and made it *the* experience of womanhood.[16]

African American women recognized that white women as well as white men racially oppressed them. Although white women fought against patriarchy, they also derived privileges from patriarchal systems and were oppressors of African American women.[17] White feminists' identification of patriarchy[18] as "the primary cause of all the oppression all women experienced"[19] was too narrow a category to embrace the reality of African American women's lives. Rather than simply dealing with patriarchy, African American women were dealing with "demonarchy," defined as "the demonic governance of black women's lives by white male and white female ruled systems using racism, violence, violation, retardation, and death as instruments of social control."[20]

Given the particular emphases of both the feminist and the civil rights movements, African American women had to choose whether they were first African Americans or women. Instead, they chose to create for themselves the opportunity to be both black and female and to work toward the liberation of all African Americans. Thus, "womanist theology arose out of the feminist movement and the Black Power/ black liberation movement."[21] Alice Walker's nomenclature furnished them with the language and framework to be who they are and pursue liberation from sexist, racist, and classist oppression.

African American women's insistence that their experience was just as valid as the experience of white women also necessitated the creation of their own theological voice. M. Shawn Copeland states, "Womanist theology claims the experiences of Black women as proper and serious data for theological reflection."[22] By reflecting on their experiences, African American women needed to and could "affirm different cultural foundations for identical assertions made by both feminists and black women."[23] Womanist theology, then, expanded Walker's definition in order to create a space in which Christian theology and the experiences of African American women could connect. As Stephanie Mitchem puts it, "Womanist theology is an opportunity to state the meanings of God in the real time of black women's lives."[24]

The "real time" of African American women's lives occurs at the nexus of gender, race, and class. Womanist theology, then, engages each of these facets of African American female life simultaneously. To neglect any area of oppression that affects their lives is to "deny the holistic and integrated reality of Black womanhood."[25] Therefore, "womanist symbolizes black women's resistance to their multi-dimensional oppression."[26]

Renita Weems asserts that it has only been within the context of the African American female interpretative community that African American women have been allowed to "hold in tandem all components of [their] identity."[27] This interpretative community includes the church and the academy, as well as civic organizations. Womanist theology creates another opportunity for African American women to occupy their particular gender, racial, and economic spaces and be wholly human.

The attention given to gender issues is evident in womanist theology, but womanists do not stop there. They are committed to the "wholeness of entire people":

> Womanists are particularly concerned with the 'isms' that oppress African American women. Our work unmasks, disentangles, and debunks religious language, symbols, doctrines, and socio-political structures that perpetuate the oppression of African American women in particular, but also African American men, children, humanity in general, and nature.[28]

The struggle of womanist theologians against oppression has to go beyond the survival, liberation, and well-being of women.[29] Gender, race, and class intersect and reinforce each other in the lives of African American women. Therefore, womanist theology does not limit itself to sexism and an "analysis of white racism," but also includes issues of class.[30]

Classism can be defined as "the systemic tendency of ruling classes to reinforce the distance between themselves and ruled classes by preventing the dispersal of power through a restructuring of wealth, privilege and access to resources and technology."[31] In her article "Racism and Economics: The Perspective of Oliver Cox," Katie Cannon explores the connection between racism and classism. Cannon's work builds upon the thought of Oliver Cox, who argued that capitalistic expansion requires the "core system to breed universal contempt for those exploited by the system," especially people of color and, specifically, people of African descent. Racism becomes the means by which contempt for African Americans is bred.[32] Lies of inferiority and media portrayals that cast people of color as "uncivilized" infer that "capitalists have the right to hold people of color in subjection until they are 'civilized.'"[33] Because "civilization" equals "White power" in this schema, people of color must permanently be held in subjection. Cannon concludes, "Racism supports the belief, conscientiously held, that poverty and ignorance sustained by force and fraud are desirable for people of color and that White power and prestige must remain at any cost."[34]

Therefore, the social, economic, political, and spiritual location of African American women necessitates a theological perspective that seriously considers gender, race, and class and the interplay among them. Consequently, womanists intentionally try to "produce a theology whose construction, vocabulary and issues [take] seriously the everyday experiences, language and spirituality of women."[35]

Womanist theology is predicated on the "experience of being black and female in the United States."[36] Coupled with experience is the appeal to scripture. Weems claims that although the Bible has been used to subjugate African Americans, it is "still extremely influential in the African American religious life."[37] One reason for the Bible's continued influence is that for African American women "the Bible still has some power of its own."[38] In other words, African American women view the Bible as authoritative for their lives.[39] Moreover, African American women have accessed meaning in the text that contradicts the racist, sexist, and classist interpretations of their oppressors. Weems writes, "Outlook plays an important role in how one reads the Bible."[40] Womanists bring a different lens to the theological and biblical enterprise by beginning with the uniqueness of their experience. This need to start from the foundation of African American women's experience was the catalyst for developing a womanist theology.[41]

Because womanist theology uses the experiences of African American women as primary sources for theological reflection, Mitchem defines womanist theology as the "systematic, faith-based exploration of the many facets of African American women's religiosity."[42] Womanist theology, however, is not merely a descriptive but also a constructive theological endeavor. By "critically draw[ing] from the many meanings of faith in the lives of black women," womanist theology can examine the "doctrinal and ecclesial constructions" for the purpose of reconstructing them in a way that is both meaningful and empowering to African American women.[43]

✎ Rethinking Traditional African American Piety

Womanist theologians have shown that traditional African American interpretations of Jesus as the divine cosufferer can reinforce rather than alleviate the suffering of African American women. In this section, I examine several "doctrinal and ecclesial constructions"[44]—Jesus, the cross, suffering, and discipleship—maintaining that the suffering of African American women is reinforced when we limit our identification with Jesus to suffering or make suffering a necessary point of identification.

Jesus Christ

Central to the theology of African American women is the person of Jesus Christ. Because Jesus is an intrinsic part of African American women's spirituality, he is also central to womanist theology. Womanists identify two primary reasons for Jesus' critical role in the theological understanding of African American women. First, womanists contend that Jesus makes God real to African American women. Second, womanists assert that the interpretations of Jesus that African American women accept will also be the interpretations they accept about their own lives and selves.

Kelly Brown articulates well the first reason for Jesus' centrality: "Jesus of Nazareth makes God real, brings God down to earth, for black women."[45] Neither Jesus' maleness nor the fact that he has been historically depicted as a white man rather than a man of color nullifies his ability to make God real for African American women. Brown asserts that African American women identify with what Jesus has done in their lives, not with how he looks.[46] Jesus is the one whom African American women refer to as healer and provider.[47]

Brown's theological analysis, while helpful in exposing African American women's connection to Jesus' ministry, overlooks a critical point. African American women believe Jesus to be a healer or provider based upon their understanding of the Bible and the meaning it gives to their lives. African American women describe Jesus as a healer and a provider because this is how the Bible portrays him. If Jesus of Nazareth makes God real to African American women, then it is the Bible that makes Jesus real. I therefore contend that a womanist Christology must be grounded in biblical exegesis.

Elaine Crawford voices the second reason for Jesus' centrality in the theology of African American women. She writes:

> For black women, the hermeneutical key or "interpretive reality" is the life of Jesus Christ. One's interpretation of Jesus bears a direct relationship to one's understanding of self. And one's understanding of self is directly related to one's understanding of Jesus.[48]

The relationship between African American women's perception of Jesus and their perception of themselves is a critical issue since Jesus as the divine cosufferer is one of their dominant understandings of Jesus. By espousing an understanding that makes suffering a sole or necessary point of identification with Jesus, African American women cast themselves into the role of perpetual sufferers. Should they escape from the context of their tridimensional suffering, they would risk disconnecting themselves from a dominant cultural understanding of Jesus. Rather than ignore the biblical testimony of Jesus' suffering, I would assert that African American women would benefit by following the lead of womanist theologians in broadening their understanding of and identification with Jesus so that their primary connection to Jesus is not based on suffering.

Womanists affirm that the "foundation [of their theology] is Jesus Christ who is inclusive, relational, particular and, yet, universal."[49] Jesus is particular in that he recognizes and affirms the particularities of who they are and what they have endured. The particularity of Jesus, I would argue, is seen in African American women's identification with him as their cosufferer. Jesus is particular in that he is familiar with the suffering of African Americans as stated in the Negro spirituals:

> Nobody knows the trouble I see
> Nobody knows but Jesus
> Nobody knows the trouble I see
> Glory, Hallelujah![50]

and

> Sometimes I hangs my head an' cries
> But Jesus goin' to wipe my weepin' eyes[51]

According to womanists, Jesus is also universal. His significance and availability are not limited, but have meaning for and are open to all. This affirmation allows us to expand African American women's identification with Jesus beyond the context of suffering. Suffering does not have to delimit the boundaries of one's relationship to Jesus. In other words, there are other ways of identifying with Jesus in addition to suffering. One's context of suffering may be a particularity of one's existence that coincides with the life of Jesus. However, suffering is not a necessary particularity for relationship or identification with Jesus. While it is a fact that African American women identify with Jesus' suffering, his suffering does not have to be the primary or sole basis for identification. Kelly Brown's work has already shown that there is also a strong cultural connection with Jesus' life and ministry. She notes that the testimonies of African American women are founded on what Jesus did during his earthly ministry: Jesus healed the sick and helped the poor and oppressed. They therefore affirm Jesus' presence in their lives to do the same for them.[52] By so doing, African American women connect with Jesus' life and ministry, not his death. Womanist interpretations of Jesus bear four basic principles in mind. First, womanist theological explorations "look beyond the static absolutism of classical Christology to discern and celebrate the presence of Jesus in the lives of the abused and the oppressed."[53] The meaning of Jesus for African American women cannot be merely theoretical postulations, but concrete affirmations grounded in the everyday experiences of their lives. This involves discovering the "presence and participation of Jesus in [their] own particular existential reality."[54]

Second, womanist Christology must dismantle interpretations of Jesus Christ that "aid and abet the oppression of black women."[55] Womanist Christology examines the ways in which traditional Christian doctrines of Jesus Christ have affected African American women in negative ways. For example, Brown notes that because they connect the significance of Jesus to maleness, many male preachers refuse to ordain women.[56] In addition, biblical texts that are held to advocate the subordination and silence of women must also be challenged by womanist scholars.[57] To meet this challenge, womanists will not only need to continue their work in theology but also need to enter the arena of biblical scholarship.

Third, womanist Christology "must also affirm black women's faith that Jesus has supported them in their struggles to survive and be free."[58] This affirmation is essential. If Jesus does not support African American women's struggles, then they are forced to either give Jesus up or fight against, rather than in solidarity with, him. Womanists, therefore, affirm his support. They affirm his support based upon a particular understanding of traditional African American women's affirmation of Jesus as the divine cosufferer.

The affirmation of Jesus as the divine cosufferer declares that Jesus is the one who is present with them and "empowers them in situations of oppression."[59] However, it is important to note with JoAnne Terrell that the divine cosufferer motif is in no way to function as a legitimization of anyone's suffering or oppression.[60] In other words, African American women are not to pursue or embrace suffering in order to be Jesus' cosufferer. Instead, they affirm that Jesus is their cosufferer. He knows their suffering and does not abandon them but rather empowers them in their struggle for freedom.

Finally, womanist interpretations of Jesus "must always make it clear that [Jesus'] ultimate significance is predicated upon . . . his sustaining and liberating activity."[61] Although African American women have a tradition of acknowledging Jesus as the divine cosufferer, womanists emphasize that his significance for them is not found in his suffering. For womanists, Jesus' significance is found in his ministry. In other words, womanists acknowledge that there are definite points of connection between Jesus' suffering and that of African American women. They recognize that African American women point to these similarities as proof that Jesus knows about and can identify with their suffering, so they can conclude that God has not abandoned them. However, womanists affirm that similarity does not automatically translate into significance. Just because African American women identify with Jesus in his suffering does not make suffering the significant aspect of who Jesus is or what Jesus did.

Delores Williams identifies the Synoptic Gospels as sources for reconstructing understandings of Jesus and the atonement that "[speak] meaningfully to black women."[62] Specifically, she points to Luke 4 as proof that "the spirit of God in Jesus came to show humans life."[63] She points to the parables, healings, exorcisms, and prayer life of Jesus as proof that "humankind is, then, redeemed through Jesus' ministerial vision of life and not through his death." Therefore, Jesus' significance is not found in his death, but his significance is found in a life that showed humanity a "ministerial vision of life in relation."[64]

Karen Baker-Fletcher also locates Jesus' significance in his life. However, she presents a more egalitarian view than Delores Williams. Baker-Fletcher posits a "diunital approach to the problem of Christology [because] it gives attention to both the life and death of Jesus Christ."[65] Rather than focusing on Jesus' life as Williams does or his death as traditional Christian understandings do, Baker-Fletcher advocates a "both/and approach."[66] She, too, recognizes the Synoptic Gospels as fruitful sources for womanist interpretations. Both womanists and African American women in general "identify Jesus by his work in the synoptic Gospels."[67] Although she believes that African Americans will always have a deep connection to the cross, Baker-Fletcher maintains that it is ultimately the lives of those who have been "crucified, lynched or bullet-ridden" that we should not forget.[68] With regard to Jesus, it is his life, not his crucifixion, that must remain foremost in our memories.

Baker-Fletcher advocates a theological stance that is based on Jesus' life. By refusing to forget Jesus' life, one operates from an ethic of risk rather than an ethic of sacrifice. An ethic of sacrifice glorifies Jesus' death on the cross. An ethic of risk recognizes that following "Jesus' ministry of resistance against evil . . . involve[s] the real risks of political persecution, character assassination and even death."[69] Baker-Fletcher's diunital approach and ethic of risk allow one to see the causal relationship between Jesus' ministry and suffering by not prioritizing his suffering. Jesus' life becomes the key to understanding his suffering and his death.

Womanist theologians use African American women's experience to produce an experiential lens that challenges both traditional African American and Eurocentric assertions about Jesus Christ. These challenges could be better waged, however, if they were grounded in the biblical text. Both Williams and Baker-Fletcher point to the Synoptic Gospels as fruitful areas for developing womanist Christology. Yet neither they nor the other womanists I reviewed capitalize on this authority for African American female life. None of the womanists produce conclusions based upon a sustained exegesis of the texts to which they refer.

The Cross

Although womanists acknowledge problems with interpretations of Jesus that emphasize his suffering and death, they still contend with the historical reality of the cross and its implications for African American women's faith.[70] In short, womanists recognize the centrality of the cross in African American Christianity, a centrality based upon African Americans' identification with Jesus and his suffering. JoAnne Terrell writes:

> Historical Christianity's focus on the cross, the experience of chattel slavery and unabated experiences of suffering and delimitation illustrate in principle the major reason cited by black theologians as to why the symbolism of the cross became and remains central in African American Christianity.[71]

As we shall see, there are womanists who reject the notion that suffering is the will of God. Consequently, they will reject any interpretation of Jesus' death on the cross as God's will. Those working from this perspective must reinterpret the cross so that the suffering of African American women and the suffering of Jesus are not sacralized. The issue for many womanists is not the inclusion of the cross in womanist theology. Williams writes, "As Christians, black women cannot forget the cross."[72] The issue is how the cross is interpreted: "The problem is not preaching 'Christ crucified,'" states Baker-Fletcher; "the problem is *how* we preach Christ crucified."[73]

I believe that there are two potential problems inherent in how we preach Jesus crucified. First, it is problematic to draw parallels between the characteristics of Jesus' and African American women's suffering without determining if there are parallels between the causes of their suffering. By ignoring the cause(s) of Jesus' suffering, we disconnect his suffering from his life and ministry. Jesus' cross, viewed in isolation from factors that caused it, degenerates into a symbol for all suffering. Therefore, when African American women suffer, they can mistakenly conclude that they are bearing the cross.

The second potential problem is in making Jesus' suffering the sole or required point of identification for African American women. This is critical given African American women's historical role as surrogates and Christian atonement theories that depict Jesus as the divine surrogate who takes the place of humanity on the cross. Delores Williams claims, "Surrogacy . . . gives black women's oppression its unique character."[74] Surrogacy is characterized by being either forced or coerced to perform roles that normally belong to others. The surrogacy of African American women has primarily involved "social role exploitation"[75] in which African American women were "pressured into some surrogacy roles" such as domestic workers, heads of households, even surrogate mothers.[76]

Williams identifies two forms of surrogacy: coerced surrogacy and voluntary surrogacy. Coerced surrogacy existed during the pre–Civil War era when African American women lived in a "forced condition in which people and systems more powerful than black women and black people forced black women to function in roles that ordinarily would have been filled by someone else."[77] Voluntary surrogacy refers to the postbellum period when African American women "could exercise the choice of refusing the surrogate role."[78] This choice, however, was often hampered by the poverty black women and families faced. In other words, African American women could resist functioning in surrogate roles circumscribed by white employers but only at the risk of further economic hardship.

These surrogacy roles and the theological justification they are given further complicate African American women's struggle for liberation. The dominant theories of atonement depict Jesus as the "ultimate surrogate figure standing in the place of someone else, sinful humankind."[79] William's concern is that African American women will compare their surrogacy roles with that of Jesus in an attempt to render their oppression sacred and thus tolerable. The acceptance of surrogacy roles is encouraged by what Emilie Townes calls the "moral valuing of loss, denial and sacrifice." These are values that Emilie Townes asserts require reexamination in light of African American women's experience.[80] I would add that this reexamination requires not only consideration of African American women's sociocultural location but also an interpretation of biblical passages that refer to these values from a womanist perspective.

In womanist theology, two seemingly opposite and yet complementary interpretations of the cross are found. On the one hand, the cross exemplifies the sin of humanity, and on the other hand, it demonstrates the love of God. Baker-Fletcher asserts that the cross is "a symbol of our capacity to sin."[81] In a similar manner, Williams writes, "The image of Jesus on the cross is the image of human sin in its most desecrated form."[82] The cross, then, is an indictment of human violence, abuse, injustice, and oppression. The cross becomes the clearest example of these sins as the one who was crucified suffered because of these sins in action.[83] Since human beings have demonstrated, in the crucifixion of Jesus, an enormous capacity to sin, the cross is also a warning. It stands to remind people of the possible consequences of fighting oppression:

> Jesus' ministry of resistance against evil and the empowerment of others involved the real risks of political persecution, character assassination and even death. The cross must not be forgotten because such persecution is a possible consequence of standing up for what is morally right.[84]

Even though womanists contend that the cross symbolizes human sinfulness, they also assert, paradoxically, that it reveals the love of God. When referring to the Negro spirituals, M. Shawn Copeland insists that the music emphasized the cross because it showed God's commitment to them. She notes, "The enslaved Africans sang [of the cross] because they saw on the rugged wooden planks One who had endured what was their daily portion. The cross was treasured because it enthroned the One who went all the way with them and for them."[85]

In a world that denied their humanity and the existence of their souls, the enslaved Africans maintained their belief in God's love and commitment to them. They believed that what Jesus endured, he endured for them, which proved that they were valued in the sight of God. JoAnne Terrell argues in similar manner.

However, Williams raises a dissenting voice. To Williams, the cross only symbolizes sin. The cross represents both "the evil of humankind trying to kill the ministerial vision of life and relation that Jesus brought to humanity"[86] and "an image of defilement, a gross manifestation of collective human sin."[87] In her desire to avoid the sacralization of African American women's suffering, Williams eliminates any reason to glorify this symbol. Consequently, she seeks to nullify cross bearing for African American women—"There are quite enough black women bearing the cross by rearing children alone, struggling on welfare, suffering through poverty, experiencing inadequate health-care, domestic violence and various forms of sexism and racism."[88]

In her article "A Crucifixion Double-Cross?" Williams describes the cross as a "reminder of what can happen to reformers who successfully challenge the status quo."[89] Yet she uses single parenting, addiction, and inadequate healthcare as examples of black women's crosses. In similar fashion, JoAnne Terrell refers to systemic racism, sexism, and heterosex-ism as crosses African Americans bear.[90] Both Williams's examples and those of Terrell are examples not so much of those who challenge the status quo as of those who suffer the effects of it. At this point, woman-ist interpretations of the cross suffer from a lack of engagement with the biblical text. Specifically, a biblical interpretation from a womanist perspective could assist them in clarifying a womanist view of the cross and defining cross bearing. I assert that just as the cross cannot be for-gotten because it is part of the biblical text, neither can the command to take up the cross (Mark 8:34) be forgotten or ignored. What is needed is a womanist interpretation of cross-bearing texts, particularly ones like Mark 8:34: "And calling the crowd with his disciples, he said to them, 'Whoever desires to follow behind me, let him/her deny him-/herself, take up his/her cross and follow me'" (my translation).

Both Williams and Terrell want to desacralize the suffering of Afri-can American women. Williams's aim is to show that "God does not intend black women's surrogacy."[91] Therefore, she attempts to clearly distinguish between God's will and sinful human action. According to Williams, Jesus' life and ministry represent God's will. His death is a "gross manifestation of collective human sin."[92] The cross is solely a reflection of human sinfulness. Because Williams views the cross as a symbol of sin, she concludes, "There is nothing divine in the blood of the cross."[93] On this point, Terrell takes issue. She asserts that there is "something of God in the blood of the cross."[94]

Terrell can only agree with Williams's statement "if she means that there is nothing of God's sanction in violence."[95] Like Williams, Terrell does not believe that God purposed Jesus' death. However, she does want to affirm the presence of God in Jesus' and, therefore, human suf-fering. Consequently, Terrell's statement maintains the affirmation of Jesus as the divine cosufferer. If one removes God's presence from the cross, one cannot affirm God's presence with African American women in the midst of their suffering. This would negate the third interpretive principle that governs womanists' understandings of Jesus, that Jesus empowers us in situations of struggle. Moreover, it would suggest that when the cross became inevitable, God abandoned Jesus. Anyone who engages in transformative ministry that results in persecution and/or execution, as Williams has described the outcome of Jesus' ministry, would incur abandonment from God. In this sense, Terrell joins with Jacquelyn Grant and Copeland in affirming the cross as a symbol of God's love. The cross does not sanction the violence committed against African American women; it is the "supreme reminder of God's with-us-ness."[96]

Womanists, such as Copeland and Terrell, therefore, continue to work within the traditional African American interpretive tradition that sees positive value in the symbol of the cross. They see no contradiction between the cross as a symbol of both human sin and God's love. The cross demonstrates God's commitment to them and a love that endures despite the sinfulness of humans. Delores Williams, on the other hand, makes us acutely aware of the potential problems of traditional interpretations of the cross. Given the opposite yet complementary womanist interpretations of the cross, one question remains: How do womanists understand suffering? Our next section will explore this question.

Suffering

A womanist theology of suffering begins with African American women's experience. It is "rooted in and draws on Black women's accounts of pain and anguish, of their individual and collective struggle to grasp and manage, rather than be managed by their suffering."[97] Copeland defines suffering as "the disturbance of our inner tranquility caused by physical, mental, emotional, and spiritual forces that we grasp as jeopardizing our lives, our very existence."[98]

She defines evil as the "negation and deprivation of good." Therefore, suffering and evil are inseparable but not identical.[99] Within this framework, the multidimensional oppression of racism, sexism, and classism that affects African American women is evil because it deprives them of good. The resulting deprivation and/or negation disturbs their inner tranquility, thereby causing their suffering.

Jamie Phelps describes African Americans' suffering as both existential and physical. Existential suffering occurs when African

Americans "question their value and worth within the society."[100] Physical suffering can be caused by "hunger, hopelessness, unemployment, ill health, drug abuse, and so forth."[101] Like Copeland, Phelps points to evil as the cause of suffering.[102] Specifically, she refers to socially constructed evil: "Socially constructed evil involves patterns of relationships that are directed toward the denial of the human dignity and value of some human beings for the benefit of other human beings."[103] The sins of sexism, racism, classism, and heterosexism are the results of socially constructed evil. These isms yield the existential and physical suffering Phelps describes.

Rather than distinguishing between evil and suffering, Emilie Townes appeals to Audre Lorde's distinction between pain and suffering. Lorde defines pain as "an event, an experience that must be recognized, named and then used in some way in order for the experience to change, to be transformed into something else."[104] Pain, then, is a "dynamic process."[105] Pain leads to transformation because by definition, it is recognized and named. Therefore, pain "promotes self-knowledge, which is a tool for liberation and wholeness."[106] Individuals who experience pain are aware of themselves and their situation and can fight against that which causes the pain.[107]

Suffering, on the other hand, is "unscrutinized and unmetabolized pain."[108] It is "reliving pain over and over again when it is triggered by events or people."[109] Consequently, suffering is a static process because it does not lead to transformation but oppression.[110] Suffering, then, can be used as a tool of oppression rather than one of liberation. It keeps people in a state of misery without reflecting on the causes of their condition or developing any plan of action to alleviate it. In effect, they are left without the "right or ability to say 'no' to their oppressors."[111] Whereas pain puts African American women in a position to actively engage and challenge the world around them, suffering leaves them always reacting to the dehumanizing and degrading onslaught of racism, sexism, and classism. Consequently, Townes advocates for the "inevitability and desirability of suffering [to be] challenged."[112]

The goal, then, is to move from suffering to pain.[113] This movement is necessary not simply because it liberates African Americans but because suffering is sinful. Townes contends that suffering is sinful for two reasons. First, "the gospel message calls for transformation."[114]

Suffering is not transformative. Second, suffering prohibits individuals from "act[ing] through [their] finite freedom on behalf of [their] liberation from sin to justice."[115] Rather than evoking the desire to fight against injustice, suffering produces a malaise in which injustice is tolerated and accepted.

Interestingly enough, Townes's discussion does not take into consideration Jesus' suffering but only his resurrection: "God has taken suffering out of the world through the resurrection of Jesus."[116] Neither does she ground her discussion in Scripture. Her distinction between pain and suffering, however, introduces the question of whether Jesus' crucifixion was an experience of suffering or of pain. The answer necessitates an examination of the biblical text to determine why Jesus was crucified. It is also necessary to explore whether his crucifixion was a named and recognized experience or one of unscrutinized, unmetabolized pain.

Although Copeland does not employ Townes's distinction between suffering and pain, she does assert that any womanist theology of suffering must be both redemptive and resistant. It is redemptive in that "black women invite God to partner with them in the redemption of black people."[117] Citing narratives of African American women under chattel slavery, Copeland notes that they endured suffering to ensure freedom for their children. In this way, they "[made] meaning of their suffering."[118] In other words, they did not suffer for the sake of suffering, but suffered as the inevitable result of pursuing a better life within a society that annihilates such endeavors by African Americans. By "managing the suffering," African American women can fight against oppression that causes the suffering, thereby making redemption possible.

Terrell agrees with Copeland's assessment of African American women's need to "ascribe meaning to their suffering and to affirm divine assistance to gain victory over it."[119] Contrary to Copeland, however, she does not believe that suffering is redemptive but that suffering can be overcome by not surrendering to it. Terrell explains, "Not that 'violence, victimization and undeserved suffering' are redemptive, but that suffering and merit are unrelated, just as love and merit are, and that we who suffer can be redeemed."[120] Terrell emphasizes that suffering does not deny one's redemption, but neither does it ensure it. With reference to the women under chattel slavery, Terrell could assert that their suffering did not ensure their children's liberation, but chattel slavery could not prevent their liberation either. They could endure the suffering by ascribing meaning or a greater purpose to it, but their suffering was no magic formula for deliverance.

Copeland, on the other hand, sees suffering as possibly containing redemptive qualities when it brings about freedom for African Americans. In similar fashion, Black theology distinguishes between suffering and redemptive suffering. In other words, suffering is the basic experiential reality of African Americans in the United States. One only needs to be black in America to suffer. However, to suffer in an effort to alleviate the suffering caused by racism, sexism, and classism is redemptive suffering. One's suffering for the cause of freedom is efficacious. Suffering affords liberation.

James Cone sees suffering in this way. According to Cone, suffering is both positive and negative. Negative suffering is that which is inflicted upon the oppressed.[121] Negative suffering includes "white people's insults," which are not to be "passively endured but fought against."[122] However, Cone sees suffering as positive when one suffers in his or her struggle against suffering.[123]

This type of approach to suffering employs what Theophus Smith calls homeopathic practices. Smith explains that homeopathic practices are those that treat illnesses by prescribing a modified dosage of the disease to cure it. The goal is to mimic the disease enough to cause the body to rally its natural defenses and destroy the disease.[124] Suffering, then, becomes a necessary ingredient for deliverance. Womanists like Phelps, Townes, and Terrell, however, consistently link suffering with evil, not redemption. Therefore, suffering is no longer required to alleviate the multidimensional oppression of African American women. Instead, self-knowledge is the tool of choice.

As seen above, there is no single definition of suffering purported by womanist theologians. What is clear, however, is that womanists agree that suffering is not to have control of their lives. To use Copeland's terminology, they are not to be "managed by their suffering." Although Copeland contends that suffering can "coax real freedom and growth,"[125] suffering is never viewed as good or positive in womanist theology. Townes puts it succinctly: "Womanist ethical reflection rejects suffering as God's will."[126]

Discipleship

I noted above that womanists locate the significance of Jesus in his life and ministry. Baker-Fletcher described Jesus' ministry as resisting evil. Williams described his ministry as one that presented humanity with a perfect vision of how to live in relationship. In the discussion of the cross, I showed that according to womanists, the cross represents both human sinfulness and God's love. The cross depicts human sin because it represents humanity's sinful attempt to stop the work of God through Jesus Christ. Consequently, the cross is the result of Jesus' ministry, not the preordained will of God. Because discipleship is based on the ministry of Jesus, the discipleship of African American women, as advanced by womanist theologians, is implicitly related to this understanding of Jesus' ministry and the cross.

According to Jamie Phelps, "Christian discipleship demands that we be willing to confront death in our struggle to transform these sinful patterns which are embodied in sinful social structures of our church and society."[127] This suggests that African American women's discipleship be characterized by resisting their multidimensional oppression. As Baker-Fletcher's ethic of risk signifies, discipleship is a dangerous endeavor.

Jacquelyn Grant notes another danger of discipleship. She contends that the very language of servanthood, which is used to describe discipleship, maintains rather than challenges "sinful social structures." Given the legacy of African American women as servants who have experienced coerced and/or voluntary surrogacy, servanthood language maintains and supports these roles. Servanthood in an African American female context equals suffering. Therefore, discipleship that is understood as servanthood degenerates into spiritually sanctioned suffering.

Consequently, Grant argues for a change of terminology when speaking about "the life-work of Christians," noting, "Servanthood language has, in effect, been one of subordination."[128] She deems this change necessary because "Black people's and Black women's lives demonstrate to us that some people are more servants than others."[129] Due to African American people's subordination within larger society, Grant believes that our language must challenge, not support, this reality. She argues that "for liberation to happen the psychological, political, and social conditions must be created to nurture the processes.

Servant language does not do this."[130] Grant, therefore, proposes three areas of consideration for reformulating theological affirmations.

First, we should refrain from using language that "camouflages oppressive reality, rather than eliminating [it]."[131] By using servant-hood language as a way of talking about the lifework of Christians, we inadvertently equate having a servant's status with having Christian virtue. In so doing, we camouflage the reality that African Americans have been continuously cast in servant roles such as domestic workers, janitors, and Pullman porters. The denial of opportunities had nothing to do with the pursuit of a higher Christian goal. Instead, its roots are found in practices that arise from the "socio-political interests of proponents of the status quo and their attempts to undergird their intended goal through psychological conditioning that arises partially with the institutionalization of oppressive language, even theological language."[132] By extolling the "goodness" of being a servant, we make it "bad" to move beyond menial work positions.

Next, we must "resist the tendency of relegating some to the lower rung of society."[133] Grant asserts a more egalitarian version of discipleship in which certain people do not bear the burden of service while others simply receive. She notes that within many Christian churches, women shoulder the brunt of service. In this way, some people are more servants than others.

Finally, we must "resist the tendency of devaluing the lives of people by virtue of who they are."[134] Relegating people to the status of servant often relegates them to a position that others perceive as less than human.[135] On the contrary, Grant argues that we must affirm humanity. Structures within the church and society that perpetuate this type of inequality can no longer be tolerated.[136] She writes, "The church does not need servants, as oppressively conceived of and experienced by many; the church needs followers of Christ—disciples."[137]

Discipleship, according to Grant, equals following Jesus. However, she does not explicate how one is to follow Jesus. Nor do the other womanist scholars. Consequently, womanist theology would benefit from a biblically based description of discipleship that considers the particularities of African American women's experience in relationship to the biblical mandate to follow Jesus that womanists have brought to light.

∞ Conclusion

Womanist analyses of Jesus, the cross, suffering, and discipleship reveal how traditional African American interpretations of Jesus as the divine cosufferer can reinforce rather than alleviate the suffering of African American women. This reinforcement occurs when African American women sacralize their suffering and surrogacy by connecting it to Jesus' crucifixion. I contend that the problem occurs when African American women make this connection based on a *particular understanding* of his suffering.

The affirmation of Jesus as the divine cosufferer becomes problematic when African American women assume that Jesus' suffering was the will of God rather than a consequence of his ministry. When suffering is viewed as the divine purpose or intention of God, the individuals and institutions that promote suffering become instruments of God. To fight against the causes of one's suffering is to fight against God. In this way, all moral responsibility for suffering is removed from human beings.

This affirmation is also problematic when African American women perceive Jesus' experience to be what Townes describes as the static condition of unmetabolized and unscrutinized pain, known as suffering. This identification with Jesus casts African American women in the perpetual role of sufferers. Moreover, it renders their existential suffering as sacred and requires that they remain in a suffering condition to be Christians. The result is an understanding of discipleship that requires suffering in order to be genuine. The same conclusion is reached when African American women identify with Jesus solely on the basis of suffering. Even if one distinguishes between suffering and pain, the issue remains. In either case, their identification rests completely on a condition that womanists insist derives from evil.

The affirmation of Jesus as the divine cosufferer is empowering to African American women when it assures black women that they are not alone during times of suffering. This connection to Jesus certifies that because Jesus' suffering was real, so too is theirs. In a modern context, this affirmation insists that the negative effects of racism, sexism, and classism that the majority society often wishes to ignore still abound and need to be remedied. Therefore, the potential exists for this affirmation to motivate African American women to challenge the causes of their suffering. If Jesus experienced pain, then one cannot identify one's suffering with Jesus, only one's pain. In other words, for Jesus to be one's divine cosufferer, one cannot simply link his or her general context of suffering to Jesus. Jesus is not a cosufferer until one moves from suffering to named, recognized pain. Consequently, womanists need to answer an essential question: Did Jesus suffer (understood as passive) or experience pain (understood as transformative)? The answer requires an examination of the biblical text.

Womanist theology affirms two primary sources: African American women's experience and the Bible. Womanists affirm African American women's experience because they seek to do theological reflection from their sociocultural context. The Bible is central to the womanist theological enterprise because it is central to many African American women. On the one hand, the Bible informs African American women's experience and their understanding of the Christian faith. On the other hand, African American women's experience also affects how they read the text. In no way do I wish to suggest that this interaction between experience and text is peculiar to African American women. What I do contend, however, is that this interaction between the text and African American women in particular represents another vantage point from which to view the Bible. This interaction is not maximized in womanist theological circles.

Granted, womanist theologians are just that, theologians. Because their work is primarily theological, however, they miss opportunities to utilize one of their primary sources—the Bible. In the review of womanist perspectives on Jesus, the cross, suffering, and discipleship, I identified areas where insights could be gained and the harmful effects of traditional African American interpretations could be challenged by critical study of the biblical text. If the womanist theological enterprise is to speak to the real time of African American women's experience, key areas of investigation such as the biblical commands to take up the cross and to deny oneself must be addressed by means of biblical interpretation.

Additionally, there is no exegetically formulated description of discipleship from an African American woman's perspective that considers these commands or the relationship between agony and discipleship. Stephanie Mitchem is correct: "Exploring black women's unique interpretations or hermeneutics of scripture will most likely lead to new expressions of womanist theologies. The area of womanist biblical scholarship has great promise."[138]

Before we engage the biblical text, two areas of womanist theology require attention. First, I will clarify womanist terminology as it relates to suffering. Second, I will use the categories of moral evil and natural evil as a means of sharpening Karen Baker-Fletcher's diunital approach.

The first task in clarifying womanists' use of suffering language is to distinguish between suffering that is the byproduct of one's oppression, on the one hand, and suffering that is the result of challenging the sources of one's oppression, on the other. Womanist scholars have articulated the tridimensional oppression that causes the suffering of African American women, as well as their unique history of surrogacy. This suffering occurs regardless of her faith commitment—whether she is a Christian or not. In addition, womanists are aware that by fighting oppression, suffering will inevitably occur. Either way, she will suffer. Yet those two experiences of suffering are qualitatively different. Suffering that arises from oppressive systems and conditions results in a static condition that will not change until its sources are confronted. Suffering that is a result of challenging the causes of one's oppression has the possibility of being eliminated. This distinction needs to be made evident.

Womanist theologians' definitions of suffering vary considerably. Copeland provides a general definition of suffering. Townes, using Lorde's distinction between pain and suffering, proposes a different understanding of suffering. Moreover, Townes's and Lorde's distinctions between pain and suffering are not clear. For example, pain is named and recognized in their view. Yet suffering is unmetabolized, unscrutinized pain. How can suffering be unscrutinized pain when pain is both named and recognized? In an effort to clarify my use of these terms and to oppose the notion of redemptive suffering, that is, suffering purported to be efficacious in and of itself, I will use Copeland's, Lorde's, Townes's, and Phelps's work to redefine the terms *suffering* and *pain*.

From this point on, I will employ three terms: *agony*, *suffering*, and *pain*. My understanding of agony is roughly equivalent to Copeland's definition of suffering as "the disturbance of our inner tranquility caused by physical, mental, emotional, and spiritual forces that we grasp as jeopardizing our lives, our very existence."[139] I use the term *agony* in the sense of Copeland's definition, with one important addition. Given Jamie Phelps's emphasis on socially constructed evil, our definition should also list social forces among those that jeopardize our lives. Therefore, my definition of agony becomes: the disturbance of our inner tranquility caused by physical, mental, emotional, social, and spiritual forces that we grasp as jeopardizing our lives, our very existence. *Agony*, therefore, will be the general term I use to describe any distress that fits the above description.

For my purposes, *suffering* and *pain* represent two types of agony. Drawing upon the work of Lorde and Townes, I define suffering as unmetabolized, unscrutinized agony. Because suffering is unmetabolized, unscrutinized agony, I maintain with Lorde and Townes that suffering is a static condition that enables one's continued oppression. I believe that the term *suffering* adequately expresses this type of agony since suffering connotes that which is endured and suggests a perpetual condition.

Pain, then, is named, recognized agony that can be transformed into something else. Pain is not static; it is dynamic. I believe that pain aptly describes this type of agony because pain connotes a temporary condition. This is not to minimize the experience of pain but to maintain the integrity of its definition. Because pain, understood in this way, is named and recognized, it is not a perpetual condition. Unlike suffering, pain is a transitioning experience because it can be transformed into something else. Just as labor pains can be transformed into the joy of childbirth and as Townes's work suggests that Jesus' crucifixion was transformed into a resurrection, pain is a process that must sometimes be experienced for the accomplishment of something else. In short, I will only use *pain* to refer to named and recognized agony that comes as a temporary result of life-affirming behavior. As seen in the discussion on suffering, womanists identify evil as the cause of suffering. Whereas Townes rejected suffering as the will of God, I reject agony as the will of God and contend that agony is not "the considered and deliberate divine purpose, intention, or determination."[140] I maintain that evil is the cause of agony and, therefore, the cause of both suffering and pain.

Theologians distinguish between two types of evil: natural and moral. Natural evil "refers to injury and suffering caused by diseases, accidents, earthquakes, fire and floods."[141] In other words, there are some forms of suffering to which we are susceptible simply because we are finite, mortal creatures. Daniel Migliore is careful to note, however, that it would be a mistake to "view vulnerability, finitude and mortality as [inherently] evil"; they represent the "shadow side" of life.[142] Douglas John Hall writes, "Challenge, struggle and *some* forms of suffering belong to the very structure of life. To insist that believers should be immune from *every* form of struggle and *every* form of suffering would be to wish not to have been created at all."[143] In short, a creaturely existence includes the possibility, and even the inevitability, of agony due to natural evil.

Moral evil, on the other hand, "refers to acts (sins) of creatures that are contrary to God's holy character and law."[144] It is the negation and deprivation of good inflicted upon human beings by other human beings. Moral evil includes both individual and corporate acts. For Jamie Phelps, "socially constructed evil" manifests itself in racist, sexist, and classist structures, behaviors, and policies.[145] Consequently, socially constructed evil is an example of moral evil that involves social groups rather than individuals. When human beings suffer or experience pain at the hands of their fellow human beings, moral evil is at work.

In neither construction of evil is God the "culprit."[146] Natural evil finds its cause in the finitude, mortality, and vulnerability of creation. Moral evil finds its root in the sinful acts of human beings who behave contrary to God's benevolent purposes. Consequently, there is a causal relationship between the moral evil inflicted by *humans* and human suffering and pain.

I believe that the category of moral evil is especially helpful in crafting a womanist lens since womanists reject suffering as the will of God and see it as a consequence of racist, sexist, and classist oppression or moral evil. Sexism, racism, and classism, then, are not divinely preordained; they are the manifestations of human sinfulness that cause the existential suffering of African American women and inflict pain on those who fight against these forces. This perspective represents how Baker-Fletcher and Williams view the life and death of Jesus. Moreover, the category of moral evil sharpens Baker-Fletcher's diunital approach. It enables one to see the relationship between Jesus' ministry and the agony of his death. The theological category of moral evil provides a way of understanding Jesus' death without asserting that his death was God's will. In other words, Jesus' life and ministry represent the will of God. His suffering and death are the results of moral evil, that is, the sinful reaction of human beings. And Jesus' resurrection is God's divine counteraction.

There are therefore two primary questions that womanist theology cannot answer on its own: (1) What is the relationship between the agony that the cross symbolizes and discipleship? (2) Is the agony of the cross suffering (passive) or pain (transformative)? I now turn to biblical scholarship, posing these questions to Markan scholars.

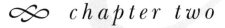

chapter two

Perspectives on Discipleship and Suffering in Mark

[BRIAN K. BLOUNT'S] DISCUSSION OF SIN AND
SUFFERING IN MARK REQUIRES RETHINKING
EXEGESIS OF THE GOSPEL BY SCHOLARS
GENERALLY, WHATEVER THEIR PERSPECTIVE.

—Pheme Perkins, review of *Then the
Whisper Put on Flesh: New Testament
Ethics in an African Context*[1]

 In chapter 1, I drew on womanist theology to show the problems and possibilities of the traditional African American understanding of Jesus as the divine cosufferer. Although womanist theology exposes ways in which this affirmation promotes suffering, it has, to date, failed to engage the biblical text. Womanists agree that it is to the Gospels that African American women turn to understand the person of Jesus Christ. For this project, I will focus on the Gospel of Mark.

Frank J. Matera summarizes the occasion of Mark's Gospel as follows: "Finally, the community has forgotten the centrality of the cross in the life of discipleship. Most importantly, then, Mark writes to remind them of the cross and the true meaning of discipleship."[2] Matera's comments highlight three important themes in the Gospel of Mark: discipleship, the cross, and the agony the cross symbolizes. These are the themes I wish to examine. I therefore pose the questions raised in chapter 1 to Markan scholars: (1) What is the relationship between the agony that the cross symbolizes and discipleship in Mark's Gospel? and (2) Is the agony of the cross suffering (unmetabolized, unscrutinized agony that enables one's continued oppression), or is it pain (named and recognized agony that comes as a temporary result of life-affirming behavior)?

Most Markan scholars do not explicitly address these questions. Like me, they have brought their own set of questions to the text. Therefore, I seek answers to my first question by determining whether the authors understand Jesus' agony to be a part of his ministry and, therefore, a requirement for discipleship or whether they understand Jesus' agony to be a consequence of his ministry and, therefore, a consequence of discipleship. In this chapter, I survey the answers gleaned from Markan scholars regarding the first question. At the end of each subsection, I engage the authors from a womanist perspective. Based on the definitions proposed in chapter 1, I posit which type of agony, pain, or suffering the authors' interpretations suggest. In this way, I answer my second question. (Although in chapter 1, I made distinctions between agony, suffering, and pain, I have maintained the authors' original terminology in the following summaries.)

Suffering as Requirement for and Consequence of Discipleship

In *Jesus and the Twelve: Discipleship and Revelation in Mark's Gospel*, Robert P. Meye seeks to "call attention to the didactic motif in Mark's narrative of Jesus."[3] He emphasizes that Mark presents Jesus as both teacher and lord. Jesus' role as teacher is essential: it is through his teaching that his disciples are prepared for the work to which he has called them. Although Mark does depict Jesus preaching, Meye gives primacy to Jesus' teaching ministry. The teaching takes precedence because Mark records only two instances when someone other than Jesus teaches (6:30; 7:7).[4] Preaching, in effect, becomes a subordinate component of Jesus' ministry because others participate in proclaiming the good news.[5]

Meye's fundamental thesis is that "Mark describes Jesus' ministry consistently with only the Twelve in view as the disciples of Jesus."[6] Discipleship in Mark's Gospel only applies to the Twelve who were contemporaries of and called by Jesus. Meye defines being with Jesus (see, by way of comparison, 3:14) as the "primary characterization of discipleship"[7] and following Jesus as the "decisive characteristic of discipleship."[8] Being with Jesus is essential for discipleship and necessitates following him. Although following is a "decisive characteristic of discipleship," simply following Jesus does not a disciple make. For Meye, "following does not automatically signify the will to abide with Jesus and to learn from him."[9] Meye therefore acknowledges that there were those who followed Jesus because "Jesus' way is open to all . . . but . . . only a few were privileged to follow him and to be with him as his disciples."[10] Thus, only the Twelve qualify as disciples.

Since the Twelve were the only ones called to be with Jesus, they are the only ones who receive the mystery of the kingdom of God (see, by way of comparison, 4:11) and the only ones called to become "fishers of men [sic]."[11] Meye links Jesus' call to Simon and Andrew in 1:17 and the call of the Twelve in 3:13-19 with Jesus' explanation of the parable in 4:10-19, concluding that the Twelve are the only ones to be given the mystery of the kingdom because they alone have received both the person and teaching of Jesus.[12] Since the Twelve alone have the mystery of the kingdom, they are the only ones able to become fishers of people: "The fullest meaning of the expression 'fishers of men,' which is to be realized in *following Jesus*, is to be found in a *work that is similar to that of Jesus.*"[13]

Meye goes on to give the ministry of the word and exorcisms as examples of these works.[14] He points out that the teaching ministry of Jesus not only is necessary for training disciples, but also plays a critical role in his death. When examining Mark 11:18, he writes, "The death of Jesus is ultimately related to the impact of Jesus' *didache* upon the multitudes."[15] In this passage, Jesus' teaching upsets the status quo of the temple system. Both his words and actions confront the practices of religious leaders and signify that their practices must come to an end. Meye confirms this interpretation by pointing to Mark 12:1-12. In this parable, Jesus criticizes the religious elite for their hard-hearted opposition to the kingdom of God as he represents it. The religious leaders realize that Jesus has taught the parable against them. The parable is, therefore, a direct cause of their desire to arrest him. It is for such a reason that "one could say that Jesus' way as teacher is for Mark a direct cause of the way of the cross."[16]

Throughout Meye's writing, he never explicates the way of the cross. For the purposes of his work, Meye only seeks to demonstrate the consistency with which Jesus teaches throughout the Gospel narrative. However, the closing section of Meye's work hints at the way of the cross. Meye notes, "The very heart of the Gospel is given over to making the point that the way of suffering ordained for the Messiah is ultimately not for the Twelve but for the many (cf. 10:45; where there is a concentration on the Twelve, it is always for the sake of the many).[17] Initially, Meye locates the cause of Jesus' suffering in the response of the religious rulers to Jesus' teaching ministry. Yet in his conclusion, Meye says that Jesus' suffering has been "ordained"—appointed by God.[18] His teaching becomes *a* cause, but not *the* cause, of his death. It seems as though Meye cannot let his original conclusion stand without at least hinting that God had a role in Jesus' suffering.

Here Meye strays from his original conclusion that Jesus' death is ultimately related to his teaching. Instead, he inserts a theological cause rather than allowing the narrative cause to stand. He implies that suffering, rather than ministry, is the way ordained by God for Jesus, the Twelve, and all who follow. Contrary to the evidence Meye himself presents, he suggests that suffering is the will of God, rather than the result of the teaching of Jesus and the result of discipleship.

 Meye's reading of Mark's Gospel initially corresponds to Karen Baker-Fletcher's diunital approach, which gives attention to both the life and death of Jesus. He begins by exploring the nature of discipleship by first examining Jesus' ministry. By looking at both the life and death of Jesus, Meye grasps the causal relationship between Jesus' ministry and death. He asserts that Mark emphasizes Jesus' teaching ministry, and it is this ministry that ultimately leads to Jesus' death. Therefore, the agony of the cross is pain. Pain, then, is a consequence of discipleship.

However, Meye does not maintain this reading. In his conclusion, Meye describes Jesus' agony as suffering. It is ordained, appointed by God. Thus, his reading contradicts the womanist affirmation that agony is not the will of God and has the potential of maintaining the agony of African American women. Since African American women identify with the agony of Jesus, any interpretation that suggests agony is the will of God also suggests that African American women should view their agony as divinely willed.

Suffering as Necessary for Discipleship

For Theodore Weeden, suffering is critical to the self-understanding of Jesus and that of his disciples. Suffering is what separates a true Christology and messiahship from a false one. Weeden, though, never explains why Jesus suffers. He simply acknowledges the fact of Jesus' suffering and argues that this component is what legitimizes a true Christology.

Weeden argues that Mark's Gospel is a "polemic against the disciples" with "two opposing Christologies" at work.[19] The disciples represent the false Christology; Jesus represents the true Christology. Although Weeden does not enumerate the characteristics of true discipleship, one can glean an understanding of it from what he calls the "three successive and worsening stages in the relationship between Jesus and the disciples."[20] Since Weeden's depiction of the Markan disciples is primarily negative, one can get at Weeden's understanding of true discipleship by looking at what the disciples do not do.

In the first stage, Weeden states that the "disciples' strange inability to perceive who Jesus is" is characteristic.[21] The disciples demonstrate their imperceptivity by failing to "detect their relationship to Jesus and his true identity."[22] The disciples do not comprehend who Jesus is despite the miracles, healings, and exorcisms performed by Jesus. A disciple, then, is one who ascertains the identity of Jesus and his or her relationship to him.

In Weeden's second stage, the disciples move from "imperceptivity to misconception."[23] Weeden points out that even with Peter's confession in Caesarea Philippi (8:27-29), he still does not understand who Jesus is. His confession of Jesus proves to be a misconception in the ensuing conversation (8:31-33). Weeden writes, "Whatever Peter's concept of Messiahship is, it is not Jesus' concept of a suffering Messiah."[24] The disciples' inability to conceive of Jesus as a suffering Messiah renders them incapable of being true followers. Citing Mark 9:33-35; 10:23-31, 35-43, Weeden concludes that a "commitment to suffering discipleship [is] demanded of disciples of a suffering Messiah."[25] By extension, a disciple is one who not only recognizes Jesus as the Messiah but also perceives what kind of Messiah he is—a suffering Messiah.

Weeden's final stage is that of rejection. Weeden traces the disciples' behavior in chapter 13 to show that Judas was not the only one to reject Jesus. The disciples' rejection of Jesus culminates in Peter's denial. For Weeden, the disciples' rejection of Jesus reflects the Markan community's rejection of the suffering Christology espoused by Jesus and advocated by Mark in favor of a *theios anēr* (God-human or divine human) Christology.

Weeden argues that the first half of Mark's Gospel (1:1—8:29) is dominated by the *theios anēr* Christology. Characteristic of this perspective is the announcement of Jesus as the Son of God in the opening of the Gospel and the "wonder-working activities of Jesus."[26] Peter's confession in 8:27-29 is consequently a confession of the *theios anēr* Christology. This is precisely what prompts his rebuke of Jesus in 8:32 so quickly after his confession. Jesus teaches that he is a suffering Messiah. However, Jesus' self-description contradicts who Peter has accepted him to be. In this stage, the disciples have moved beyond imperceptivity and misconception to a refusal to accept who they now know Jesus is. Thus, true discipleship is one that embraces Jesus as the suffering Messiah.

In Weeden's work, one can construct a definition of discipleship that includes an understanding of who Jesus is, the kind of messiahship he embodies, and the necessity for one to accept him as the suffering Messiah. He writes, "The only authentic characteristic of Messiahship is that of suffering, a suffering and humiliation that leads to death."[27] Therefore, suffering is the dividing line between true and false messiahship in Weeden's reading. Suffering then becomes the determining factor between true and false discipleship. As noted above, Weeden alleges that suffering discipleship is not only necessary but also demanded of those who follow a suffering Messiah. The *theios anēr* Christology is wrong from a Markan perspective precisely because of its stance on suffering. It is a Christology "pitted against the suffering Messiahship of Jesus."[28] Therefore, suffering is the identifying mark of discipleship, for it is the only genuine characteristic of messiahship.

For Weeden, suffering is as much a part of Jesus' identity as is his commission as Messiah, the Son of God, in his baptismal scene (1:9-13). And yet he posits no reason for Jesus' suffering. Because Jesus' suffering is integrally linked to the suffering of his disciples, we are therefore left with no explanation or understanding of the disciples' suffering. One has no indication how to live, except to suffer, since according to Weeden, one must be committed to a suffering discipleship. Simply stated: discipleship is suffering.

Weeden's use of the term *suffering* comes closest to its womanist counterpart. The suffering that characterizes Weeden's version of discipleship is unmetabolized, unscrutinized agony. His interpretation, therefore, is highly problematic for African American women. It confines African American women's understanding of Jesus as the divine cosufferer *only*. No other points of identification with Jesus are necessary. As long as one suffers, she or he is a disciple. Consequently, African American women become disciples simply based upon their existential context of suffering. Should they seek to understand the agony they endure and fight against it, they would no longer be disciples or in relationship with Jesus. Weeden's interpretation maintains the perpetual suffering of African American women by making suffering their only point of connection with Jesus.

∞ *Dei* in Mark 8:31 as Divine Necessity

Several scholars have interpreted Mark's use of the term *dei* as divine necessity, which for them involves the idea that God wills suffering both for Jesus and for his disciples.

Joanna Dewey

In *Disciples of the Way*, Joanna Dewey defines a disciple as "one who learns, a pupil, an apprentice, or more generally speaking, an adherent, a follower."[29] Contra Robert Meye, Dewey expands the number of disciples in Mark's Gospel to include "the inner core of three (or four), 'the twelve,' and a larger group who followed Jesus and/or participated in his ministry."[30] Dewey is able to expand the number of disciples because she argues that the basis of discipleship is following Jesus.[31] Following is the "first step on the way" and is a necessary component of discipleship: "It is only by following Jesus that we can come to understand what the gospel is, the nature of the kingdom and of Jesus."[32] Whereas Meye argued that being with Jesus necessitated following, Dewey contends that following is what allows the disciples to be with him.[33] Following and being with Jesus produce a "greater knowledge of Jesus,"[34] thereby equipping the disciples to "engage in the same activities as Jesus,"[35] namely, preaching and teaching. A disciple, then, is one who follows Jesus, is with Jesus, and participates in the same ministry activities as Jesus.

Dewey, however, does note another element of discipleship: suffering. She sees suffering as God's will for Jesus and part of discipleship. She contends that according to 8:31 the suffering and death of Jesus are "according to the will of God."[36] The result is that God has already determined the suffering of Jesus as foreshadowed in 3:6. The rejection of the religious elite and the plotting of the Pharisees and Herodians become a part of God's divine plan: "It is according to God's will that Jesus must suffer and die."[37]

Suffering, however, is not reserved for Jesus only. Dewey states that suffering is "a condition of discipleship" that happens to "true disciples."[38] Suffering, by her own admission, is a condition rather than a consequence of discipleship. Interestingly enough, Dewey does acknowledge the hostility of the world toward Jesus' ministry and that of his followers. She admits that since "the world has power," it will cause the followers of Jesus to suffer.[39] Yet she insists on subsuming the world's actions under God's intent. She does not posit a connection between Jesus' ministry and his suffering and death. Because her interpretation does not acknowledge moral evil, it divests the world of all responsibility and places it squarely on God's shoulders.

Ernest Best

Ernest Best claims that the purpose of Mark's Gospel is to show "what true discipleship is."[40] By chronicling the successes and failures of Jesus' disciples, Mark presents the readers with examples to follow and behaviors to avoid.[41] Best notes two critical elements for understanding discipleship: an understanding of Jesus and one's relationship to him[42] and an understanding of Jesus' death and resurrection.[43] For Best, a disciple can only be a disciple if she or he has a correct understanding of who Jesus is. Referencing Mark 8:27-33, he concludes that discipleship is linked to confession.[44] However, confession in and of itself is not enough because the disciple is drawn into not a static but a dynamic relationship with Jesus in which she or he embarks on a journey under his command.[45]

Best employs the language of the Gospel, *following*, to articulate the idea that disciples take their lead from Jesus, even though they may not be required to perform in the same way as Jesus. Best does not start with being with Jesus or include this in his definition of following. In this way, he opens up discipleship for those who do not experience the physical presence of Jesus.

Following Jesus is obeying the will of God and the demands of Jesus (see, by way of comparison, 1:16-18).[46] By so doing, the disciples attach themselves to Jesus. "Taking up their crosses" and "deny[ing] themselves" characterize this attachment.[47] For Best, "the rule of discipleship is: Jesus. As Jesus was, so the disciples must be."[48] Yet he maintains that Jesus is always unique in that "disciples of Christ never become Christs or have their own disciples."[49] Consequently, Best argues against any attempt to define discipleship solely in terms of imitation.

For Best, "the nature of discipleship becomes apparent only in light of the cross."[50] He describes the cross in Mark's Gospel as that which is not "thrust on disciples; it does not represent difficult sets of circumstances which they cannot evade; it means they move forward of their own freewill into such difficult situations."[51] The cross, then, is a choice that stems from the disciples' decision to follow Jesus. The suffering of the disciple is connected to his or her decision to follow Jesus and, therefore, carry the cross. Best states, "To take the cross is to take an active step in the direction of suffering and endurance."[52] Given Jesus' instructions in Mark 8:34, this is a necessary step on the road of discipleship. In this sense, discipleship includes being prepared to suffer. In fact, one chooses suffering.

Best presses this point further in his explication of Mark 8:31—9:1. He asserts that the failure of the disciples at the end of the Gospel is implicit in chapter 8 because it is here that "discipleship is defined as suffering and they have shown themselves unable to appreciate suffering as God's way."[53] Best sees suffering as God's way because he interprets the *dei* in 8:31 as divine necessity: "The 'must' is the 'must' of divine necessity, not that of human chance or human political reckoning that defiance of the authorities will lead to their powerful opposition. As we move towards the death this predestined element becomes more explicit."[54] As noted above, Best acknowledges human political reckoning but does not connect it to Jesus' suffering. Jesus' suffering is predestined. He suffers as the result of a divine plan that the religious authorities unwittingly follow.

Likewise in *Mark: The Gospel as Story*, Best addresses the element of suffering as it is linked to discipleship in the Gospel. He concludes that Christians live "in two modes of existence, one of suffering [and] risen life."[55] Thus, he states that the "goal might more adequately be described as Jesus himself rather than the cross or even the cross and the resurrection."[56]

The goal of discipleship, then, is not so much the replication of Jesus, for that would suggest imitation. Instead, it is obedience to Jesus, the decision to do things God's way. However, Best has already asserted that suffering is God's way. Therefore, discipleship, which is obedience to Jesus and doing things God's way, becomes suffering in Best's interpretation. Although it is not necessary for the disciples to suffer in the exact way Jesus did (for this would be imitation), suffering is necessary. By interpreting *dei* as divine necessity, suffering becomes the purpose or goal rather than a consequence of discipleship in a hostile world.

Augustine Stock

Augustine Stock, like Werner Kelber and Robert Tannehill (see discussion below), situates his discussion of discipleship primarily in Mark 8:21—10:45.[57] He states that the majority of Jesus' teaching occurs after Peter's confession at Caesarea Philippi and is "devoted especially to discipleship."[58] From this section, he identifies several characteristics of discipleship: "to deny oneself, to go take up one's cross, to lose one's life, to be last and least, to drink the cup that Jesus is to drink, and to be baptized with Jesus' baptism."[59]

Discipleship also includes service[60] and a commitment to preach the good news to others.[61] These characteristics find their purpose in Jesus. Stock argues that "discipleship cannot be built around a self-fulfillment scheme; the goal of life is [Jesus], not self."[62]

Because Jesus is the goal of discipleship, "Jesus leads the way and the disciples are to follow him."[63] Following is necessary in order for a disciple to know who Jesus is and to gain an understanding of who she or he is.[64] However, following Jesus is not without risks.[65] In his explication of Mark 8:31, Stock declares that in his response to Peter's confession, Jesus equates his own ministry with suffering: "Immediately Jesus goes on to say that to be the Christ means to suffer."[66]

Because Stock interprets *dei* in 8:31 as divine necessity, he makes the same interpretive move in 14:36, asserting that "in the Garden, Jesus came to terms with the necessity of his suffering."[67] By accepting "the cup" in his prayer, Jesus "allows for the divine plan of passion."[68] Jesus suffers because it is God's plan for him to do so. Since Stock argues that the goal of discipleship is Jesus and states that Jesus equates his identity as the Christ with suffering, to be a disciple means to suffer. Stock follows this line of thought when he writes, "Then Jesus goes on to say that to be a Christian means to suffer."[69] Like Weeden, Stock believes that suffering is a key, if not a defining, feature of discipleship.

Morna Hooker

In *The Message of Mark*, Morna Hooker writes, "Mark's Gospel is the good news about Jesus Christ. But it is also a story about discipleship."[70] She then begins to trace the theme of discipleship throughout the narrative. Upon reaching Mark 8:27—10:45, she notes that the theme of discipleship is only beginning. For within this section, not only is there a "great deal of teaching on discipleship," but also "the meaning of discipleship is spelt out clearly."[71] Hooker points to Mark 8:34 for the definition of discipleship: "Those who wish to be Jesus' disciples must deny themselves, take up the cross and follow him."[72]

Hooker consistently identifies discipleship as *following*. She affirms that discipleship should be understood in terms of following as imitating Jesus: "Commentators frequently shy away from suggesting that discipleship is seen in terms of the imitation of Christ in the New Testament, but there is no doubt that Mark sees it in these terms in the chapters that follow."[73] She grounds her argument in the third passion prediction (Mark 10:32-45), in which James and John request seats on the left and right of Jesus. When Jesus states that they will drink from the same cup and share in his baptism, Hooker interprets this saying as a call to imitate him. She notes, "Those who are called to be rulers of the Christian community must follow the example of their master."[74] Yet she does acknowledge that in this passage Jesus' death and resurrection are unique because Jesus does these things for them in a way that cannot be copied.[75]

Hooker seeks to hold together the unique identity and work of Jesus and the call to imitate him. What Jesus does is done on behalf of or for others in a way that the actions of his disciples are not. At the same time, following Jesus does require the disciples to imitate him, to do as he has done. She refers to this as a "complementary truth that he is our example that discipleship means following him and suffering with him."[76] However, the connection is morbid. She writes, "In some mysterious way, which is not spelt out, the sufferings of one man are used by God to bring benefit to others."[77] Jesus' suffering accomplishes something that benefits others, whereas the disciples suffer only to imitate Jesus.

Hooker states that Mark "links the death of Jesus with the suffering of others, both before him and after him."[78] She shows the connection between the fate of John the Baptist and that of Jesus. She points to the three passion predictions followed by Jesus' teaching on discipleship to demonstrate the link between Jesus' death and the suffering of those after him. For Hooker, discipleship and suffering go hand in hand since discipleship is predicated upon Jesus' suffering and death.

Hooker further enforces this point by noting that Jesus' death is not a substitute for his disciples but rather the pattern for them.[79] She states, "Mark has emphasized the link between the sufferings of Jesus and the demands he makes of his disciples."[80] The passion predictions followed by Jesus' lessons on discipleship bear witness to this claim. Because Jesus suffers, the disciple who follows him must suffer also. Suffering, therefore, is necessary. "The cross is the mark of the Christian," she writes.[81]

Hooker goes on to posit three reasons for the death of Jesus.[82] First, Jesus' death is part of God's divine plan in that the Son of Man must suffer (Mark 8:31). Second, Jesus is obedient to God's will and goes the way of suffering and death. Third, there is the refusal and rejection of human beings who desire to destroy him. Thus, the suffering of Jesus lies within the will of God and the rejection of humans.

For Hooker, the divine plan is that Jesus suffers and dies. Human beings reject him; however, their rejection is part of the divine plan. Based on her assertions that the theme of imitation is found throughout Mark's Gospel, especially in the discipleship section of 8:27—10:45, and that Jesus' death is a pattern for his disciples, it would stand to reason that it is also the will of God for the followers of Jesus to suffer. In Hooker's interpretation, discipleship becomes suffering because of an imitative pattern that follows Jesus to his death.

Jack Kingsbury

Jack Kingsbury defines a disciple as "one who is a committed follower of Jesus."[83] For Kingsbury, this could be the Twelve or others who follow him. However, a disciple is not merely a follower, but one who "join[s] oneself to Jesus in total allegiance."[84] That allegiance is articulated in the language of Mark 8:34: carrying the cross and practicing self-denial. The characteristics of discipleship found in this passage form the "essence of discipleship."[85] Moreover, discipleship is about servanthood.[86] A disciple is one who engages in ministry directed toward others. This focus is primarily mission oriented, for disciples are called to be "fishers of men [sic]."[87]

Kingsbury also makes the reader aware of the context of discipleship. He writes, "Mark's story of Christ is a story of conflict between Jesus and Israel."[88] Thus, discipleship consists of following Jesus in a ministry marked by opposition that will culminate in Jesus' suffering and death. Kingsbury defines the "heart of his ministry" as suffering and death.[89] He notes that in Mark 8:31, Jesus "teaches his disciples . . . that it is God's will that he suffer and die."[90] He, too, interprets *dei* as divine necessity. Whereas discipleship is defined in Mark 8:34, Jesus' ministry is "defined by the passion predictions and centers on his suffering and death."[91]

For both Jesus and his disciples, servanthood is a necessary part of ministry. Kingsbury describes the servanthood Jesus espouses as "submission to suffering and the taking of his life."[92] Kingsbury therefore articulates Jesus' purpose as follows:

> God sent Jesus not only to preach, call disciples, teach, heal and exorcise demons but also to suffer and die (and rise). Sent by God to suffer and die, both God and Jesus will Jesus' death, for by it he establishes a new covenant and accomplishes atonement for sins and universal salvation.[93]

Thus, Kingsbury understands the ministry of Jesus in terms of his suffering and death, both of which are Jesus' primary purposes.

The suffering and death of Jesus are both the will of God and the will of Jesus. In addition, the religious authorities play a role in Jesus' demise. Kingsbury writes, "Utterly convinced they are doing the will of God, the authorities do whatever is necessary to bring Jesus to the cross."[94] The authorities act in response to Jesus' ministry. Therefore, it is Jesus' commitment to doing God's will by preaching, calling disciples, teaching, healing, and exorcising demons that necessitates the cross. Yet Kingsbury's reading does not connect the religious elites' opposition to Jesus' ministry and his suffering.

In bringing Jesus to the cross, Kingsbury states that the religious elites "unwittingly oppose God by repudiating the Son and King he sent them."[95] There is an apparent contradiction in Kingsbury's rationale for Jesus' suffering and death. He argues consistently that Jesus' ministry is based upon his suffering and death. His suffering and death are the will of God and the very purpose for which he is sent. Yet when the religious authorities bring about the suffering and death of Jesus, which both God and Jesus will, they are said to oppose God. Since God wills Jesus' suffering and the religious leaders cause Jesus' suffering, the religious leaders actually support God by killing Jesus.

What is clear in Kingsbury's interpretation is that the suffering and death of Jesus are ultimately the will of God and the choice of Jesus. Jesus lives out his sense of servanthood by submitting to the suffering willed by God and the taking of his life. Because discipleship requires the same kind of servanthood, discipleship is also characterized by submission to suffering and the losing of one's life. In this interpretation, the suffering of the disciple has no purpose. Jesus' suffering is redemptive. However, the disciple suffers because this is what God and Jesus will. The disciple, therefore, is left to suffer like Jesus without being able to achieve the same purpose as Jesus.

A Womanist Perspective on Dei as Divine Necessity

The above interpretations are inadequate from a womanist point of view because they advance a mode of discipleship that requires agony, the disturbance of our inner tranquility caused by physical, mental, emotional, social, and spiritual forces that we grasp as jeopardizing our lives, our very existence. By insisting that *dei* expresses divine necessity, the agony discussed by these authors is suffering. The suffering espoused here depicts a static condition in that to stop suffering is to forsake the way of God and terminate one's discipleship. This line of thought requires one to continually suffer in order to be a disciple. Therefore, one's suffering cannot be transformed into something else without fundamentally changing one's identity as a follower of Jesus. The above interpretations once again limit suffering to African American women's identification with Jesus. Jesus as the divine cosufferer is no longer a dominant understanding; it must become *the* understanding if African American women are to be disciples.

Because Dewey, Hooker, and Kingsbury do not employ the category of moral evil, they do not posit human culpability for the death of Jesus or the agony of his disciples. Each of them positions the religious rulers who plot to kill Jesus on the side of God. They are part of the divine plan. Their interpretations suggest that to oppose the status quo is to oppose God's way. Consequently, they offer no understanding of discipleship that encourages resistance to the dehumanizing conditions that affect African American women's lives. Through the lenses offered by Dewey, Hooker, and Kingsbury for viewing Mark's Gospel, African American women's suffering is the will of God, and to resist suffering is to resist God.

The Interpretive Priority of Mark 8:31—10:52

Several interpreters have contended that the central passage in Mark regarding suffering is 8:31—10:52. Among them are Robert Tannehill and Werner Kelber.

Robert Tannehill

In "The Disciples in Mark's Gospel: The Function of a Narrative Role," Robert Tannehill performs a narrative reading of the Gospel. He contends that "close attention to the composition of the Marcan narrative can guide us to a better understanding of the disciples' role in Mark."[96] This reading is possible because "Mark narrates a single, unified story."[97] By performing a narrative reading, Tannehill can point out the contradictions found in Weeden's work. He argues that Weeden places Jesus in opposition to himself. For Weeden, the Jesus depicted before 8:31 represents the *theios anēr* Christology, while the Jesus depicted after 8:31 represents the true Christology. In effect, Jesus after 8:31 must nullify the work of the Jesus before 8:31 in order to assert the true Christology. The only basis by which to do this is suffering.[98]

Tannehill also refutes Meye's limitation of the disciples in Mark to the Twelve. While acknowledging the Twelve as having a special relationship with Jesus, Tannehill argues that the disciples include those around Jesus because there are some "common characteristics which define the group" and are broad enough to include others besides the Twelve.[99] His criterion for determining who is a disciple is twofold. A disciple is one who has "responded positively to Jesus and his message" and is "bound to Jesus in a continuing bond."[100] Both of these criteria equal *following*. Tannehill notes that those whom Jesus healed responded positively, but not all had a continuing relationship with him.[101] As with Dewey, his definition of discipleship affirms that following enables them to have a continuing relationship or be with Jesus.

The basis of Tannehill's understanding of discipleship is grounded in his interpretation of Mark 8:31—10:45. He refers to this section as the "authoritative commentary on discipleship."[102] Tannehill highlights two aspects of discipleship that he derives from this section. The disciple is to follow Jesus in his suffering and become a servant.[103] Therefore, Jesus places "special importance [on] the issues of suffering and desire for status" in his teachings.[104] Jesus is not only the teacher but also the model for the disciples. Tannehill writes, "Jesus represents the positive alternative to the failure of the disciples. He not only calls the disciples to save their lives by losing them and to be servants, but he follows this way himself."[105] The primary emphasis for discipleship, then, is suffering and servanthood.

Although Tannehill does a narrative reading, he makes the same mistake as Weeden: he does not read 8:31—10:45 in light of what precedes it. While he does not place Jesus in contradiction with himself, Tannehill does not read the narrative consistently to develop a picture of discipleship that defines servanthood and suffering in reference to Jesus' ministry. Consequently, Tannehill never explains why Jesus suffers. He simply refers to suffering as something Jesus chooses.[106] Jesus, then, teaches his disciples how to suffer: "The teaching points to Jesus' suffering as a model for Jesus' followers (esp. 8:34-35 and 10:45)."[107]

Tannehill misses the point of Meye's work that emphasizes ministry, specifically teaching, as a major choice of Jesus. Although he does not follow through on his original conclusion, Meye notes that Jesus' *ministry* choices are what evoke the anger and violence of the ruling authorities. If Meye is right, when Jesus chooses to suffer, he does so only because he chooses ministry, and that ministry upsets the status quo. Because Tannehill's emphasis on 8:31—10:52 ignores this point, discipleship degenerates into a form of suffering servanthood.

Werner Kelber

In *Mark's Story of Jesus*, Werner Kelber states that the "Gospel of Mark serves as an example of the deliberate integration of the realities of suffering and death."[108] He points to the reason for Jesus' suffering by identifying his objective and purpose. The principle objective is to overcome the powers of evil that impede the realization of God's kingdom. This is evidenced by the Spirit-driving Jesus into the wilderness to be tempted by Satan (1:12-13).[109] Thus, Jesus' purpose is to "bring the Kingdom of God."[110]

Kelber notes that what Jesus proclaims and practices is in contradiction to the status quo. The first controversy cycle (2:1—3:6) demonstrates this fact. The charge of blasphemy in 2:5-7 foretells the charge that will "seal Jesus' death sentence (14:64)."[111] Because the religious authorities accuse Jesus of blasphemy as a result of his healing the paralytic, their persecution of Jesus will arise from their attack on his ministry. Yet Kelber ignores this narrative flow that his own work suggests. Instead, he stresses that suffering and death are precisely what give meaning to Jesus' life: "[Jesus] spares no effort to make them see the meaning of his life. He is going to be a suffering and rejected person, tormented, spat upon and killed."[112]

Kelber sees Markan discipleship as "unambiguously [defined] in terms of following a suffering Jesus."[113] He argues that the lessons on discipleship are "modeled after a suffering Jesus who is on his way to the cross."[114] Using Mark 8:22—10:52, Kelber characterizes discipleship as "carrying the cross," being the "first in service," and demonstrating a "willingness to suffer."[115] Following Jesus comprises these three components. Kelber therefore concludes his interpretation by stating that a Christian is one who follows Jesus (and is therefore willing to suffer), "drinks the cup of suffering" (actually endures suffering), and is "concerned with the salvation of others."[116] Moreover, suffering is a positive attribute of discipleship because suffering, toil, and pain are the prerequisites for reward and success. Without suffering, toil, and pain, reward and success cannot be achieved, for there is "no reward without toil and pain" and "no success without the suffering that precedes it."[117] Unfortunately, the disciples "fail to accept the suffering Jesus and the concept of suffering discipleship."[118]

Kelber's interpretation of Mark's story places great emphasis on suffering. It is the basis of both messiahship and discipleship. Based on his own work, however, Kelber has shown that the opposition to Jesus' ministry in Mark 1 is connected to his death in chapter 13. Consequently, Kelber does not follow his own research to its logical conclusion: Jesus' life gives meaning to his death.

A Womanist Perspective on the Interpretive Priority of Mark 8:31—10:52

Both Tannehill and Kelber miss the causal connections in Mark's Gospel. A diunital approach would aid in exposing the connections between Jesus' ministry and his death, thereby shifting the context of interpretation from suffering to pain. In similar manner, discipleship would be seen in relation to pain rather than suffering. Therefore, agony would not be a constant state but a temporary stage toward the eradication of suffering. As their interpretations stand, suffering is a necessary and therefore constant part of discipleship. Consequently, their interpretations are insufficient because they offer support for the maintenance rather than the elimination of Black women's suffering.

Old Testament Allusions as Explanations of Suffering

Among those who interpret Mark's theology of suffering from Old Testament perspectives are Sean Fréyne, Norman Perrin, and Joel Marcus.

Sean Fréyne

Sean Fréyne devotes very little attention to exploring Jesus' ministry. He does note that the disciples are to "carry on a mission very similar to that of Jesus himself, preaching and casting out devils."[119] Whereas Meye emphasizes teaching, Fréyne points to Jesus' preaching. Both limit the disciples in Mark's Gospel to the Twelve.[120] Fréyne does, however, acknowledge the possibility, if not probability, of future disciples.

He posits that Jesus' "real purpose" was to "reveal fully the mystery that is hidden and to open the way to true discipleship for those who are prepared to follow Jesus from the slavery of sin and ignorance."[121]

Using the Twelve as examples, Fréyne identifies three characteristics of discipleship. The first is to be with Jesus. Being with Jesus is essential to discipleship because it is only in the presence of Jesus that they receive special instruction.[122] The disciples are to "be with Jesus to learn from him, to learn about him."[123] They have been given the mystery of the kingdom that Fréyne defines as "primarily the proper understanding of the person of Jesus."[124] Armed with this understanding, their task is not only to receive the mystery but also to share it with the community of faith.[125]

Because the disciples' task is to share the mystery with the community of faith, Fréyne concludes that their "special function is to 'preach.'"[126] They must proclaim the good news that both is preached by and centers on Jesus.[127] Within the narrative purview of Mark's Gospel, this task is never fulfilled. When the Twelve are sent out, they "preached that men should repent" (6:12, Freyne's translation). Fréyne argues that their proclamation did not include an announcement of the good news (see, by way of comparison, 1:15) and was therefore "confined to the preliminary aspect of preaching repentance."[128] In any case, the disciples are called to continue the work of Jesus. As Fréyne puts it, "They are to be the projection and extension of the mission of Christ in the post-resurrection era."[129]

This mission will include not only preaching but also an attack on the powers of Satan.[130] Just as Mark links preaching and exorcisms in Jesus' ministry, he does the same for the disciples. From the beginning, Jesus' ministry opposes satanic forces. Fréyne specifically notes that "on one occasion Satan is ready to make Peter his tool to try to prevent Jesus from going his road of suffering (8:32), but Jesus is able to rebuke him and ward off the danger."[131] According to Fréyne's reading, *Satan* opposes Jesus' suffering. If Jesus' road of suffering is opposed by Satan, God must affirm it. This brings us to our third characteristic of discipleship: suffering.

For Fréyne, the nature of discipleship is that those who are disciples "must be prepared to suffer if they wish to be followers of Jesus."[132] In his exposition of Mark 8:27—10:52, Fréyne posits that the "idea of suffering" is "central" to this section and concludes that "Mark wants to indicate that the true disciple must be prepared to take the road of suffering, following the Master."[133] He believes that Mark pushes this idea of suffering one step further in that a disciple "must be prepared to follow even to death."[134] Therefore, Fréyne writes, the "idea of a suffering Messiah is presented to them and the need for 'following' him in his suffering to be really his disciple is stressed."[135] The suffering of the disciples is connected to the suffering and death of Jesus, following the Master. Following Jesus is following in the way of suffering and death.

Unlike Meye, who focuses on Jesus' ministry and at least acknowledges the connection between his ministry (that is, teaching) and suffering, Fréyne links Jesus' suffering and death exclusively to God. He interprets Jesus' passion in light of one Old Testament passage. In his discussion of Mark 14:27, 50, he notes Mark's use of Zech 13:7[136] to interpret the abandonment of Jesus by his disciples. Fréyne writes, "In this way the desertion of the 12, like the death of Jesus itself, is shown to be God-willed."[137] He therefore locates the cause of Jesus' suffering primarily in the person of God. To be with Jesus, in Fréyne's reading, is to follow him on the path of God-willed or -ordained suffering.

Although Fréyne acknowledges Jesus' ministry as presenting an attack on satanic powers, he does not connect this to Jesus' suffering and death. Rather, Satan stands in opposition to Jesus' suffering while God supports it! Neither does he point out the obvious conflict between Jesus and the religious leaders. Rather than exploring the Gospel narrative for an explanation of Jesus' suffering and death, Fréyne opts for a theological reason grounded in the interpretation of a single Old Testament passage.

Norman Perrin

Norman Perrin asserts that Mark uses the "Son of Man" designation for Jesus to teach about the "true nature" of Christian discipleship and messiahship[138]; it is all about suffering. He grounds his interpretation in a "passion apologetic" in Mark 9:12 and 14:21 based on a Christian exegetical tradition of Psalm 118, which aids in "stressing the scriptural necessity for Jesus' suffering."[139] Like Fréyne, Perrin looks to the Old Testament for his explanation. However, Psalm 118:18 specifically states, "The LORD has punished me severely, but he did not give me over to death." Perrin uses a scripture that says God did not give the psalmist over to death to assert the scriptural necessity of Jesus' death. In Mark's Gospel, Jesus is given over to die. By appealing to this tradition, Perrin identifies God as the cause of Jesus' suffering.

Perrin tries to bolster his interpretation by connecting Mark 8:31 to Psalm 118: "*Dei* must be seen as a reference to the divine necessity for the passion revealed in scripture and 'be rejected' . . . is a reference to Ps. 118."[140] Because Perrin claims Jesus' suffering and death are divinely necessitated, as suggested by *dei*, he assumes Psalm 118 supports his reading. He then joins Mark 8:31 to Mark 10:45.

According to Perrin, 10:45 is the "climax to the section 8:27—10:52, which we all recognize is intended as the introduction of the passion and the vehicle for the suffering sayings."[141] In Perrin's opinion, Mark 10:45 represents a movement from "scriptural necessity to the idea of soteriological significance [which is] in fact at the heart of Mark's theological enterprise."[142] In effect, Perrin has woven together an Old Testament allusion with Mark 8:31 and 10:45 to conclude Jesus' suffering was divinely intended to fulfill the Scriptures.

Perrin alleges that Mark is correcting a false Christology, demonstrated by the disciples, with a true Christology, taught by Jesus. According to Perrin, Mark uses the "Son of Man" reference in 2:28 to "give content to the conception of Jesus as Son of God"[143] and in 8:31 to "introduce the notion of the suffering element into the Son of Man Christology."[144] It is in the first passion prediction (8:31) and the two successive ones (9:35; 10:38) that Mark presents his understanding of discipleship.

Perrin identifies three key elements that demonstrate the nature of discipleship. First, a disciple must be "prepared to take up the cross."[145] Second, one must be "prepared to be last and servant of all."[146] Third, Jesus explicates servanthood in 10:45 as "giving [one's] life as a ransom for many."[147] Every element must include suffering, as true discipleship is "the way to glory through suffering."[148] This coincides with his understanding of true messiahship as "including suffering and glory."[149] Perrin therefore reaches a conclusion similar to Weeden: not only is it necessary for Jesus to suffer, but the "necessity for suffering is laid also upon the disciples."[150] Whereas Weeden offered no explanation for Jesus' suffering, Perrin grounds it in an allusion to Psalm 118 and connections he draws to Mark 8:31 and 10:45.

Joel Marcus

In *The Way of the Lord*, Joel Marcus reads Mark's Gospel against the backdrop of the Jewish Roman War and the Old Testament. He states, "Where Jesus acts, there God is acting."[151] Consequently, the way of Jesus is the way of the Lord.[152] Referencing Mark 8:31, Marcus describes the way of the Lord as the "path to suffering and death . . . foretold in the scriptures."[153] Apparently, Marcus assumes that Old Testament prophecies do not simply foretell the future but represent the will of God. Marcus knows Jesus' suffering is divinely willed because he assumes that the Scriptures necessitate rather than predict his suffering. For Marcus, foreknowledge equals predestination. In other words, the Old Testament requires that Jesus *must* suffer rather than foretelling that Jesus *will* suffer. This is the same logic he uses to interpret Mark 10:45.

Marcus argues that the way of the Lord is a "journey up to suffering and death," which is a "victorious assault of the divine warrior on the resistant cosmos."[154] Jesus achieves this victorious assault through his atoning death. His death has atoning value because Mark 10:45 and 14:24 allude to Isaiah 53.[155] By connecting the Markan passages to Isaiah's suffering servant, Marcus concludes that the Gospel posits an atonement theory. However, even Marcus admits that his interpretation is questionable. He notes that "the Deutero-Isaian Servant Songs in the Markan passion narratives are not as pervasive as the allusions to the Psalms of the Righteous Sufferer."[156]

The allusions to the Psalms of the Righteous Sufferer in the Markan passion narrative portray a very different picture of Jesus' suffering. Marcus acknowledges that the "New Testament present[s] the idea that the righteous one must suffer on account of his righteousness, but that he will be glorified at the eschaton."[157] Within this framework, the righteous suffers precisely because she or he is righteous. Because one's works evidence one's righteousness, righteous action will incur suffering. Since the Psalms of the Righteous Sufferer are more strongly connected to the passion narrative than the Suffering Servant Songs, one would think the text better supports a reading that Jesus' suffering is the result of his righteous ministry rather than an atoning work.

Marcus defines discipleship as "following Jesus in the way of the cross (8:34, 10:52) or being with Jesus (see, by way of comparison, 3:14)."[158] Because suffering characterizes Jesus' ministry, and his ministry is understood primarily as atonement, suffering also characterizes discipleship. Jesus' ministry requires suffering. To follow him or to be with him places his disciples in the midst of that suffering.

In addition, Marcus ascribes value to the suffering of the disciples. After asserting the salvific nature of Jesus' suffering and death, Marcus goes on to question whether the disciples' suffering is salvific. Referencing Mark 8:34, he concludes that they are called to participate in Jesus' suffering, and as long as their suffering is linked to his, it will be efficacious.[159] Thus, suffering is the only thing that has value because it is through suffering that salvation is wrought. There is no discipleship apart from suffering; only through suffering can a disciple add anything meaningful to the work of the kingdom.

Like Fréyne, who reads Jesus' passion (Mark 14:27, 50) in terms of Zech 13:7, Marcus does not take into consideration the preceding portions of the Gospel. He allows the Old Testament allusions to overshadow the New Testament text. In other words, Marcus sets the Gospel within the context of the Old Testament allusions rather than setting the Old Testament allusions within the context of the Gospel. The result is that Jesus and his disciples suffer because God purposes that suffering. Suffering becomes a condition rather than a consequence of discipleship.

A Womanist Perspective on Old Testament Allusions as Explanations of Suffering

The above interpretations are inadequate for addressing womanist concerns because they conclude that suffering is the will of God and, therefore, a condition of discipleship. Rather than interpreting Jesus' death within the narrative details of his life, they seek meaning in Old Testament allusions. Consequently, they miss the causal connections that a diunital approach exposes.

I contend that these authors do not give adequate attention to the role of the religious rulers in the death of Jesus. As a result, their interpretations demonstrate no awareness of moral evil. What happens to Jesus is what God wanted to happen to Jesus. Within the sociocultural context of African American women, these interpretations affirm that their condition is the way God has willed it. By combining the affirmation of Jesus as the divine cosufferer with Marcus's assertion that suffering is efficacious when linked with Jesus' suffering, we are left with a toxic interpretation that ascribes positive value to African American women's existential suffering. Thus, the interpretations of Fréyne, Perrin, and Marcus posit a relationship between suffering and discipleship that womanists cannot support.

∞ Suffering as a Consequence of Discipleship

Ched Myers, Mary Ann Tolbert, Donald H. Juel, and Brian K. Blount variously interpret suffering in the Gospel of Mark as a consequence of discipleship.

Ched Myers

In *Binding the Strong Man*, Ched Myers employs a socio-literary methodology to perform a political reading of Mark's Gospel.[160] A distinctively different portrait of Jesus emerges. This is due primarily to his methodological approach. Myers states, "A socio-literary method stipulates that the gospel narrative must be interpreted whole, not in isolated parts."[161] Consequently, Myers is able to see narrative connections that previous authors either missed or failed to carry to their logical conclusions.

Myers notes that from the onset of the Gospel, "Jesus' kingdom project is incompatible with the local public authorities and the social order they represent."[162] He characterizes Jesus' ministry as one that "brings wholeness and liberation to the poor."[163] Referencing the controversy cycle in 2:1—3:6, Myers acknowledges Jesus' tenacious commitment to his ministry. Jesus is consistent in "critici[zing] every social code that serves to institutionalize alienation."[164] It is this commitment that will bring about his death.

Based upon his reading of the earlier portion of the Gospel, Myers is able to break away from his predecessors' interpretations of 8:31. Whereas previous works interpreted what has been translated "must" in 8:31 as divine necessity, Myers interprets it as "political inevitability."[165] Jesus' ministry "necessarily comes into conflict with the 'elders and chief priests and scribes' (8:31)."[166] In no way does God intend Jesus' suffering or send him for that purpose. The passion predictions do not express divine intention; rather they are "portents concerning his political fate."[167]

Yet Myers's interpretive stance wavers at Mark 8:34. He defines the command to take up the cross (8:34) as an "invitation to share the consequences facing those who dared to challenge the ultimate hegemony of imperial Rome."[168] Consistent with his understanding of suffering as a consequence of Jesus' ministry, Myers asserts that cross bearing is not about enduring divinely willed suffering. He posits that cross bearing is being willing to endure suffering as a result of following Jesus. Next, he connects self-denial to cross bearing. Self-denial "is the antecedent for cross-bearing," which he defines as risking one's life. [169] According to Myers, Jesus invites his disciples to share the consequences of his ministry and commands them to risk their lives. Moreover, since self-denial is the antecedent of cross bearing, Jesus is commanding the disciples to risk their lives in order to share in his political fate. Although Jesus' suffering is not divinely willed, the suffering of the disciples is commanded.

Because Myers reads Jesus' ministry in strictly political terms, he casts discipleship in the same hue. There are two key themes of discipleship in Myers's view: repentance and resistance. Repentance is "the concrete process of turning away from the empire."[170] Resistance is "shaking off the power of sedation of a society that rewards ignorance and trivializes everything political."[171] In effect, a disciple must be converted to the point that his or her political orientation is changed. The empire and the kingdom of God cannot peacefully coexist. Therefore, disciples must have a change of mind and resist the trappings of a society in opposition to the kingdom of God. Discipleship, then, is "a specific social practice and political engagement."[172]

Myers's work is helpful in establishing the links between Jesus' ministry and his death. His consistent reading of the narrative guards against an erroneous understanding of suffering. Moreover, it suggests that suffering is not a requirement or goal, but a consequence of discipleship.

Mary Ann Tolbert

In *Sowing the Gospel: Mark's World in Literary Perspective*, Mary Ann Tolbert seeks to "articulate at least one possible 'consistent interpretation' of 'the Gospel in all its parts.'"[173] Rather than focusing on 8:31—10:52, she uses the parable of the sower in chapter 4 and the parable of the tenants in chapter 12 as the keys for interpreting the Gospel. Tolbert, like Myers, represents a major shift in Markan scholarship in that she utilizes a narrative approach to read the entire Gospel rather than a particular aspect of the Gospel.

Tolbert's discussion of both passages provides insight into her understanding of Jesus' ministry, suffering and death, and discipleship. Tolbert first notes the *exousia* (power, authority) of Jesus, which is demonstrated in his "performative utterance: what he says, happens; his word performs an act."[174] This kind of power is central to Jesus' ministry and is necessary for his mission, which Tolbert defines as "the preaching of the good news with the authority that effects changes in people's lives."[175] By chapter 4, the reader knows that Jesus is the sower in the parable, and his ministry is to sow the word. Discipleship, then, can be seen as the faithful reception of the word that enables the individual to participate in the transforming activity of Jesus. A disciple is one who will follow Jesus by "do[ing] as he does and teaches."[176]

It soon becomes evident that following Jesus is risky business. In the parable of the tenants, Tolbert posits an explanation for the suffering and death of Jesus. Jesus is the heir, the beloved son, who comes to receive the fruit of the vineyard. "Both his mission and John's are to demand a change of heart and the release of the fruit from the vineyard."[177] Just as the son in the parable is seized, killed, and thrown out of the vineyard,"[178] so too is Jesus. The suffering and death of Jesus, therefore, does not come about because God sends Jesus for the purpose of suffering. She writes:

> God did not send Jesus in order that he might die; rather, the lord of the vineyard sent the final messenger, the beloved son, in the divinely foolish hope that the tenants would revere the son (12:6) and experience a change of heart.[179]

Within this context, we can assume that Mark 8:31 expresses inevitability rather than divine necessity. Jesus is killed for "challenging the authority of the present tenants."[180] It is within this narrative framework that one must interpret Mark 10:45.

Contra Marcus, Tolbert rejects any idea that Jesus is an "innocent sacrifice . . . [that is] to atone for the sinful nature of humankind."[181] Jesus gives his life "for the sake of the Gospel."[182] And a disciple "must emulate" this behavior "for the gospel must be preached."[183] The point of identification between Jesus and the disciple is preaching. Tolbert's reading suggests that Jesus gives his life in his living—not simply his dying—by preaching a gospel that results in his death.

For Tolbert, the suffering and death of Jesus are the result of ministry to "this generation."[184] Jesus' death is a reminder to all who follow him of the opposition that they too will face. Those who follow him will encounter the same resistance. As with Elizabeth Struthers Malbon, Tolbert's work affirms that discipleship is not easy.[185] Yet Tolbert never expounds upon the command to deny oneself, and she speaks about cross bearing only once: "[The] sowing of the word will inevitably bring upon them the wrath of the corrupt authorities of this world and thus their preaching too must be a taking up of their crosses in faith."[186] What, then, is Tolbert's understanding of cross bearing and its relationship to preaching/discipleship?

By following the narrative, she clearly shows suffering as a result of Jesus' ministry in a world that opposes him. Because Jesus suffers as a result of his ministry, one can expect his disciples to encounter the same. Within this framework, suffering is a consequence, not a condition, of discipleship.[187]

Donald H. Juel

Donald H. Juel contends that disciples "are called to be with Jesus and share his ministry of preaching and healing."[188] He describes Jesus' ministry as one that transgresses ritual boundaries that order Jewish life.[189] Mark depicts Jesus as refusing to abide by the limitations of the law as interpreted by the religious authorities. Jesus' ministry, therefore, stands in opposition to the established tradition. Consequently, "followers must be prepared to take up their crosses and follow even all the way to death," for the death of Jesus is the logical result of his ministry.[190]

Unlike Best, Dewey, and Tannehill who see Jesus' suffering and death as divine necessity, Juel agrees with Tolbert and Myers that Jesus suffers because of the rejection of humans.[191] He writes that looking for "the 'necessity' of his death begin[s] not by looking at ultimate reality from God's point of view, but 'from below.'"[192] Mark's narrative provides ample evidence to begin investigating the causes of Jesus' suffering among human beings. Juel points to the boundary-breaking ministry, noting that the religious and political authorities must kill Jesus out of their "need to live within the bounds of the law."[193] Thus, Jesus dies not because God requires it. Human beings require Jesus' death, and God allows it.[194] Juel states, "For God to reclaim a captive creation there must be a battle. And Jesus will be the casualty."[195] Juel follows Mark's narrative to assert that Jesus' suffering and death are a result of his ministry and, by extension, a result of discipleship.

Brain K. Blount

Brian K. Blount, like Juel, identifies boundary breaking as the hallmark of Jesus' ministry. He argues that God desires to "remake Israel" and does so through the economic, political, cultic, and ethnic boundary-breaking ministry of Jesus.[196] Jesus employs preaching as the "tactical representation of God's future kingdom."[197] Those who follow Jesus are to "do what Jesus did."[198] Therefore, discipleship can be understood as "transformatively attacking [boundaries] with manifestations of kingdom preaching."[199]

Blount refers to Jesus' followers' actions as "imitative interventionist attempts to establish the boundary-breaking conditions for a new covenantal relationship with God."[200] However, Blount does not envision discipleship as imitation in the sense of Hooker. Instead, he views the disciples as following in the ministry of Jesus. Like Best, who argues that there will never be more Christs,[201] Blount writes, "Only Jesus represents the kingdom in his person."[202] Both Blount and Best maintain the uniqueness of Jesus' person while seeing him as the example of ministry for his disciples. Jesus' ministry example also shows the disciples the consequences of discipleship.

Blount, along with Myers, Juel, and Tolbert, affirms that the rejection of Jesus' ministry by the religious leaders causes his suffering and death. He asserts that the conclusion drawn from Mark's Gospel is that "Jesus' boundary-breaking kingdom way led directly to the cross."[203] Blount maintains that even though Jesus' kingdom way "all but guaranteed suffering and even death, it was God's way."[204] Consequently, he argues for reading the necessity language in Mark 8:31 in the context of the narrative and argues that one should not conclude "that his suffering is an objective on par with preaching."[205] Similarly, Blount rejects the understanding that the command to take up the cross (Mark 8:34) is a "call to suffer."[206] Although he severs the connection between cross bearing and a call to suffer, Blount remains silent about the first command. Like Myers, Juel, and Tolbert, Blount locates the reasons for Jesus' suffering and death within the narrative. He concludes that suffering is inevitable, but so too is "God's transformative kingdom power and salvation."[207] By so doing, Blount shows the reader that Jesus' suffering and, therefore, the suffering of his disciples will be the result of following the ministry of Jesus.

A Womanist Perspective on Suffering as a Consequence of Discipleship

This final section presents an investigation of the text that corresponds to a diunital approach. These authors employ the presuppositions of narrative criticism to read Mark's Gospel as a consistent and coherent story. Each of the authors interprets both the life and death of Jesus within the context of the Gospel's story world. Moreover, they demonstrate an awareness of moral evil by tracing the causal connections between the backlash of the religious rulers and the death of Jesus. The *dei* in Mark 8:31 expresses inevitability rather than divine necessity. Suffering, then, is a consequence, not a condition, of discipleship. Consequently, their understanding of suffering coincides with our womanist definition of pain.

However, the consistency of this group's interpretations breaks down at Mark 8:34. I have shown in chapter 1 the need to understand cross bearing and self-denial in ways that do not promote the suffering of African American women. When cross bearing is understood as bearing the crosses of others and self-denial equals neglecting one's need for the good of others, these interpretations maintain the surrogacy roles of African American women. To avoid such interpretations, I believe a distinction needs to be made between pain and suffering. This distinction is necessary for establishing a context from which to interpret the commands to take up the cross and deny oneself. If one interprets these commands within the context of one's existential suffering, then cross bearing and self-denial will maintain the present conditions of African American women. African American women will continue to bear the cross of their triple oppression and assume surrogacy roles. I opine that this is why Delores Williams stated that there were enough African American women bearing crosses.[208] If, however, one interprets these commands within the context of pain, one has the possibility of empowering African American women to reject understandings of cross bearing and self-denial, as well as understandings of Jesus as the divine cosufferer, that maintain their suffering, shame, and surrogacy.

∞ Conclusion

This review of Markan interpreters discloses the potential of seeing agony as a result of following Jesus. It also demonstrates the effectiveness of the diunital approach. Moreover, this chapter reveals that Mark 8:31, 34 contain the critical elements of our discussion—the cross, agony, and discipleship. However, the interpretations of Markan scholars do not fully attend to womanist concerns.

The majority of Markan scholars equate suffering with discipleship. Because they do not employ a diunital approach, they insist that according to Mark 8:31, Jesus' suffering was divinely preordained. Consequently, suffering becomes a condition of discipleship. Both cross bearing and self-denial are interpreted within this context of suffering (Mark 8:34). Discipleship becomes a static condition of unmetabolized, unscrutinized agony. This mode of discipleship reinforces the affirmation of Jesus as the divine cosufferer in a way that limits our identification with Jesus and our understanding of how discipleship relates to suffering. Since suffering is the will of God and not the result of moral evil, one must challenge God rather than sinful individuals and institutions for one's deliverance. Moreover, should one escape from his or her suffering, one must relinquish his or her self-identification as a disciple, because to be a Christian means to suffer.

A small group of Markan commentators reach the opposite conclusion. They employ a diunital approach that enables them to assert that Jesus' suffering was not the preordained will of God. It was an inevitable consequence of a ministry that challenged corrupt institutions and the individuals who sustained them. Therefore, Mark 8:31 depicts inevitability rather than divine necessity. They conclude that suffering is a consequence, not a condition, of discipleship. Disciples will experience agony because of moral evil. Thus, their interpretations offer us the possibility of seeing discipleship from the perspective of pain rather than suffering.

These scholars, however, do not maintain their interpretive stance so consistently in their examinations of Mark 8:34. Three of the four scholars neglect the first command—"Let him/her deny him-/herself" (my translation). This portion of verse 34 bears directly upon African American women because the positive moral valuing of loss, sacrifice, and denial turns their self-denial into surrogacy. Consequently, these interpretations overlook an important part of the text that is relevant to African American women. Without sustaining the interpretive context of pain (named and recognized agony that comes as a temporary result of life-affirming behavior) throughout this pericope, African American women's perception of discipleship degenerates into suffering, shame, and surrogacy.

The need remains for an interpretation that integrates the distinctions I have made regarding agony, suffering, and pain language. In addition, Mark 8:34 awaits a womanist exploration that situates these commands within the context of pain. In short, this chapter demonstrates the need to examine the entire pericope, Mark 8:31-38,[209] through a lens crafted by the experience of African American women. I now turn to a methodology that can enable biblical interpretation from a womanist perspective.

chapter three

A Model
for Womanist Reading

THE THEORY PRESENTED HERE IS AN
INSTRUMENT FOR MAKING DESCRIPTIONS, AND
HENCE INTERPRETATIONS, DISCUSSABLE. THAT,
NOT OBJECTIVITY OR CERTAINTY, "BEING RIGHT"
OR "PROVING WRONG," IS THE ISSUE.

—Mieke Bal, *Narratology*[1]

In chapter 1, I examined the sociocultural context of African American women and explored womanist perspectives on Jesus Christ, the cross, suffering, and discipleship. This exploration raised questions about the relationship between agony and discipleship. Chapter 2 showed that the questions raised from an African American female context were not questions Markan scholars were asking. I therefore needed a methodology that would enable me to explore the biblical text from an African American female perspective and answer the questions raised in chapter 1: (1) What is the relationship between the agony that the cross symbolizes and discipleship? (2) Is the agony of the cross suffering or pain? Brian K. Blount's cultural interpretation model provides the methodological framework for my interpretation of Mark.

Blount's methodology is a sociolinguistic approach to biblical interpretation. Sociolinguistics is the "study of language in relation to society."[2] Sociolinguists not only examines the internal structure of the language, as a linguist does, but also its social context. The context is "the total environment in which the text unfold[s]" and "in which [it is] to be interpreted."[3] There are two contexts in which the text is interpreted—the context of culture and the context of situation. The context of culture is "the broader background against which the text is interpreted."[4] It includes "the cultural background and the assumptions that have to be made if the text is to be interpreted."[5] The context of situation is "the immediate environment in which the text is actually functioning."[6] This context is embedded in the text. Therefore, one can ascertain the context of situation through the language of the text itself.[7]

Blount expands the sociolinguistic program by considering both the context (situation and culture) of the text *and* the context of the interpreter and/or interpretive community. His contribution allows me to integrate the sociocultural context of African American women and womanist perspectives, thereby creating a womanist cultural lens through which readers can view the text. Because this methodology defines a text as "language that is functional,"[8] it allows me to consider how the language of the text functions in both the biblical context and the sociocultural context of African American women.

∝ A Sociolinguistic Model

Cultural Interpretation: Reorienting New Testament Criticism is Brian K. Blount's challenge to European biblical interpretation that has dominated the church and academy. Blount maintains, "The text—indeed, all of the New Testament text—must have meaning that is not confined to a single interpretive ideology," that is, the "perspective of standard white European values."[9] Because text interpretation is done according to white European perspective, people working with a different set of values must either adopt these values or remain outside of the interpretive endeavor. The fact that one must adopt a certain set of values to interpret biblical texts "correctly" reveals the obvious: that biblical interpretation is not governed by universal criteria but by the established norms of the Euro-American community. These norms appear to be universal because the Euro-American community has the power to advance them to the exclusion of those that are interpretively significant for other reading communities. Cultural interpretation, therefore, "contest[s] the requirement that marginal members of society adapt their understanding of the text to Eurocentric values and norms already in place."[10] The alternative model for text interpretation that Blount proposes is a composite approach based on Enrique Dussel's liberation theology, M. A. K. Halliday's sociolinguistic theory, and Rudolf Bultmann's existentialism.

Blount appeals to Dussel's sociological model in order to show the power dynamics at play in interpreting a text.[11] He notes that according to Dussel, "all perspectives are not equal when a determinative interpretation is being formulated."[12] Some interpretations are validated and therefore deemed "official" or "scientific" while others are not.[13] Those interpretations that lie outside the "official" one are given the status of "nonbeing, nothing, barbarity, nonsense."[14] Blount then turns to M. A. K. Halliday's sociolinguistic theory to show how meaning is accessed from a text based on the interpreter's background, not purely textual or ideological concerns.

Halliday's sociolinguistic theory is a functional approach to the study of language. His primary thesis is that language is "shaped and determined for what we use it for."[15] Language not only "evolve[s] in the service of functions"; these functions are socially prescribed.[16] He writes, "There will be no bureaucratic mode of discourse in a society without a bureaucracy."[17]

The functional evolution of language is both a societal and individual phenomena. Halliday explains that as individuals mature, their use of language becomes more complex. The primary difference between the language of children and that of adults is one of function. A child's utterance serves only one function at a time. There is a one-to-one ratio between the utterance and its function. The adult, on the other hand, is capable of expressing more than one function in a single utterance. At the adult level, the linguistic system becomes a "grammar"[18] that "provides the mechanism for the different functions to be combined in one utterance in the way that the adult requires."[19]

Because language is functional, Halliday posits three functions or macrofunctions that language performs: the textual, ideational, and interpersonal.[20] These macrofunctions are the foundation of the adult grammatical system. The textual macrofunction is the "grammatical component." It "enables the speaker to organize what he [*sic*] is saying in such a way that it makes sense in context and fulfills its function as a message."[21] The textual macrofunction enables one to create texts rather than simply form strings of words unrelated to each other.[22] The ideational macrofunction "express[es] content in terms of the speaker's experience."[23] This macrofunction enables one to "relay information efficiently and express experiences."[24] Finally, the interpersonal macrofunction is "language as the mediator role."[25] It is "all that may be understood by the expression of our own personalities and personal feelings on the one hand, and forms of interaction and social interplay with other participants in the communication situation on the other hand."[26]

Within this functional model of language theory, Halliday and Ruqaiya Hasan define text as "language that is functional."[27] The textual and ideational macrofunctions "establish boundaries for [a text's] meaning."[28] A text cannot mean whatever an interpreter wants the text to mean. It has limitations. However, each word within the text has a range of possible meanings. The range of possible meanings may be expanded, contracted, or changed when words are linked together to form phrases, colloquial expressions, sentences, and paragraphs. This results in a text with the possibility of multiple interpretations rather than a single interpretation that is deemed "right." This is why Halliday defines language as "meaning potential: that is, as sets of options or alternatives in meaning that are available to the speaker-hearer."[29] The speaker-hearer, then, must determine meaning from among the options and alternatives circumscribed by the ideational and textual macrofunctions. This decision is an *interpersonal* decision and requires the third macrofunction of the adult grammatical system: the interpersonal macrofunction.

The interpersonal macrofunction "alerts us to the fact that language is social."[30] As Blount notes, "Meaning in language must be determined as much from its social context as from its internal structure."[31] In other words, the interpreter chooses a particular meaning from the range of possible meanings based upon his or her understanding of how language functions. Because language is the result of socially prescribed functions, the social context of the interpreter influences the interpretive choices he or she makes. Blount therefore argues that it is the interpersonal macrofunction that enables one to access meaning from the text. [32] The background of the interpreter affects interpretation because the interpreter "determines which elements of the potential are utilized and transcribed as meaningful."[33] In short, the textual and ideational macrofunctions limit what the text can mean; the interpersonal macrofunction determines what the text does mean.

By pointing out that interpretation is based upon interpersonal decisions, Blount challenges claims to universality. There can be no universal interpretation in that there is no universal context. If interpretation involves a relationship with others in a social environment, changes in the social environment will affect the act and, therefore, the conclusions of the interpretive process. I have argued that it is precisely this change in the social environment that causes me to address the issue of suffering differently than my supervised-ministry pastor or the Markan scholars I have surveyed.

The interpersonal macrofunction performs another critical role in that it "establishes one's relationship with others in the social environment."[34] This relationship with the social environment consists of one's participation in, and one's distinctiveness from, that environment.[35] Because the interpersonal macrofunction deals with the interactions of persons in their particular social environment, it operates on two levels: the level of the text and the level of the interpreter. In order to distinguish these two levels, Blount subdivides Halliday's interpersonal macrofunction into two components: the macrointerpersonal component and the microinterpersonal component.

The macrointerpersonal component operates at the level of the text. It is the interpreter's "scholarly attempt to uncover the interpersonal factors involved in the original setting of the work."[36] The macrointerpersonal component, therefore, ascertains the interpersonal factors involved in the original setting of the text.[37] The interpreter attempts to "recreate the biblical world" and interpret it against the backdrop of this reconstructed first-century context. [38]

The microinterpersonal component corresponds to the level of the interpreter. It identifies interpersonal factors at work in the interpreter's act of interpretation.[39] For example, the particular questions that an interpreter brings to the text are microinterpersonally driven. The interpreter will need a methodology that will enable him or her to ask and answer these queries. Therefore, the microinterpersonal component influences the interpreter's decision in selecting a methodology for the macrointerpersonal component.[40]

Blount turns to Rudolf Bultmann to nuance the macro- and the microinterpersonal components. Bultmann's existentialist framework presents two elements that can be interpersonally understood: life-relation and preunderstanding. The life-relation is the "relation of the interpreter to the subject matter that is (directly or indirectly) expressed in texts."[41] The preunderstanding is "a specific understanding of the subject matter of the text, on the basis of a life-relation to it."[42]

Blount further subdivides the macro- and microinterpersonal components using Bultmann's definition of life-relation and preunderstanding. In other words, each interpersonal component consists of a life-relation and a preunderstanding. The macrointerpersonal life-relation is the methodology used to recreate the linguistic context of the biblical speech event. The preunderstanding is composed of the assumptions of that particular methodology. The microinterpersonal life-relation involves the relationship between the interpreter's particular sociohistorical community and the subject matter.[43] It is "the scholar's form of research [that] has a methodological encoding that helps determine the conclusions reached."[44] The preunderstanding reflects the interpreter's "internal interests that influence his or her interpretation."[45]

Now that I have explicated Blount's sociolinguistic model for biblical interpretation, I will show how this framework enables me to do a sociolinguistic reading through a womanist cultural lens.

Using a Sociolinguistic Model for Womanist Biblical Interpretation

One of the salient features of Blount's program is its exposition of the interpersonal macrofunction and its role in interpretation. Specifically, Blount's model shows that all interpretation is microinterpersonally driven. Everyone enters the interpretive process with questions and preunderstandings:

> No exegesis is without presuppositions, inasmuch as the exegete is not a tabula rasa, but on the contrary, approaches the text with specific questions or with a specific way of raising questions and

thus has a certain idea of the subject matter with which the text is concerned.[46]

Blount's model reveals that the questions and presuppositions of the interpreter are the byproducts of his or her life-relation to the subject matter.

In chapter 1, I raised two primary questions: (1) What is the relationship between the agony that the cross symbolizes and discipleship? (2) Is the agony of the cross suffering or pain? My microinterpersonal life-relation, that is, womanist theology, is the context out of which these questions arise.

In chapter 2, I concluded that the majority of Markan scholars' answers to these microinterpersonally driven womanist questions did not attend to womanist concerns. They affirmed suffering as the will of God and, therefore, a condition of discipleship. The review of Markan scholarship also revealed another group of interpreters who employed a methodological strategy that considered both the life and death of Jesus. These interpreters were able to identify causal connections between Jesus' ministry and his crucifixion. Consequently, they posited suffering as a consequence of discipleship. As an interpreter, I am drawn toward a methodology that can reveal these causal connections that coincide with the womanist understandings of Jesus Christ, the cross, suffering, and discipleship articulated in chapter 1. The womanist perspectives outlined in chapter 1 are the bases of my microinterpersonal preunderstanding.

The microinterpersonal life-relation for this project was also delineated in chapter 1. Part of the microinterpersonal life-relation is the diunital approach of womanist theologians. A diunital approach considers both the life and death of Jesus as significant for interpretation. As noted in the conclusion of chapter 2, the diunital approach advanced by womanist scholars in chapter 1 corresponds to the narrative-critical principles of coherence, causation, and contextualization assumed in the work of the final category of Markan scholars in chapter 2. In the macrointerpersonal preunderstanding section, I will show the correspondence between the narrative-critical principles revealed in chapter 2 and sociolinguistics. We shall see that sociolinguistics enables me to maximize the causal connections in the text while also attending to the contexts of the Gospel and the interpreter.

Sociolinguistics allows me to combine the narrative-critical principles of coherence, contextualization, and causation (principles the final set of Markan scholars utilized) with a womanist life-relation and preunderstanding. Moreover, this methodology forms a bridge between biblical criticism and womanist theology. Womanist theology gains a methodology for interpreting the biblical text that coincides with its mandate to examine both the life and death of Jesus. Biblical scholarship gains another lens, crafted by the experience of African American women, through which to view the text.

Finally, I will use the insights from chapter 1 to construct the microinterpersonal preunderstanding. I posit this microinterpersonal preunderstanding as a template for a womanist biblical hermeneutic. In this way, I will link my particular sociocultural perspective to a critical biblical methodology. The result is a methodology that enables me to do biblical interpretation from a womanist perspective.

The Macrointerpersonal Component

Mark 8:31-38 is a narrative. Narratologist Mieke Bal has a very expansive definition of narrative that includes not only texts but also imagery, buildings, and sound. According to Bal, narrative works are not limited to written texts but include *any* text "in which an agent relates ('tells') a story in particular medium: such as language, imagery, sound, buildings, or a combination thereof."[47] At the very least, a narrative is "any work of literature that tells a story."[48] Robert Scholes and Robert Kellogg push this definition one step forward by asserting that every narrative must have a story and a storyteller.[49] Fowler corrects Scholes and Kellogg by adding that there must also be an audience for the story and storyteller. Any definition of narrative must not neglect the participation of the one who receives or hears the story, namely, the *reader*.[50] For our purposes, we will uphold Robert Fowler's important addition. Therefore, our working definition of narrative is a written text that tells a story to a reader. For this reason, our methodology must take into consideration the context of the interpreter.

Chapter 2 has shown there are three important assumptions of narrative criticism that bear directly upon the work at hand—coherence, causation, and contextualization. Each of these presuppositions is a part of the sociolinguistic model. I will first present these assumptions from the perspective of narrative criticism, then detail the corresponding sociolinguistic components. In this way, I will show that our sociolinguistic model includes the key narrative critical elements exposed in chapter 2 and accommodates the sociocultural context of the interpreter. For these reasons, the sociolinguistic model is the best choice for this project.

Narrative critics presuppose that a narrative is unified and coherent.[51] They affirm that the text is self-sufficient and, therefore, a complete entity. The narrative is finite, having a beginning and an end.[52] In addition, the narrative is a "sequential composite" with each event connected to another.[53]

Seymour Chatman notes that within classical literature, events are linked together by cause and effect. Coherence then is predicated upon causation. Cause followed by effect continues until the final effect.[54] According to the principle of causation, the reason for events that occur within the narrative can be found in the narrative.[55] Chatman argues that causation is a powerful tendency within human beings, who will "connect the most divergent events."[56] He writes, "Our minds will inverately seek structure, and they will provide it if necessary."[57] The narrative critic, however, will seek structure within the story world of the text rather than outside of the narrative, because she or he assumes an "internal rationale."[58] Accordingly, she or he will "look for the logical progression of cause and effect."[59]

The assumption of an "internal rationale" is a natural outgrowth of the presuppositions of coherence and causation. There is an internal rationale or reason for what occurs in the narrative because the narrative is a series of events linked together by causation. These connections organize the story world and unify the narrative.[60] Narrative critics therefore assert that the "primary explanatory grid [is] an internal literary or narrative one."[61] In other words, one does not look outside of the narrative to explain what is going on within the story world. One should begin with the story itself. Similar to New Criticism's minimization of authorial intent,[62] narrative critics "are wary of interpretations based on the elements external to the narrative."[63] This would also include underlying theological assumptions that are not borne out in the text.

In similar fashion, sociolinguists affirm the principle of coherence. They assert that coherence is what characterizes a text. In other words, the text can be understood because it "hangs together."[64] Sociolinguists identify three types of cohesive ties or "two terms tied together through some meaning relation."[65] These ties—co-referentiality, co-classification, and co-extension—are what hold a text together.

Co-referentiality is a "relationship of situational identity of reference."[66] For example, in the sentence, "I do not have the money; I gave it to John," the terms "money" and "it" are co-referents. They refer to the same thing. The same money that I do not have is the same money that I gave to John.

Co-classification occurs when the two terms refer to the same class but are not identical.[67] The sentence, "I teach each Tuesday and my friend does, too," is an example of co-classification. My friend and I are both teaching. We participate in an activity that shares the same semantic class. However, the two teaching events occur in two different situational contexts. We are both teaching, but the "teaching" refers to two distinct contexts and teachers.

Co-extension is a semantic relation in which "both [terms] refer to something within the general field of meaning."[68] The following sentence exemplifies co-extension: "I do not like green eggs and ham."[69] "Green eggs" and "ham" do not share a co-referential relationship because they do not refer to the same thing. Neither are they an example of co-classification because they are not identical things that occupy different situational contexts (like "teaching" in the last example). "Green eggs" and "ham" are related because they both belong to the general field of things "I do not like."

As demonstrated above, the linguistic orientation of sociolinguists causes them to focus on semantic terms. This is understandable, given the fact that sociolinguists are not limited to narrative texts as narrative critics are. Therefore, sociolinguistic theory must focus on the greatest common denominator that is a word. I contend, however, that when interpreting narrative texts, these same ties can be found among characters, events, and behaviors. Moreover, there is room within the sociolinguistic program to add causation to the list of possible cohesive ties.

Halliday and Hasan write, "At any point after the beginning [of a text], what has gone before provides the environment for what is coming next."[70] The text, then, is simultaneously text and context. The internal rationale that narrative critics recognize is the result of what sociolinguists call "internal expectations."[71] Because the text is coherent, these expectations are both raised and met by the text itself. One appeals to the *con*text, the text "with" the text, to discover reasons for particular choices or events narrated within the text. Thus, a sociolinguistic reading would also militate against interpreting the Gospel of Mark based on underlying theological assumptions, such as theories of atonement that are not borne out in the text.

Finally, both sociolinguistics and narrative criticism are contextualized interpretations. No single reading is final or authoritative, but rather "partial and contextualized," because the reader can never completely relinquish his or her preunderstanding while reading.[72] As a result, both methodologies acknowledge multiple interpretations of the same text. There are, however, limits to interpretation. In other words, the text cannot simply mean whatever one wishes it to mean. The text can mean many things, but it cannot mean everything. As Powell notes, "The text itself sets parameters for interpretation."[73] Using the terminology of Halliday, I agree with Blount that it is specifically the ideational and textual macrofunctions of the adult grammatical system that set the parameters for interpretation. Therefore, both narrative critics and sociolinguists can agree that "textual analyses only *clarify the potential of the text* rather than determine its absolute meaning."[74] Mieke Bal expresses this point succinctly: "An interpretation is never anything more than a proposal."[75] The sociolinguistic model enables the interpreter to integrate intentionally the sociocultural context of the interpreter into this kind of narrative biblical critical methodology. It is to this context that I now turn.

The Microinterpersonal Component

According to Blount, the microinterpersonal component refers to the interpreter's participation in the act of interpretation. This component examines the presuppositions of the interpreter that are the byproducts of the interpreter's sociocultural background and experiences. It also reveals how these presuppositions influence interpretation, because they raise certain questions and necessitate a particular methodology to answer them.

Chapter 1 detailed my microinterpersonal life-relation. My life-relation is what led me to the diunital approach. This approach corresponded to the principles of narrative criticism employed by the last group of Markan scholars in chapter 2. The macrointerpersonal section detailed the correspondence between sociolinguistics and narrative criticism. Both methodologies assume coherence, causation, and contextualization. However, it is only the sociolinguistic model that enables me to integrate a womanist preunderstanding and life-relation into the methodology. Therefore, sociolinguistics is the methodology that will be used.

Below, I attend to the microinterpersonal preunderstanding. My preunderstanding consists of the presuppositions I bring to the interpretive process. These presuppositions are derived from the sociocultural context and womanist reflections presented in chapter 1.

Koala Jones-Warsaw defines the task of womanist biblical hermeneutics as "discover[ing] the significance and validity of the biblical text for black women who today experience the 'tridimensional reality' of racism, sexism, and classism."[76] For African American women, the significance and validity of the Bible are founded in its affirmation of God's solidarity with and commitment to them. Specifically, it is God's commitment to their survival and wholeness, a commitment that womanists uphold in their theological formulations and praxis. Whereas some feminists employ a hermeneutics of suspicion,[77] I would suggest that a womanist biblical hermeneutic be characterized as a hermeneutics of wholeness. Intrinsic to our understanding of wholeness are both survival and liberation. Using the four interpretive principles identified in the section on Jesus Christ, I posit the following tenets for a womanist biblical hermeneutic. These tenets also comprise the preunderstanding that I bring to the biblical text.

First, a womanist hermeneutics of wholeness must promote the wholeness of African American women without prohibiting the wholeness of others. Stated negatively, a womanist biblical hermeneutic cannot aid or abet the oppression of African American women or anyone else. Womanists recognize the interrelatedness of all people. Therefore, African American women will not accomplish individual or community wholeness by the destruction or bondage of others. Womanists are "committed to the wholeness of an entire people."[78] This commitment extends across racial, gender, and class lines. In this way, womanists will reflect the nature of Jesus, whom we describe as "inclusive, relational, particular and, yet, universal."[79]

Second, our interpretive procedure must be grounded in the concrete reality of African American women's lives. It is grounded in that it does not simply postulate theoretical formulations, but it also seeks to assist African American women in living out the gospel message and addresses issues that affect them. This requires that any methodology employed take seriously the unique perspective African American women bring to the text as well as the situations to which they will apply the interpretation. It is for this reason that I began our discussion by describing the sociocultural context of African American women.

Third, I affirm that God supports African American women in their commitment to and struggle for wholeness. God in the person of Jesus Christ exemplifies this commitment. I affirm this commitment based on the testimony of Gospel accounts that depict Jesus' ministry as ministry to the "least of these." Therefore, the biblical record is indispensable for womanist reflection. I agree with womanists—Jesus makes God real to African American women. However, I maintain that it is the Bible that makes Jesus real.

Finally, a womanist interpretation asserts that Jesus' significance is his life and ministry. I advocate a diunital approach that considers Jesus' life and ministry but does not exclude his suffering and death. In chapters 1 and 2, I presented the traditional African American understanding of Jesus as the divine cosufferer and the potential harm this interpretation inflicts on African American women. For too long, African American women have identified primarily with the suffering of Jesus. Therefore, I do not accept suffering as a divinely necessitated part of Jesus' ministry. However, I do acknowledge pain as an inevitable consequence of following Jesus. Consequently, a womanist hermeneutics of wholeness affirms that we will endure pain rather than forsake following Jesus, in order to bring about transformation in ourselves, our homes, our churches, our communities, and the world.

∞ Conclusion

Blount's subdivision of Halliday's interpersonal macrofunction demonstrates the microinterpersonal influence that affects one's choice of methodology. It therefore provides points of connection between the interpreter's biblical critical methodology and background. Blount's model has enabled me to link together two academic disciplines: biblical scholarship and theology. I now have a methodology that makes a womanist interpretation of the biblical text possible.

However, we cannot perform a sociolinguistic reading without establishing both the context of the interpreter and the context of Mark's Gospel. In this chapter, I reviewed the language macrofunctions employed by sociolinguists. All of these macrofunctions either reveal how language functions or help us to establish the context of the interpreter. Both the macro- and the microinterpersonal components explicated in this chapter refer to the relationship between the interpreter and the text. Therefore, the next chapter will elucidate the context of Mark's Gospel.

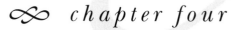

∽ *chapter four*

Establishing Mark's Social Context

WORDS AND PHRASES IN THE BIBLE NOT ONLY
HAVE "THEOLOGICAL" MEANING BUT THEY HAVE
A SOCIAL MEANING AS WELL: THEY FUNCTION IN
A SOCIAL CONTEXT.

—Halvor Moxnes, *The Social World of
Formative Christianity and Judaism*[1]

 As noted in chapter 3, there are two social and cultural contexts to be taken into consideration in the interpretation of texts: the context of the Gospel and the context of the interpreter. I used womanist theology in chapter 1 to construct an African American female sociocultural context for womanist biblical interpretation. Now, building on the work of others, I posit a cultural context for interpreting the Gospel of Mark.

First, however, I suggest what I believe is the most probable historical setting for the Gospel. The general consensus among Markan scholars is that the Gospel was written somewhere in the Roman Empire between 66 and 70 C.E. Among those who propose a specific locale, Rome,[2] Galilee,[3] and southern Syria[4] are the top choices. Markan scholars identify several characteristics of the Gospel that

Mark's setting should account for, namely, Latin, Hebrew, and Aramaic words and phrases, the explanation of Jewish traditions, the author's and audience's familiarity with the Old Testament, and Jesus' ministry to Gentiles. In the first section of this chapter, I examine each characteristic with reference to the views of Markan scholars about the Gospel's original audience. Assessing this information, I arrive at the probable setting for the Gospel and then proceed to describe Mark's context of culture.

The cultural context does not escape the influence of the microinterpersonal component discussed in chapter 3. The presuppositions that comprise the microinterpersonal component affect one's understanding of Mark's social world. Donald Juel acknowledges that we know very little about Mark's original setting. In order to reconstruct a probable audience for the Gospel, his suggested course of action is to "make note of what [Mark's] audience can be expected to know and to what concerns the narrative is directed."[5] However, Mark's original audience no longer exists. Therefore, our best understanding of his original audience is filtered through the lens of a particular contemporary community. Because Mark's social location cannot be definitively determined, Markan scholars are actually arguing probabilities. And in that stretch of probability lays potentiality. In other words, Markan scholars are reconstructing the social location of the Gospel according to how well the meaning potential of the Gospel, accessed through the lens of their particular sociocultural contexts, fits a particular setting.

Likewise, I can only make note of what Mark's original audience might know based on clues apperceived through a womanist lens. The sociocultural background of African American women influences my understanding of Mark's context of culture. It focuses a womanist lens on the meaning potential in Mark's social context (as others reconstruct it) that corresponds to the African American female experience of suffering, shame, and surrogacy.

Every society is ordered by symbolic systems that correspond to social experience.[6] Each society has a symbolic order, that is, norms and values that govern social life. Based on our discussion in chapter 1, I contend that the pursuit of wholeness and the eradication of suffering, shame, and surrogacy are the values that comprise a womanist symbolic order. In the second section of this chapter, I use this womanist symbolic order as the lens through which to access meaning potential in Mark's setting in order to postulate a symbolic order for Mark's community. Having posited a setting and symbolic order, I will then describe Mark's context of culture.

The Provenance of Mark

Although the Gospel is written in Koiné Greek, the narrator is also familiar with Latin, Aramaic, and Hebrew words and phrases.

Latinisms

Mark's Gospel reveals little familiarity with Latin, the use of which is generally limited to governmental or military terms (*legiōn*, 5:9, 15; *kentyriōn*, 15:39), measurements (*modion*, 4:21; *xestōn*, 7:4), and money (*dēnariōn*, 6:37; 12:15; 14:5).[7] Although the presence of Latin words in Mark has been used as evidence for a setting in Rome, they provide insufficient grounds for such a conclusion.[8] A basic knowledge of Roman coinage, military troops and soldiers, and measurements was common throughout Roman-occupied territories. Werner Kelber has argued that what is conspicuously absent from Mark's Gospel are Latin words that refer to the social, domestic, and/or religious spheres of Roman life, which strongly suggests a location somewhere within the Roman Empire rather than a Roman province.[9]

Although the Latinisms point to a location within the Roman Empire, there is not enough evidence to establish a Roman origin for the Gospel. The most one can say is that the Latin terms employed by Mark are general enough to occur within any Roman-occupied territory.

Use of Hebrew and Aramaic

Mark shows evidence of knowing both the sacred language (Hebrew) and common language (Aramaic) of first-century Jewish people. In Mark 7:11, the narrator transliterates and provides an interpretation for the Hebrew word *korban* (gift, offering). Likewise, in Mark 11:9-10, he transliterates the Hebrew *hosanna*. Moreover, there are five instances in which the narrator transliterates *and* translates Aramaic words or phrases (5:41; 7:34; 14:36; 15:22, 34).

The use of Hebrew and Aramaic provides information about both the author and audience of the Gospel. First, the author is proficient enough in the languages used by Jewish people to both translate and explain them. This proficiency in Hebrew and Aramaic suggests that the author is Jewish.[10] Second, the fact that the majority of the Hebrew and Aramaic employed by the author is translated or explained implies an audience that includes Gentiles. Third, the fact that the author includes both Hebrew and Aramaic words and phrases rather than opting to employ the Greek translations alone intimates a Jewish presence among the Gentile audience. The author's decision to place the languages of the Gentiles and the Jews side by side implies that Mark's community was composed of both Jews and Gentiles who lived side by side.[11]

Both Rome and the southern portion of Syria had such an audience. The largest foreign population in Rome during the first century was the Jewish population.[12] In southern Syria, near the borders of Israel, there existed communities of Jews living in separate quarters among the Gentile inhabitants of the city.[13] Galilee, on the other hand, does not match our evidence. Galilee, unlike Rome and Syria, was an "overwhelmingly Jewish area in the first century."[14]

Explanation of Jewish Traditions

In Mark 7:3-4, the narrator explains the Jewish practice of hand washing and the washing of utensils and containers. Mary Ann Tolbert observes a "notable lack of clarity" about the tradition.[15] This lack of clarity leads her to conclude that the author and audience "were at some distance from the more established practices of Judaism."[16]

However, the lack of clarity could also imply that the Gentile population in Mark's community outnumbered the Jewish occupants. Therefore, the narrator only provided as much information as he thought was required to make sense of the story. A predominantly Gentile community with a smaller number of Jews (who did not embrace these practices) would not need a detailed account of this tradition.

A predominantly Gentile audience seems probable when we compare Mark 7:3-4 to the Matthean parallel (15:2). In Matthew's account, there is no explanation for the tradition of the elders. Daniel Harrington notes that Matthew "could use Jewish rhetoric and themes without explanation" because he was writing primarily, but not exclusively, to a Jewish audience.[17] Again, the fact that the narrator takes the time to explain this tradition of the "Pharisees and all the Jews" (7:3) reinforces the Gentile presence in Mark's community. The inclusion of this explanation militates against a Galilean origin.

Familiarity with the Old Testament

Mark's Gospel reflects both the author's and the audience's familiarity with the Old Testament. The author includes twelve references to the Hebrew Scriptures that are incorporated into nine out of sixteen chapters (1:2-3; 4:12; 7:6-7; 10:6-8, 19; 11:17; 12:10-11, 36; 13:24-26; 14:27, 62; 15:34). The narrator assumes his audience's knowledge of the Scriptures. Although Mark provides explanations of Jewish traditions, he does not explain even one Old Testament scripture. His audience is expected to know the Hebrew Bible or, at the very least, accept its meaning as consistent with his good news. An audience situated in Rome, Galilee, or southern Syria would have had those among them with this base of knowledge.

Ministry to the Gentiles

In Mark's Gospel, Jesus' ministry reflects an intentional inclusion of Gentiles.[18] Jesus' first excursion into Gentile territory occurs in Mark 5:1-20 when he enters the region of the Gerasenes and exorcises a demon from an unnamed man. After being delivered from the demons by Jesus, the former demoniac begs to accompany him (5:18). Jesus refuses his request. Instead, Jesus commands him to return home and tell "what the Lord has done for [him]" (5:19, my translation). The exorcism story concludes with the former demoniac obeying the instruction of Jesus and preaching in the Decapolis (5:20).

The Gospel of Luke follows Mark's lead (Luke 8:26-39). According to Luke, the man begs to go with Jesus and Jesus refuses his plea (8:38). Luke ends his account with Jesus commissioning the man to proclaim "how much God has done for you" and the man preaching in the Decapolis in obedience to Jesus' word (8:39).

Although Matthew includes this story (8:28-34), his Gospel differs from Mark in three notable ways. First, the Matthean account is substantially shorter than the Markan and Lukan parallels. Second, Matthew's version records two demoniacs instead of one. Finally, Matthew does not recount either demoniac begging to go with Jesus nor Jesus sending them home to proclaim their deliverance from the demons.

The first and third deviations from the Markan text can be attributed to Matthew's audience. Matthew writes to a predominantly Jewish community. He therefore does not advocate the proactive inclusion of the Gentiles. Luke, on the other hand, is writing to a Gentile community. Consequently, it is important for him to show his audience that Jesus intended their participation in his ministry. The fact that Mark and Luke show such similarity suggests that they are writing to a similar audience: Gentiles.

We also see Mark's openness to Gentiles in 7:24-37. In this section, Jesus travels into the Gentile regions of Tyre (7:24), Sidon (7:31), and back to the region of the Decapolis (7:31). Mark's narration begins with Jesus healing the daughter of a Syrophoenician woman (7:24-30). He then continues his ministry to the Gentiles by healing a deaf and mute man in the Decapolis (7:31-37).

Again, Matthew's portrait (15:21-28) differs from Mark's. Most notably, for our purposes, is that Matthew does not include the healing of the deaf and mute man. He reports no ministry in the region of the Decapolis. According to Matthew, Jesus leaves the region and returns to Jewish territory after healing the woman's daughter (15:29).

Even in Mark's Gospel, however, Jesus' ministry to the Gentiles does not seem to be a part of his original plan. The narrator informs the reader that Jesus came to the region not wanting anyone to know he was there (7:24). He entered Gentile territory not to minister but to escape notice. In Matthew, Jesus follows that plan. Once he is found out by the woman, he returns to Israel.

In Mark, however, Jesus' plans change. His encounter with the Syrophoenician seems to compel him to intentionally extend his ministry into Gentile territory.[19] Jesus takes a very circuitous route through Gentile territory back to Israel. Donahue notes that Jesus' excursion "compass[es] the whole of the southern Phoenician territory prior to his journey to Jerusalem in 8:22—10:52."[20] Commentators therefore have concluded that Jesus' journey as recounted by Mark is historically inaccurate.[21] However, Mark is making a theological rather than a historical point. This journey "symbolical[ly] embraces the entire Hellenistic neighborhood surrounding Galilee."[22]

Mark's inclusivity of Gentiles highlights the presence of a Gentile audience. Galilee does not make a likely candidate for the Gospel's origin[23] unless one, like Werner Kelber, includes the Gentile territories of Tyre, Sidon, and the Decapolis as a part of Galilee.[24] However, Joel Marcus, following the lead of G. Stemberger,[25] refutes "such elastic definitions of Galilee."[26] Southern Syria and Rome, on the other hand, have a large Gentile population regardless of where the boundary lines are set.

❧ Mark's Social Location

In view of the above considerations, Galilee is the most unlikely place of origin of the Gospel of Mark. The translation and explanation of Hebrew and Aramaic words as well as the explanation of Jewish traditions and Mark's openness to the inclusion of Gentiles point to a predominantly Gentile audience. Such an audience would not have been found in Galilee. Howard Kee observes that although the author knows Galilean place names, Mark lacks familiarity with Galilean topography. Kee concludes that "a Syrian provenance could account for this state of affairs."[27]

Rome and southern Syria remain as possible settings for Mark's Gospel. Each locale had a large Gentile population with a significant Jewish faction. A community with this ethnic composition would explain the incorporation of Hebrew and Aramaic words in Mark's text, the explanation of Jewish traditions, and Mark's receptivity to Gentiles. A Syrian locale, however, is more convincing than Rome. First, the Latinisms do not support, but rather argue against, a Roman origin. The lack of words referring to the social, domestic, and/or religious spheres of Roman life points more strongly to a location within the Roman Empire but outside Rome.

Joel Marcus additionally identifies a clue in Mark 7:26 that favors a Syrian origin. The description of the woman as Syrophoenician serves to distinguish her from other Syrians. Citing Strabo, who divides Syrians into Coelo-Syrians, Syrians, and Phoenicians, Marcus claims that a Syrian origin would explain why Mark included this particular description of the woman.[28] Namely, Mark wishes to differentiate among the various Syrian ethnicities. A Syrian origin would explain the detail and attention given to the particularities of Syria's inhabitants.[29]

Syria is a strong candidate for an additional reason. Mark 5:1-20 and 7:24-30 not only highlight the tensions between Jews and Gentiles but present a mitigated version of the hostility between the Jews and Gentiles in Syria. Mark's account of the people's response to the Gerasene demoniac's healing illustrates a form of Gentile resistance to the ministry of Jesus. Likewise, Jesus' initial response to the Syrophoenician woman's petition portrays Jewish resistance to a ministry by Jesus that includes the Gentiles.

The fact that Mark identifies the woman as a Syrian and locates this story in Tyre is not without significance. Josephus informs us that Tyre was both Gentile and hostile to Jews during the time of the Jewish War. Moreover, he describes the inhabitants of Tyre as enemies of the Jews.[30] During the outbreak of the revolt against Rome, the occupants of the Syrian villages near Caesarea Philippi slaughtered and imprisoned Jews.[31] In retaliation, groups of Jews raided and pillaged the Syrian villages including the Tyrian village of Kedasa.[32] Thus, the first year of the revolt was characterized by fighting between Jews and their Syrian neighbors, not Jews and Romans. U. Rappaport therefore contends that this conflict was what led to the revolt.[33]

Although I contend that Mark was written in Syria rather than Galilee, I do not agree with Marcus that the Gospel was written in an urban setting. Marcus concludes that the Gospel was written in Pella, because Pella was one of the Hellenistic cities Josephus says was attacked at the beginning of the war and had a predominantly Gentile community negatively predisposed toward Jews. Moreover, Marcus cites sources that recount the flight of Judeans to Pella before the fall of Jerusalem, which he links to the warning in Mark 13:14.[34] Instead, I concur with Herman Waetjen that Mark presupposes an agrarian or rural setting.[35] Chapter 4 contains the largest section of sustained instruction from Jesus. Each of the parables is founded on agricultural examples (4:2-7, 26-29, 30-32). The commonality among the parables is the use of examples from rural life to explain the kingdom of God. Mark ends his account of Jesus' teaching by informing the reader that Jesus spoke to them with "many such parables" (4:33), suggesting that this pattern continued in the remaining parables Jesus told but were not recounted.

Mark's use of agricultural examples in the parables of the sower (4:2-7) and tenant farmers (12:1-9) is especially significant. In *Sowing the Gospel*, Tolbert insists that these two parables function as plot synopses for the entire Gospel. By examining each of them in light of their surrounding material, she hopes "to explore in greater detail how the various parts of the narrative merge together to present a unified, consistent, and peculiarly Markan story."[36] Thus, Mark uses the experiences of rural rather than city life as a means of arranging his presentation of the gospel.

Finally, Mark locates the majority of Jesus' ministry in the villages, towns, farms, and countryside (1:38; 6:56; 8:27; 11:1, 2, 11, 12; 14:3).[37] This is not to say that the city (*polis*) is not featured as a location in the Gospel. On the contrary, Mark uses the word *polis* eight times. However, there are only three instances when Mark specifically tells the reader that Jesus was in the *polis* at the time he was ministering (1:33; 6:56; 11:19). In Mark 6:56, *polis* is not the only location specified. Mark informs us that Jesus healed the sick in the villages (*kōmas*) and countryside (*agrous*) as well.

Moreover, three out of the eight uses of *polis* refer to the presence of others besides Jesus in the city. On two occasions *polis* refers to Jerusalem, where Jesus instructs his disciples to prepare for the Passover (14:13, 16). The city is also the setting for the former demoniacs preaching (5:14). Mark also uses *polis* to identify the origin of the people who journey into the countryside to follow Jesus (6:33). In addition, the reader is informed that Jesus could not enter the city (*polis*) because of his fame (1:45). Because Mark consistently places Jesus' ministry outside of the cities and in the towns, countryside, and deserted places, a rural Syrian locale rather than an urban Syrian or Roman setting is most plausible.

Howard Kee asserts that Mark's Gospel was "written in close proximity" to the revolt and "in all likelihood before it came to an end."[38] Marcus agrees with Kee in that the Gospel was written in southern Syria near the Galilean border. He differs on the time and, following the lead of Gerd Theissen, dates the Gospel "shortly after the destruction of the Temple in AD 70."[39]

Marcus does note that although there is no consensus about the location of the Gospel, with proposals for Syria being the most recent among them, there is more scholarly agreement about the date of the Gospel. The general consensus of Mark scholars regarding the date of origin is that Mark wrote either right before the fall of the temple or shortly after its demise.[40] Either date places Mark's audience within the context of the Jewish War.

Mark's Gospel, whether written before or after the fall of the temple, "arose at least in part as a response to the Jewish War."[41]

Richard Horsley acknowledges the messianic tones, which pervaded first-century Palestine during the time of Jesus, stating, "By the time of the great Revolt of 66–70, of course, popular hopes for an anointed king must have been widespread."[42] The widespread nature of this hope manifested itself in messianic movements. The emergence of this form of social protest in an environment familiar with banditry and riots suggests that "there had to have been a certain critical level of religio-political consciousness."[43] Adela Collins points out that by the onset of the revolt there had already been several false messiahs and prophets, as reflected in Mark 13:6, 22.[44] Likewise, Brian K. Blount describes Mark's cultural context as a "messianically tinged, combative socio-political background."[45] Read within this context, Mark's "good news of Jesus Christ" (1:1) declares Jesus to be the true Messiah among messianic pretenders. This message, however, would fit a date before and after the fall of the temple since false messiahs arose before and after the temple's destruction.

To narrow the date of Mark's origin, the arguments of Markan scholars hinge primarily on their interpretation of Mark 13:2, 14. Mark 13:2 describes the total destruction of the temple: "Not one stone will be left here upon another." Marcus states that both Gerd Theissen and Rudolf Pesch have pointed out the similarity between the "no stone upon a stone" description of Mark and that of Josephus.[46] Because Josephus recounts rather than foretells the razing of the temple in these terms, Pesch, Theissen, and Marcus date Mark after the fall of the temple.

Mark 13:14 refers to the "desolating sacrilege standing (*estēkota*) where he ought not" (my translation). The masculine participle *estēkota* refers to a person. There are two individuals whom scholars propose as Mark's referents: Titus and Eleazar. Titus entered the temple at the end of the revolt as the temple was being destroyed. Therefore, scholars who maintain that Titus was the person who was standing where he ought not date the Gospel after the destruction of the temple.[47]

Joel Marcus, on the other hand, identifies the desolating sacrilege as Eleazar, who occupied the temple in the winter of 67–68. He contends that a reference to Eleazar would make more sense than one to Titus since Mark 13:14 admonishes the Judeans to flee to the mountains when the desolating sacrilege occurs. Eleazar's occupation of the temple occurred in enough time for the people to flee Judea before

Titus crushed the revolt. If Titus's entry to the temple was the signal to leave, it would have already been too late.[48] Although Marcus contends that the desolating sacrilege took place earlier than 70 C.E., he still dates Mark after the temple's destruction.

While I find Marcus's proposal for the desolating sacrilege more convincing than those who point to Titus, his identification of Eleazar, by itself, suggests a date for Mark's Gospel prior to 70 C.E. Marcus admits that farsighted people could have believed the temple would be destroyed. This would especially be the case if Eleazar's occupation of the temple was interpreted as the desolating sacrilege. However, the similarity between the language Mark and Josephus use to describe the temple's destruction is too compelling to ignore. Therefore, I date Mark shortly after the fall of the Jerusalem temple. Thus, the social location for Mark that I will use to describe a context of culture for the Gospel is a village in southern Syria near the Galilean border shortly after the fall of the Jerusalem temple. My next task is to explore a symbolic order that may have been operative in this setting.

∞ Honor and Shame: A Symbolic Order

The eradication of suffering, shame, and surrogacy and the pursuit of wholeness are values that constitute a womanist symbolic order. The suffering, shame, and surrogacy of African American women have roots in the experience of chattel slavery. Cheryl Gilkes asserts that the institution of slavery was the "first step in the devaluation or labeling process that shaped attitudes and actions towards Black women."[49] The attitudes and actions toward women of African descent were negatively shaped through the propagation of ideology that alleged persons of African descent were beings above the higher animals but lower than humans.

The racist ideology of black inferiority was compounded by the claim that slavery saved African people from spiritual darkness. For women of African descent, racism took on a sexual character. As white colonizers embraced a self-righteous form of sexual morality, African women were cast as sexual heathens.[50] The supposed natural inferiority and hypersexuality of the Negro race were used as the justification for their enslavement and perpetual subordination within the social order. The tautological definition of African Americans became "servants."[51]

I have already referred to Jacquelyn Grant's dissatisfaction with the theological use of servanthood language based on the factors highlighted above. Grant asserts that servanthood language camouflages rather than eliminates the oppressive reality of African American people in general and African American women in particular.[52] I concluded in chapter 1 that suffering, shame, and surrogacy characterize the oppressive reality of African American women. Suffering, shame, and surrogacy mutually reinforce one another and function to keep African American women in their place: subordinate to persons of European descent.

To describe the cultural context of African American women as one characterized by suffering, shame, and surrogacy is to assert that their cultural context is both physically and mentally deleterious. However, the present reality is not reflective of the womanist goal. Womanism promotes the wholeness of a people. It advocates the recognition of human worth as well as the societal maintenance and support of human life, not its debilitation or destruction.

Within New Testament studies, scholars have uncovered meaning potential in the sociocultural background of the New Testament writings that corresponds to the womanist values of wholeness and the eradication of suffering, shame, and surrogacy: honor and shame. Bruce J. Malina insists that the "social system undergirding the New Testament is that of the Eastern Mediterranean of the first century A.D."[53] He asserts that honor and shame were pivotal ancient Mediterranean values.[54]

Malina arrives at his conclusion based upon the macro- and microinterpersonal components involved in his investigation. At the macro-interpersonal level, he employs a social-science approach. This methodology focuses on the "culturally common and generic."[55] He therefore looks for cultural patterns and generalizations, not uniqueness or details.[56] Using models derived from anthropological studies of modern Mediterranean culture, he identifies the circum-Mediterranean region as a "diffusion sphere" or an area that "shares a common set of cultural institutions that have persisted for long periods of time."[57] This diffusion sphere, which encompasses the New Testament world, forms a "cultural continent."[58] Because the cultural institutions have persisted over long periods of time, the present Mediterranean region is a "living laboratory" for the study of the cultural context of the New Testament.[59]

Malina's macrointerpersonal component (social-science methodology) is influenced by his microinterpersonal life-relation and preunderstanding. The sociohistorical context from which he operates (life-relation) is contemporary Mediterranean society. The primary assumption that forms his microinterpersonal preunderstanding follows: "Given the persistence of many of the characteristics of culture areas over long periods of time, the modern Mediterranean world is far closer to the world of the Bible than North America has been during *any* period of its history."[60] It is through a modern Mediterranean cultural lens that he views the New Testament world and performs a social-science reading.

The reconstructed New Testament world with its symbolic order of honor and shame is not presented as the only context from which to read the New Testament. On the contrary, it is one possible vantage point. In the introduction to *Biblical Social Values and Their Meanings: A Handbook*, Bruce Malina and John Pilch write, "The best way to use this Bible resource is to accept the words and values as presented at face value and to use them as a set of new lenses with which to read familiar Bible passages."[61] By looking through the lenses of contemporary Mediterranean culture, Malina accesses meaning potential in the New Testament that corresponds to his social location. However, he does acknowledge that the modern Mediterranean world and that of the New Testament "are not exact equivalents."[62]

The similarities that Malina believes exist between modern Mediterranean culture and ancient Mediterranean culture is what Clodovis Boff calls a *correspondence of relationship*.[63] A correspondence of relationship occurs when the "interpretive situation of scripture and its context is *like* the interpretive situation that surrounds and activates our [contemporary] exegetical process."[64] This correspondence does not assume a one-to-one relationship between the interpreter's present context and that of the text; these contexts are not identical. A correspondence of relationship only asserts that the context of the interpreter resembles the context of the text. For Malina and those who propose a symbolic order of honor and shame, the Mediterranean core values of honor and shame exposed by contemporary Mediterranean anthropologists correspond to the honor/shame issues seen in the New Testament. Their contemporary cultural lens accesses honor/shame meaning potential in the Bible.

Bruce Malina, Anthony Saldarini, David DeSilva, and John Pilch agree that within the context of first-century Mediterranean society, honor was the value human beings sought to embody. Honor is a "claim to worth that is publicly acknowledged."[65] According to Malina, honor "surfaces especially where the three defining features of authority, gender status, and respect come together."[66] He defines *authority* as the "socially recognized and approved ability to control the behavior of others."[67] In other words, one's honor is actualized when others acquiesce to one's wishes or demands. A person's submission does not depend on physical force or strength because authority is a "symbolic reality."[68]

Moreover, a person has honor because society acknowledges his or her behavior as conforming to gender-specific social norms (gender status).[69] She or he has done what is "ideally acknowledged in the society as valuable and meaningful" by behaving in a way that is consistent with what one "ought" to do.[70] This claim to worth is significant in that honor translates into societal maintenance and defense.[71] An honorable person is entitled to "certain social treatment."[72] Persons are not only thought to be honorable; they are treated by society in a way (respect) that recognizes their claim to worth.

While honor is that which one seeks to embody, shame is what one seeks to avoid. Shame is the opposite of honor. Its corresponding characteristics are "weakness, cowardice and lack of generosity."[73] Whereas honor is worth that is publicly acknowledged, shame is a "claim to worth that is publicly denied and repudiated."[74] In ancient Mediterranean society, this repudiation of worth was tantamount to a death sentence because the shamed individual or group was no longer worthy of societal maintenance or support.[75] Just as persons with honor was treated by society in a way that acknowledged their claim to worth, shamed or dishonored persons would be treated in ways consonant with their lack of honor.

I believe that womanists, given their symbolic order of wholeness and the eradication of suffering, shame, and surrogacy, would relate to honor/shame issues. The ancient Mediterranean concept of honor and the womanist ideal of wholeness are similar in that both are predicated upon the recognition of human worth and societal maintenance. Likewise, the ancient Mediterranean concept of shame and the experience of suffering, shame, and surrogacy identified by womanists both deal with rejection by one's society and the devaluing of the individual. In short, scholars who propose a social environment characterized by honor/shame issues have accessed meaning potential in Mark's background that resembles the cultural context of African American women. Like the honor/shame proponents, womanists would also see a correspondence of relationship between their cultural context and that of Mark's community.

It is important to point out that while a womanist lens and that of the honor/shame proponents would access similar meaning potential, there are three key differences that are the result of their particular microinterpersonal components. These differences between the honor/shame proponents and our womanist perspective highlight areas where our womanist lens will enable me to access meaning potential in Mark's cultural context as well as the Gospel that others have missed.

The first difference involves the values of honor and wholeness. The cultural value of honor is seen as a limited good because increasing one's honor status requires dishonoring another.[76] The womanist hermeneutic of wholeness, however, affirms the wholeness of African American women *without* prohibiting the wholeness of others. Wholeness, then, is an unlimited good. Therefore, we shall use our womanist lens to ascertain if there is meaning potential that shows honor to be available to all.

The second difference is that our womanist lens seeks to make explicit the connection between shame and agony. It is not enough for womanists to merely define and identify shaming practices. A womanist reading of the text must also expose the agony that results from society's repudiation of one's honor or wholeness, thereby showing societal repudiation to be the shameful act.

Finally, our womanist lens has been crafted by experiences of racism, sexism, and classism. The collusion of these forces places African American women in surrogacy roles. For this reason, our womanist lens focuses in on social class structures and how these structures are maintained. Therefore, a womanist reading of Mark's social context will direct our attention to social class stratification and how the symbolic order of honor and shame maintains it.

In *Go Preach! Mark's Kingdom Message and the Black Church of Today*, Brian K. Blount claims that a correspondence of relationship exists between the African American church and the Gospel of Mark.

This correspondence of relationship is a contextual one. Specifically, the cultural similarity that the Black church and the Gospel share is colonial oppression.[77] I agree with Blount that this contextual correspondence exists. However, our womanist lens, refracted by the experience of suffering, shame, and surrogacy and the womanist value of wholeness, reveals that colonial oppression is not the only cultural similarity. There is also a contextual correspondence between our womanist symbolic order and the honor/shame codes of first-century Mediterranean society.

Blount states that contextual correspondence is important because it "forms the foundation for interpretive access of Mark's text."[78] Therefore, he contends that for Mark's kingdom language to "impact the world that the African American church serves," this language should be accessed through the cultural context of colonial oppression.[79] Similarly, the contextual reality of suffering, shame, and surrogacy experienced by African American women with its pursuit of wholeness finds a point of access through the honor/shame context of first-century Mediterranean society. For Blount, colonial oppression "bring[s] the potentiality of Mark's kingdom language to meaningful imperative life."[80] I assert that the honor/shame codes viewed through a womanist lens will bring the potentiality of Mark's agony and cross language to life.

∞ A Cultural Context for Reading Mark's Gospel

In 66 B.C.E., Syria became a Roman province. Since Syria was a territory occupied by Rome, its people were subject to the same colonial oppression as its southern Palestinian neighbors. Economic oppression and exploitation characterized the social circumstances of northern Palestine and southern Syria.[81] Economic hardship was most acutely felt by the farmers (both small landowners and tenant farmers), day laborers, and artisans who constituted the common people.

Ched Myers identifies the common people of first-century Palestine as peasants who constituted 90 to 95 percent of the population.[82] For the most part, the peasant class lived in abject poverty.[83] Although land was the key to wealth, the majority of landowners had small plots while a few owned large tracts.[84] From their small plots of land, a peasant farmer had to produce enough crops to pay taxes that totaled 30 to 70 percent of the harvest.[85] These taxes included tribute to Rome and its local regime, tithes to the Jerusalem Temple (for the Jewish population), as well as local taxes the farmers paid to sell their produce at the markets.[86]

A peasant family had to produce enough food not only to pay their taxes but also to feed the family, have enough seed for the coming year's crop, and have surplus to lend neighbors in need.[87] The surplus allowed the peasant to participate in "reciprocity and redistribution systems."[88] In other words, a peasant family needed to produce extra so that if a neighbor came to them for a loan, they could provide it. Providing for their neighbor during times of hardship meant that they had someone to go to during their time of economic distress. Whereas reciprocal relationships were advantageous for elite members of the society and enabled them to advance themselves, reciprocal relationships among the common people were necessary for survival.[89] This system was necessary because "those who controlled credit were the very rulers of the system that placed the difficult economic demands in the first place."[90]

The economic burden borne by the poor was the result of Rome's practice of aligning the interests of the subjected aristocracy with their own.[91] Because the aristocracy was dependent upon the Romans for power, position, and wealth, its members remained loyal to Rome. Their loyalty to Rome and "taste for the style and values of Hellenistic culture" widened the gap between the ruling class and the peasants. Moreover, the disparity among the social classes was exacerbated by the fact that the Roman government held the local aristocracy accountable for the "steady flow of tax revenues and societal maintenance."[92]

The large number of peasants combined with the high rate of taxation meant that the peasant class's labor primarily benefited those who ranked higher than them on the social ladder. The peasant class's labor supported both the governing class (1 to 2 percent of the population) and the retainer class (5 percent of the population).[93] The governing class was composed of "hereditary aristocrats."[94] The retainer class "served the needs of the ruler and governing class."[95] Their connection to the governing class allowed them to live at a level higher than the peasant class but afforded them none of the power of the ruling class.[96] Their interest was that of the governing class. Without the governing class, there were no retainers. Because the governing class was loyal to Rome, so, too, were the retainers.

Unlike the retainer class, the common people did not benefit from any association with their economic or social superiors. By the time of Herod the Great, many peasants had to forfeit their land due to high levels of debt. These persons became day laborers.[97] Others became tenant farmers.[98] In the years preceding the revolt, the economic vulnerability and loss of land due to the economic exploitation of the common people by both Rome and the Jewish aristocracy gave rise to social banditry.[99] Groups of brigands "were active in northern Galilee . . . raiding primarily along the border with Syria."[100] Social bandits were often supported by the peasants because the bandits were also from among the poor. Both groups were therefore aligned against the upper classes that benefited from Roman rule.[101]

The symbolic order of honor and shame functioned to maintain social stratification and the peasant class's social and economic vulnerability because honor represented a "mode of social ranking."[102] Social stratification resulted from the honor/shame codes because wealth, purity, and humility were the "means values" for honor.[103] Each of these means values for honor had economic implications.

Herman Waetjen observes that in agrarian societies such as first-century Palestine, "land was the primary source of wealth and power."[104] Wealth enabled a person to acquire honor.[105] Because the majority of land was held by a small percentage of the people, honor was limited to this group. Consequently, those who had access to land and power were those considered most honorable in the society. Wealth enabled these individuals to uphold their social status. It was especially important in helping them to maintain boundaries between clean and unclean persons, places, and tasks.

The means values of purity and humility are about the maintenance of boundaries. Purity codes uphold physical boundaries between clean and unclean. These physical distinctions translate into social ordering. What is unclean is rejected and therefore of lesser value than what is clean. Purity has economic implication because those who constituted the lower class were not able to maintain the purity codes. Poverty therefore inhibits people's ability to "maintain their dignity and honor."[106] Just as honor is limited, so also is wealth. When the poor are deprived of wealth, they are also "deprived of the honor due them."[107]

Such was the case of the "degraded" and the "expendables"—those who occupied the lowest level of the peasant class. Considered ritually unclean, the degraded were unskilled laborers or persons who worked in professions that violated the purity codes. The expendables were persons such as lepers, beggars, and outlaws. By societal standards, they were both "deprived and dehumanized."[108] They were dishonored and therefore bereft of societal maintenance and defense.

The cultural value of humility is also concerned with social boundaries. In ancient Mediterranean society, humility was not about individual self-effacement but rather about remaining in one's social place.[109] Each person inherited the honor ascribed to their group as well as their group's social status. To remain at the level of this social status was humble and therefore honorable. The ironic result is that a peasant's primary means of acquiring honor was by remaining poor. George Forster writes, "All of the desired things in life . . . *exist in finite quantity* and *are always in short supply* as far as the peasant is concerned. . . . There is *no way* directly with peasant power to increase the available quantities."[110] Since the acquisition of wealth was beyond the peasant's ability and the type of work peasants did left them ritually unclean, humility would have been the only means value they could access. However, it was a means value that required they remain poor.

As the occupants of the lowest rung of the social ladder, the members of the peasant class had no authority. There was no group beneath them whose behavior they could control. For the most part, their behavior was under the control of others because they were either forced or coerced by the economic factors of their lives to participate in a system that did not benefit them. Their economic vulnerability prevented the acquisition of wealth. Their agrarian lifestyle militated against the observance of purity rituals. Humility functioned to keep them in their place, thereby maintaining the honor and corresponding social status of their religious and political leaders. Although the peasant class represented the majority of the society, they possessed the least amount of honor.

If we view Mark's story against this cultural background, we see that the social class stratification present in first-century Mediterranean society is "mirrored in the story world of [Mark's] Gospel."[111] Mark portrays Pontius Pilate, Herod Antipas, and the high priest as persons who occupy the highest social strata. Jesus' fate is sealed in a court over which the high priest presides and in which Pilate's decision to release Barabbas to the crowd occurs. In a society ordered by honor and shame, these would be the characters in Mark's story world with the most honor.

Mark places the chief priests, elders, and some of the scribes in the governing class. The elders, chief priest, and scribes are the only groups Mark situates in the company of the high priest (14:53), suggesting that their social ranking and honor status are directly below those of the highest class. Mark shows them to be men of authority; they have the authority to send others to do their bidding. They send the Herodians and Pharisees to trap Jesus (12:13) and a crowd armed with swords and clubs to arrest Jesus (14:43). In addition, their dependence on the temple system that establishes their position in society is revealed in chapter 11. It is only after Jesus drives out the money changers, buyers, and sellers from the temple (11:15-16) that they personally question his actions (11:27-28). The chief priests, elders, and scribes' questions about Jesus' practices suggest that they have a vested interest in the financial practices of the temple system. Their involvement in the temple also implies that they are able to maintain the purity codes. Consequently, Mark shows this group to possess the means values of wealth and purity that reinforce their social rank.

The Herodians, Pharisees, and local scribes belong to ranks of the retainer class. The Herodians were most likely officials, courtiers, slaves, or servants of Herod. It is also probable that were simply supporters of Herod's regime.[112] According to Mark, neither the Herodians nor the Pharisees could succeed in a plot to kill Jesus apart from the members of the governing class. They serve the governing class by following orders and going where they have been sent.

Anthony Saldarini contends that Mark "reproduce[s] the dominant social pattern of ancient society and places the Pharisees at the edges of the governing class."[113] Since the Pharisees were retainers in the Palestinian society, on the edges of the ruling class is exactly where they would be situated. Josephus asserts that the Pharisees were "extremely influential among the townsfolk."[114] In Mark's Gospel, the Pharisees seek to maintain their influence over the crowd by competing with Jesus. Their influence among the common people ensured their position in society as "middlemen" for the upper class.[115]

Saldarini notes that the scribes performed different roles in different regions.[116] This would explain their portrayal in Mark's Gospel as members of the council and local officials. Although the scribes wielded some power and influence, at least enough to make authoritative interpretations of Scripture, they still remained "subordinate to and dependent on the priests and leading families in Jerusalem."[117] The scribes relied on the leading families because they had the financial means to both employ and educate them.[118] The scribes' dependence on leading families connects them to the elders, and their dependence on the priests connects them to the chief priests. Consequently, the scribes are not an "autonomous group with its own power and continuous agenda."[119] As depicted in the Gospels, their interests are aligned with those of the elders and chief priests.[120]

The Herodians, Pharisees, and scribes were economically dependent on those above them. However, their service to the upper classes kept them in close proximity to those whose lifestyles adhered to the societal notions of purity. In this way, they could realize the means values of wealth and purity. Although they were not as wealthy as the aristocracy or governing class, they were able to live at an economic and social level that was higher than that of the peasants.

Finally, the crowds in Mark's Gospel coincide with the peasant class in Mediterranean society. The narrative describes them as "sheep without a shepherd" (6:34). Mark records two occasions in which Jesus must feed them (6:34-44; 8:1-9), stating in Mark 8:1 that they "had nothing to eat." Mark highlights the poverty of the crowd by showing that they could not even provide for their own basic needs. The fact that they could follow Jesus as he ministered throughout the villages and countryside suggests that they were dispossessed farmers with no land to tend. Without land and connections to the society's elite, the crowd is economically and socially vulnerable. Moreover, the chief priests' ability to coerce the crowd to choose Barabbas over Jesus (Mark 15:7-11), despite Jesus' ministry to the crowd, shows them to be a group under authority rather than persons with authority.

Now that we have a probable setting, symbolic order, and social class structure, we can sketch a possible description of Mark's community. If we posit a location in a rural village in southern Syria, the majority of Mark's community would be composed of peasant landowners, tenant farmers, and artisans who were most likely dispossessed landowners. These persons probably lived at a subsistence level with their daily labors profiting those who occupied the upper strata of society. Because the peasants worked the land, the governing and retainer classes did not. Instead, they reaped the benefits of the peasants' efforts without being put in a position to violate the society's purity norms. In effect, the peasants took the places of the members of the governing and retainer classes by supplying the economy that made their lifestyles possible. From a womanist perspective, the peasants were voluntary surrogates. Their economic vulnerability and their inability to access the means values of purity and authority made it necessary to remain where they were to survive.

Mark's community operated according to the symbolic order but did not benefit from it. They were devoid of honor primarily because they lacked economic resources. The lack of honor resulting from a lack of money translates into a lack of societal maintenance, because dishonored individuals lack human worth. John Gager writes:

> Money, like cargo, represents wealth, power, and above all a symbolic measure of human worth. Thus, the . . . hoarding and control of money by a colonial power in a monied land (the situation of Palestine under Roman rulers) creates a crisis not just of finance but of human dignity as well.[121]

When we set Mark's community with its socioeconomic disparities against the backdrop of the Jewish War after the fall of the temple, we have an environment in which people live with the expectation of divine intervention.[122] They expect an "imminent reversal whereby the socially devalued, but religiously esteemed, are economically and socially vindicated."[123] If we look at Mark's story of Jesus through a lens shaped by this social context, we will see that Mark portrays Jesus as introducing this reversal through his ministry. Moreover, our womanist lens will show honor to be an unlimited good. In a society where the majority of the inhabitants were deprived of honor, the Gospel of Mark provides a means value for honor that is accessible to all: discipleship.

∞ Conclusion

Ched Myers expresses the uniqueness of Mark's Gospel and its significance for this project when he writes, "Mark's story of Jesus stands virtually alone among the literary achievements of antiquity for one reason: it is a narrative for and about the common people."[124] Although the Gospel was originally directed to Mark's audience, which was comprised of the common people, it speaks poignantly to the common people of today. If we view Mark through a womanist lens, the crowds in Mark's Gospel do not mirror the common people in ancient Palestinian society only. Their position also bears a striking resemblance to that of African American women. There is a contextual correspondence.

Like the common people in ancient Palestine, African American women in the United States have been economically exploited to the benefit of their social and economic "superiors." The experience of chattel slavery is a clear example of economic exploitation. The fact that African labor was free precluded any accumulation of wealth by African Americans. After slavery, the economic security of African Americans remained precarious as we endured various forms of voluntary surrogacy.[125] This economic vulnerability continues. The 2002 U.S. census reports that the official poverty rate for the United States was 12.1 percent. For African Americans, the poverty rate was between 23.9 and 24.1 percent, almost twice the rate of the national average.[126]

Historically, societal notions of purity did not apply to women of African descent. In the United States, the concept of purity was primarily connected to sexual chasteness. During and after slavery, purity was a value reserved for white women. Bell Hooks notes that although black and white girls were taught the value of purity, the reality for black girls was that "no social order existed to protect them from sexual exploitation."[127] One of the ways white people subordinated and tortured black people was by "defiling" black women.[128] After slavery, African American women were primarily employed as domestic workers. Many women found out that they had to "choose between sexual submission and absolute poverty for themselves and their families" because of the sexual advances of their white male employers.[129]

In *From Mammy to Miss America and Beyond: Cultural Images and the Shaping of US Social Policy*, Sue Jewell explores the origins and use of African American female stereotypes in influencing social policy.

Two of the three predominant stereotypes (the mammy/Aunt Jemima, Sapphire, and Jezebel) depict African American women as either inherently "sinful/evil" (Sapphire)[130] or sexually aggressive (Jezebel)[131] and therefore impure. Jewell notes that these images persisted in popular culture until the 1980s as the "foregoing images [that were] systematically presented as symbols of African American women."[132]

Humility in both its ancient and modern context is about remaining in one's position of subordination and assuming the appropriate submissive attitude. For African American women, humility is expressed by not being too "uppity," thereby remaining in one's place. The place of African American women in a racist, sexist, and classist society in which white male experience is normative is one of subordination. A subordinate position means that those who occupy it remain under the authority of another. The introduction of Africans to the United States as slaves clearly shows that people of African descent were never intended to have authority over themselves or others.

The points of similarity between Mark's audience and African American women are none to be envied. However, if Mark's story of Jesus is good news to its ancient hearers, it also offers good news to a corresponding contemporary community. It is to this Gospel that we now turn.

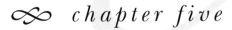

chapter five

Discipleship and the Cross in Mark

By consciously fashioning a preunder-standing of Mark different from those generally held by biblical scholars, we should expect a somewhat different view of the Gospel to emerge.

—Mary Ann Tolbert, *Sowing the Gospel*[1]

I began with an overview of womanist theology and womanist perspectives of Jesus Christ, the cross, suffering, and discipleship, showing that womanists identify agony, shame, and surrogacy as critical issues for African American female life. This has led some womanists to reject suffering as the will of God. The sociocultural context of African American women, characterized by agony, shame, and surrogacy, provides another lens through which to view Jesus and the cross. Through this lens, womanists see a causal connection between Jesus' ministry and his death on the cross. They attribute Jesus' agony and death to the sinful actions of human beings.

Although womanist perspectives are not grounded in an exegesis of the biblical text, womanists do appeal to the

Synoptic Gospels to substantiate their work. However, the sparsity of womanist biblical scholars has meant that portions of the Bible that bear directly upon the agony, shame, and surrogacy that affect African American women, like the biblical commands to deny oneself and take up the cross, have yet to be interpreted from a perspective sensitive to these issues. Consequently, in this chapter I raise two primary questions with respect to the Gospel of Mark that womanist theology cannot answer on its own: (1) What is the relationship between the agony that the cross symbolizes and discipleship? (2) Is the agony of the cross suffering or pain (as defined in chapter 1)?

In chapter 2, I suggested that Mark's Gospel contains the critical elements involved with these questions: agony, the cross, and discipleship. These elements, as well as the biblical commands to deny oneself and take up the cross, occur in a pivotal passage, Mark 8:31-38. However, Markan scholars were not asking the questions raised in chapter 1, nor did they posit an interpretation of self-denial or cross bearing reflective of womanist concerns. In short, womanist theology and Markan scholarship, when used independently of each other, are inadequate for answering my primary questions. This project required a methodology that could help mine the biblical text for answers to our questions.

In chapter 3, I posited sociolinguistics as the methodology for this project, one that takes into consideration the sociocultural context of both the original audience of the Gospel and its present readers. I therefore now offer a sociolinguistic reading of Mark 8:31-38 through a womanist cultural lens, a lens that corresponds to ancient Mediterranean honor/shame codes. I maintain that if we read Mark 8:31-38 through a womanist cultural lens, we can attend to womanist concerns and expose aspects of the text that previous Markan scholars have missed.

The following sociolinguistic analysis examines the Gospel of Mark with respect to three metafunctions. The first, the *field of discourse*, refers to what is happening in the text. The second is the *tenor of discourse*, which bears on the nature of the participants, referring to who is taking part and the roles and relationships of the participants. The third metafunction, the *mode of discourse*, refers to the part that language plays.[2]

∞ The Field of Discourse

The field of discourse focuses on what is happening in the text. Three verses—Mark 8:31, 34, 38—are our interpretive anchors and will be examined in detail. The surrounding verses also will be interpreted in light of our findings. In this way, the anchor verses will serve as one of the contexts for the succeeding verses. Our task is to employ our womanist cultural lens to access meaning potential that will enable us to answer our key questions.

Mark 8:31-33

Our field of discourse begins with Mark 8:31. The narrator opens this section with "Then he began to teach" (*kai ērxato didaskein*). Mark uses *ārcho* plus the infinitive twenty-six times. Gundry explains that this is a feature that "Mark likes to use and in which the notion *of* has no independent significance but makes some ado about the new thought of the following infinitive"[3] (emphasis added). If he is right, this formulaic expression signals a new teaching. Indeed, here for the first time, Jesus teaches about his passion. He reveals to his followers his impending fate, one that will include agony, rejection, execution, and resurrection. Moreover, Jesus informs them that these things "must" (*dei*) take place. In order to answer the questions raised in chapter 1 and asked of Markan scholars in chapter 2, our first course of action is to discover why Jesus *must* experience the things he has predicted. Only after we establish why these events must occur can we determine if the agony Jesus foretells is suffering (unmetabolized, unscrutinized agony that enables one's continued oppression) or pain (named and recognized agony that comes as a temporary result of life-affirming behavior). Although the formulaic opening of this section signals a new teaching, it does not introduce content so novel as to be unrelated to what precedes. Jesus begins a new teaching because of what has previously taken place. Jesus' teaching is in response to Peter's pronouncement of his identity. In other words, Mark 8:27-30 serves as part of the co-text for this pericope.[4]

In Mark 8:29, Peter declares that Jesus is "the Messiah" (*ho christos*). From the onset of the Gospel, the narrator has let the reader know who Jesus is (1:1). However, this is the first time a character within the narrative acknowledges what the reader knows to be the true identity of Jesus. Jesus' new teaching is a direct result of Peter's declaration.

Weeden argues that Peter rebukes Jesus in verse 32 because Peter's conception of the Christ does not coincide with "Jesus' conception of a suffering Messiah."[5] Similarly, William Lane writes, "The primary purpose of this section is to explain what it means for Jesus to be the Messiah and what it requires to be identified with him."[6] Lane goes on to say that Jesus' messianic destiny includes the necessity of suffering. Both Weeden and Lane conclude that this passage communicates that suffering is a necessary qualification for messiahship. In other words, Peter's confession was only partially true. Jesus is the Messiah, but one cannot truly understand him to be the Messiah unless one knows him to be a suffering messiah.[7]

There is meaning potential in Mark's Gospel that shows Mark 8:31-38 is not about the qualifications for being the Messiah but about the consequences of Jesus' messianic ministry. When we read 8:30 against the backdrop of 1:34 and 3:12, we expose meaning potential that leads us to a different conclusion than that of Weeden and Lane. There is a similarity between Jesus' rebuke of Peter (and the disciples) in 8:30 and his rebuke of the unclean spirits (1:25, 3:12). In both instances, the purpose of the rebuke was to command silence, not correct the identification that the speaker made. He commands the speaker to be silent precisely because what they are saying is correct. Jesus' rebuke of the unclean spirits in Mark 3:12 is most telling: "He sternly ordered them not to make him known" (my translation). Jesus rebukes them so that they do not make him known. He employs the same practice in Mark 1:34 and silences the demons, which he casts out, "because they knew him."

Jesus' rebuke of Peter (and the disciples) in 8:30 functions in the same way as his rebuke of the demons. Peter, like the demons and unclean spirits, knows who Jesus is. The disciples are privy to Peter's answer, so they now know who Jesus is. For this reason, Jesus rebukes all of them.

Most important for my purposes is that Peter's declaration of Jesus as the Christ occurs without Peter ever witnessing Jesus experience agony. Agony has played no part in characterizing Jesus as the Christ. Matthew, unlike Mark, ascribes Peter's confession to a revelation from God (Matt 16:17). The only evidence Mark offers for Peter (and the reader) to assess Jesus' identity is Jesus' ministry. Rather than witnessing an agonizing Messiah, Peter has witnessed a teaching (4:1-34; 6:2, 34), preaching (1:34), healing (5:23-43; 7:32-37), exorcising (1:23-26; 3:11; 5:1-20; 7:26-30), praying (1:35; 6:46), miracle-working (6:30-44; 8:1-10) and forgiving (2:5) Messiah. Peter concludes that Jesus is the Christ based upon Jesus' ministry, not his agony.

Agony (whether suffering or pain), then, is not a prerequisite for messiahship. Peter's declaration confirms that before Jesus' passion, Jesus is already the Anointed One. If agony is the only authentic characteristic of messiahship, as Weeden asserts, then there is no way Peter (or the demons and unclean spirits) could have recognized Jesus' true identity without it. In other words, Peter understands who Jesus is. What he does not understand, nor like, are the consequences of Jesus' messianic ministry. This becomes apparent when Mark details Peter's reaction (8:32) to Jesus' prediction about his fate (8:31).

The first thing Jesus tells his disciples in 8:31 is that his fate is somehow necessary (*dei*). Wilbur Bennett identifies four ways in which *dei* has been understood in Markan scholarship.[8] In the first case, Jesus' agony is necessary for his role as the Messiah. Jesus understands himself to be a "combination of the apocalyptic Son of Man and the figure of the Suffering Servant found in Isaiah 52.12*ff*."[9] Rudolph Otto[10] exemplifies this perspective. The second option is that Mark casts Jesus in the role of the righteous man as depicted in the Old Testament, particularly Isaiah 53. Thus, Jesus' agony is the necessary prelude to his exaltation.[11] In the third instance, Jesus' passion is set within an eschatological context. Certain things must take place that signal the last days. Jesus' passion is such an event and therefore *must* occur. Finally, Jesus must experience agony and die because it was foretold in the Scriptures. Although Bennett employs the work of Ethelbert Stauffer[12] and H. E. Tödt[13] to demonstrate this perspective, the writings of Joel Marcus, Sean Fréyne, and Norman Perrin could also represent this category.

Bennett's entire system places *dei* under the rubric of divine necessity, that is, "the considered and deliberate divine purpose, intention, or determination" of God.[14] Each of the categories prioritizes a cultural location that would situate *dei* in a Jewish context that would read in light of either an Old Testament understanding of Isaiah 53 or Psalm 118 or first-century apocalypticism. I do not dispute a cultural context for the Gospel that suggests that first-century hearers/readers of the Gospel would access Mark's meaning based on a preunderstanding of Old Testament allusions. Nor do I disagree that Mark's Gospel emerges out of a context of apocalyptic expectation as our context of culture points out. What I do assert is that every text has both a context and a co-text to consider. If we perform a sociolinguistic reading through a womanist lens of the text, a methodology that considers both the co-text (as our methodology requires and the final group of Markan scholars in chapter 2 demonstrate) and the context, there is another framework by which to interpret this word; one that expresses inevitability, an unavoidable event brought about by the actions of humans.

It is important to note at this juncture that *dei* is a neutral term. Grundmann explains that *dei* "expresses the 'character of necessity or compulsion in an event,'" that "the term itself does not denote the authority which imparts this character. It is thus given precise significance when joined with this power."[15] Thus, the variety of interpretations for *dei* arise because Jesus' passion prediction does not make explicit the authority that imparts the character of this word. Although Grundmann reads *dei* within this passage as "divine necessity," he concedes, "In most cases [*dei*] bears a weakened sense derived from everyday processes. It thus denotes that which in a given moment seems to be necessary or inevitable to a man [*sic*] or group of men [*sic*]."[16]

I believe that this is the sense in which Mark uses *dei* in 14:31. Upon hearing Jesus' prediction of his denial, Peter responds, "Even if I must die with you, I will not deny you" (14:31, my translation). Peter does not convey that it is divinely necessary for him to die with Jesus. On the contrary, his response expresses inevitability. In effect, Peter is telling Jesus that if it becomes inevitable that he die with him rather than deny him, he will choose death. Peter's denial of Jesus in verses 66–72 confirms that his death is not divinely necessitated. It is inevitable if, in the moment he is questioned about his association with Jesus, he answers in the affirmative.

Unlike Bennett and the majority of the Markan scholars reviewed in chapter 2 who interpret *dei* in Mark 8:31 as divine necessity, Ched Myers exposes meaning potential that allows one to interpret *dei* as an expression of inevitability. Myers begins by reading *dei* against a semantic field that he insists is apocalyptic. He then connects the *necessity* of Jesus' suffering with his ministry. According to Myers, what is "necessary" is for Jesus to "challenge the highest powers and be exe-cuted by them."[17] Jesus' challenge of the highest powers will mean that he will "*necessarily* come into conflict with the 'elders and the chief priests and the scribes.'"[18] Therefore, he concludes, "This is not the discourse of fate or fatalism, but of political *inevitability*."[19]

In light of Bennett's and Myers's differing interpretations of *dei*, my first task is to examine Mark 8:31 and its surrounding co-texts to see if they provide clues for understanding why Jesus claims his passion must take place. In this way, we shall see whether our womanist lens accesses meaning potential that reads the necessity of Jesus' passion as divine necessity or inevitability. Let us begin with analysis of Mark 8:31 before proceeding to its co-texts.

At this point in our investigation, there remains uncertainty about how we are to understand and therefore translate *dei* in Mark 8:31. In order to maintain the ambiguity of *dei* until we can see whether our womanist lens exposes meaning potential that charac-terizes Jesus' suffering as divinely necessitated or inevitable, I will translate *dei* as "it is necessary." There also remains uncertainty about how we shall render *pathein* (usually translated as "to suffer"). Our womanist cultural lens provides three options for its interpretation: agony, suffering, and pain. Since *agony* is our most general term, and suffering and pain are types of agony, I will render *pathein* as agony until a determination is made. Our translation proceeds as follows: "So Jesus began to teach them that it is necessary for the Son of Man to experience agony and to be rejected by the elders and the chief priests and the scribes, and to be killed, and after three days, to rise" (my translation).

There are four events that Jesus describes as necessary. These events are expressed by the four successive aorist infinitives that follow *dei*: *pathein* (to suffer), *apodokimasthēnai* (to be rejected), *apoktanthēnai* (to be killed), and *anastēnai* (to rise). Bennett advises, "It is extremely important to understand that the infinitives dependent upon *dei* are of equal weight. There is, in the syntax, no emphasis on one event over another."[20] Although the syntax suggests no prioritizing of one event over another, there are two semantic relationships that exist among the terms.

Both of the semantic relationships we will explore are cohesive chains. A cohesive chain is a "set of items each of which is related to the

others by the semantic relation of co-reference, co-classification and/
or co-extension."[21] The first semantic relationship we will explore is
known as an identity chain. An identity chain consists of items that are
co-referent. In other words, each of the items refers to the same thing.[22]
In other words, the "it" in "it is necessary" refers to Jesus' suffering,
being rejected, being killed, and rising: *pathein, apodokimasthēnai,
apoktanthēnai,* and *anastēnai.* Thus, the "it" that is necessary is made
explicit by the four infinitives. We know what is necessary because each
of the infinitives that follows gives content to what "it" is. Therefore,
each of the events signified by the infinitives is necessary.

In addition, each of the infinitives is connected to the others by means
of a similarity chain. Similarity chains are a set of items that are linked
to each other by a relation of either co-classification or co-extension.[23]
Pathein, apodokimasthēnai, apoktanthēnai, and *anastēnai* share a relation
of co-extension. Each of the semantic units "refers to something within
the same general field of meaning."[24] These four verbs all share in the same
general class of events that are necessary. (I shall determine later whether
our womanist lens sees this necessity as divine necessity or inevitability.)
The infinitives are not co-referential in that one infinitive does not equal or
mean the same as another. However, they do share a relationship because
they each make explicit the "it" that is necessary. Consequently, all of the
events referenced by the infinitives will be either divinely necessitated or
inevitable. Let us now explore the co-text to see if Mark provides clues
within the narrative that will enable us to answer why Jesus *must* experience agony, be rejected, be killed, and rise.

The only explicit reference to Jesus' death prior to 8:31 is found
in Mark 3:6. The controversy cycles that began in chapter 2 culminate
in the Herodians' and the Pharisees' plot to destroy Jesus. Our womanist cultural lens helps me to mine the meaning potential in these
verses. As stated in chapter 1, shame, surrogacy, and suffering are critical issues for African American women. In chapter 4, we saw that the
cultural context of African American women corresponds to ancient
Mediterranean culture, which is characterized by honor and shame.
I will therefore situate Mark 8:31 within an honor/shame context of
culture and use our womanist lens to help illumine this section.

The Mediterranean world is characterized not only by the values of honor and shame but also by the perception of limited goods.
Honor is one of the resources that a first-century Palestinian would

have viewed as a limited commodity. Within this environment, every social interaction that occurs outside of the family is a "contest of honor."[25] And every social exchange houses the "potential for gaining, losing or retaining" honor.[26]

What Mark 2:1—3:6 reflects is the scribes' and Pharisees' attempts to gain honor at the expense of Jesus.[27] In short, they challenge him.[28] The religious leaders try to "trip up Jesus, to cause him at first to lose face (and with it, his followers)."[29] To maintain his honor, Jesus must meet the challenge. Both the challenge and the response must be witnessed. Public opinion is the determining factor in deciding who emerges from the challenge-response with honor and who emerges with shame.[30] Each of the incidents narrated by Mark in 2:1—3:6 occurs in a public setting.

The first episode takes place in Jesus' home (2:1). The crowd that converges upon his house is so large that there is no room outside of the door (2:2). Therefore, the friends of the paralytic dig through Jesus' roof to get the crippled man to him (2:4). Rather than command his healing, Jesus offers the man forgiveness (2:5). Although the challenge to Jesus is not verbalized to the persons within the story world, it does occur in a public setting. Because Mark tells the reader what the scribes are thinking, the reader becomes part of the court of opinion in this episode. Within the story world, Jesus' response intimates and answers the unspoken questions of the scribes—"Who is able to forgive sins except God alone?" (2:7, my translation). Jesus' response is: "But in order that you may know the Son of Man has authority to forgive sins upon the earth"—he said to the paralytic, "Rise, take up your bed and go to your house" (2:10-11, my translation).

The main issue that the scribes wrestle with concerns the amount of authority Jesus has. According to the scribes, only God can forgive sins. Jesus has overstepped the boundaries that the scribes assume apply to everyone including Jesus. Their questions attempt to undermine his authority—a means value of honor. Authority is the "socially recognized and approved ability to control the behavior of others."[31] The issue is not Jesus' power—the "ability to exercise control over the behavior of others."[32] The exorcisms are proof that he has the ability to control behavior; however, his power has not been socially sanctioned. Accordingly, Jesus has no legitimate claim to the authority he seeks to wield and is, therefore, a blasphemer.

This is precisely why Jesus responds as he does. By healing the paralytic, Jesus publicly and successfully answers the scribes' challenge, confirming both his power and his authority. The crowd validates Jesus' success by glorifying God and declaring, "We have never seen anything like this! (2:12)" Reading from a womanist perspective, we can see that issues of honor and shame lie at the heart of this story.

In the three succeeding events, questions are raised that continue to challenge Jesus' ministerial practices and therefore his honor. The scribes of the Pharisees question his table fellowship with sinners and tax collectors (2:16). A group of people question his disciples' lack of fasting (2:18), after which the Pharisees question his group's adherence to the sabbath laws because the disciples have plucked heads of grain to eat (2:23-24). On each occasion, Jesus meets the challenge and silences his accusers. The result is that in every encounter Jesus' challengers lose honor, and Jesus gains it.

The final episode in this series reverses the usual pattern. In each of the preceding incidents, Jesus' opponents questioned him. They were the initiators of the challenge, and Jesus was the respondent. However, Mark 3:1-6 depicts Jesus as the challenger and the Pharisees (or, at the very least, part of Jesus' audience) are the recipients of Jesus' challenge: "Is it lawful to do good or to do evil, to save life or to kill?" (verse 4, my translation). Now the Pharisees must counter Jesus' question to maintain their honor. They fail in this challenge-riposte because they do not respond at all. In the absence of their response (3:4-5), Jesus uses his healing power to display the appropriate answer. Just as he healed the paralytic as a means of verifying his authority to forgive sins, the healing of the man's withered hand confirms that he is the Lord of the Sabbath, at least for the crowd. Moreover, Jesus' power to heal confirms that he has the authority to determine what is acceptable Sabbath behavior and observance, namely, to save life. The reaction of the Pharisees is ironically one of deadly determination: "[They] went out and immediately conspired with the Herodians against him, how to destroy him (*apollymi*)" (3:6, my translation).

Mark 3:6 narrates the conspiracy of the Pharisees and Herodians against Jesus. Their plot to destroy Jesus stands in stark contrast to Jesus' life-affirming interpretation of the Sabbath. The contradiction between Jesus' words and the actions of the Pharisees and Herodians highlights the sinfulness of the religious and political leaders. This passage, seen through our womanist lens, is an example of moral evil. If their plot is successful, Jesus' destruction will be the direct result of human acts "that are contrary to God's holy character and law."[33]

At this point (Mark 3:6), the narrative provides a reason for Jesus' destruction: the murderously negative reaction of the religious and political leaders to his ministry. Both the power and the authority that Jesus wields are means values for honor. The "court of reputation," which for the Pharisees and Herodians are the crowds,[34] publicly approve of Jesus' ministry and follow him.[35] These means values are the manifestations of Jesus' ministry. Therefore, the only way to halt Jesus' realization of honor is to stop his ministry. They must destroy (*apollymi*) him.

Our womanist lens enables us to uncover meaning potential in Mark 3:6 that shows a two-pronged understanding of the destruction (*apollymi*) that the Pharisees and Herodians plan. In Mark 3:6, the narrator uses the verb *apollymi* to describe what the Pharisees and Herodians conspire to do to Jesus. Yet in verse 4, the narrator uses *apokteinō*: "Is it lawful . . . to save life or to kill?" (my translation).Although the primary meaning of *apollymi* is "to destroy utterly," it also means "to kill."[36] Both *apollymi* and *apokteinō* occupy the same semantic field in that they share the same basic meaning: "to kill." They function in Mark's narrative as synonyms. *Apollymi* corresponds to *apokteinō*; it conveys the physical destruction of Jesus.

In light of the honor/shame undertones in this section, I contend that the conspiracy of the Pharisees and Herodians is also a desperate attempt to regain lost honor and ensure the future security of their honor status. Within an honor/shame context, it is extremely important for Jesus' rivals to shame him in every way possible. Even if they succeed in killing him, they must prevent his followers from viewing him as an honorable man, or else Jesus' followers may continue to follow his example rather than theirs. For these reasons, they plot to "utterly destroy" Jesus—physically *and socially*.

If they can shame Jesus socially and kill him physically, then there is no way for Jesus to regain or increase the honor he now possesses or maintain a following after his death. It is important to understand that in an ancient Mediterranean context, social destruction, or the shaming of an individual was tantamount to death. Malina explains:

Again, publicity, witnesses are crucial for the acquisition and bestowal of honor. Representatives of public opinion must be present, since honor is all about the tribunal or court of public opinion and the reputation that court bestows. Literally, public praise can give life and public ridicule can kill.[37]

When we read this passage through a womanist lens that accesses meaning potential through its correspondence with the honor/shame codes, we see that the "utter destruction" that *apollymi* signifies can have a physical and social component.

When we read Mark 8:31 in light of Mark 3:6, three important similarities emerge. First, both passages acknowledge human culpability for the death of Jesus. Mark 3:6 identifies the deadly opposition of the Pharisees and Herodians. Mark 8:31 identifies the elders, chief priests, and scribes as those who will reject him. Given that both *apodokimasthēnai* (to be rejected) and *apoktanthēnai* (to be killed) are in the passive voice, it would not be unreasonable to assume at this point that the persons who reject Jesus will also have a hand in Jesus' execution.

Second, the conspiracy to destroy Jesus coincides with Jesus' prediction of his rejection and death. Earlier in our discussion, I pointed out the similarity chain between *pathein* (to suffer), *apodokimasthēnai* (to be rejected), *apoktanthēnai* (to be killed), and *anastēnai* (to rise). I noted that each of the items shared the same general field of meaning. Therefore, this similarity chain is composed of items in a relation of co-extension. Relationships of co-extension can be subdivided into at least three categories based on the traditional sense relations of synonymy, antonymy, and hyponymy.[38]

Upon closer examination of our similarity chain—*pathein*, *apodokimasthēnai*, *apoktanthēnai*, and *anastēnai*—we can see two more semantic relationships. The first relationship is hyponymy, that is, a "relation that holds between a general class and its sub-classes."[39] In a hyponymous relation, one item (the superordinate) refers to a general class. The remaining items correspond to subclasses and are known as hyponyms.[40] I believe that the meaning potential we have accessed in Mark 3:6 and Mark 8:31 is similar because that meaning potential reveals a hyponymous relation between *pathein*, *apodokimasthēnai*, and *apoktanthēnai* that corresponds to the two-pronged meaning of *apollymi* (to destroy).

Wilhelm Michaelis insists that *polla pathein* (to suffer many things) cannot "be related to the accompanying circumstances of *apoktanthēnai*, i.e., to the suffering in dying, since the two sayings are separated by *apodokimasthēnai*."[41] However, our womanist lens, and specifically the work of Jamie Phelps, enables us to access meaning potential to draw the opposite conclusion. Phelps asserts that there is an existential and a physical dimension to agony. The existential dimension manifests itself in the questioning of one's value or self.[42] The existential dimension of agony identified by womanists corresponds to the social dimension of shame identified by New Testament scholars. The physical dimension of agony corresponds to the physical dimension of shame.

When we read Mark 3:6 in its narrative and cultural context, we saw that there is meaning potential within the semantic field of *apollymi* that posits a social and a physical component to the destruction that the Pharisees and Herodians plan. Likewise, our womanist lens reveals a hyponymous relation in 8:31 that exposes meaning potential in the semantic field of *pathein* that reflects a physical and an existential facet of agony. In this hyponymous relation, *pathein* is the superordinate of the set that includes *apodokimasthēnai* and *apoktanthēnai*. *Pathein* refers to the general class, agony. *Apodokimasthēnai* and *apoktanthēnai* are subclasses or types of agony. *Apodokimasthēnai* specifies the social (existential) dimension of *pathein* that will be manifested in the rejection of Jesus. *Apoktanthēnai* communicates the physical side of *pathein* that will be manifested in the execution of Jesus. *Apodokimasthēnai* and *apoktanthēnai*, then, correspond to the physical and social dimensions of shame. And the social and physical destruction that the Pharisees and Herodians plan corresponds to the agony Jesus predicts.

In other words, our womanist lens shows that the primary goal of the Pharisees and Herodians is to discredit or shame Jesus. They plot against Jesus as a means of repudiating his claim to honor. The rejection of the elders, chief priests, and scribes functions in the same way. *Apodokimasthēnai* means "to be found lacking or unsuitable after examination."[43] Whereas *apoktanthēnai* refers to Jesus' physical destruction, *apodokimasthēnai* expresses the social destruction they wish to accomplish. Just as *apollymi* conveys the physical and social dimensions of Jesus' destruction in Mark 3:6, the hyponymous relation between *pathein*, *apodokimasthēnai*, and *apoktanthēnai* in Mark 8:31 exposes the same meaning potential.

In light of the hyponymous relationship between *pathein*, *apodokimasthēnai*, and *apoktanthēnai* and the connections I have drawn between Mark 3:6 and 8:31, Jesus will experience agony for the same reasons the Pharisees and Herodians plot to destroy him. The only narrative rationale Mark provides for Jesus' passion prior to 8:31 is his ministry. Although Mark 8:31 informs the reader that Jesus is well aware of the consequences, Jesus will inevitably continue his ministry of healing (10:46), exorcisms (9:25), teaching (11:18; 12:35), and prayer (14:35, 39) after his prediction in 8:31. In response to his ministry, Jesus' opposition will try to destroy him socially by rejecting him and physically by killing him. According to the narrative presentation as I read it, what will happen to Jesus is inevitable. Whereas Ched Myers describes Jesus' agony as political inevitability, I would describe Jesus' agony, rejection, and execution as ministerial inevitability. He must experience agony because he will continue to minister.

The meaning potential we accessed in our examination of Mark 2:1—3:6 and 8:31 reveals that Jesus will experience agony as a result of his ministry. The question remains whether Jesus' agony is suffering or pain. In chapter 1, I defined suffering as unmetabolized, unscrutinized agony. Suffering is a static condition that perpetuates oppression. Pain, on the other hand, is named, recognized agony. Pain connotes a temporary condition that comes as a result of life-giving and/or life-sustaining behavior. In order to see whether our womanist lens accesses meaning potential that shows Jesus' agony to be suffering or pain, I examine the two instances of *pathein* that occur outside of Mark 8:31[44]—5:26 and 9:12. I then evaluate the meaning potential to determine whether suffering or pain is the most appropriate rendering of *paschō* (suffer) in 8:31 from a womanist perspective.

In Mark 5:26, the woman with the hemorrhage is described as having "endured much under many physicians" (*polla pathousa hypo pollōn iatrōn*). In other words, the woman's agony is a result of her life-sustaining behavior on behalf of herself. She seeks her own healing. In her attempt to be healed, she experiences agony at the hands of her physicians. The woman's presence in the crowd reinforces her desperation; she understands her condition all too well. She obviously believes, too, that it is a condition that can be transformed. Her only hope for healing is Jesus.

The woman's experience exemplifies every facet of our womanist definition of agony.[45] She is socially alienated because she and all that she touches are unclean (Lev 15:19-24). She is physically depleted, having grown worse rather than better under the care of her physicians (Mark 5:27). She is financially bankrupt. Finally, she has been separated from the community of faith for twelve years. According to Lev 15:25, she is unclean until seven days after the hemorrhage ceases. After her ailment is cured (with no help from the spiritual leadership), she can then come to the temple. The priest will then make an offering for her sin and atone for her uncleanness (Lev 15:29-30). Given Mark's description of her situation, one can reasonably assume that her illness and society's response to it have taken a mental and emotional toll on her.

However, the woman remains proactive in her stance toward wholeness. She has spent all that she had in pursuit of a cure (5:26). It is precisely this proactive orientation that Mark details in chapter 5. The woman takes the initiative. She "[comes] up behind him in the crowd" (5:27). Mark narrates her intention, "I will be made well" (5:28). Like Jesus, she disregards the socioreligious boundaries that would prevent wholeness. The result is that her experience of much pain, although prolonged for twelve years, is not a permanent condition.

The second instance of *paschō* outside of 8:31 occurs in Mark 9:12. As in Mark 8:31, *paschō* refers to Jesus. However, it is also connected to the agony of John the Baptist (Elijah). Mark connects the agony of the Son of Man with the death of John the Baptist. Jesus informs his disciples that Elijah has indeed come and "they did to him whatever they pleased" (9:13). Mark uses this statement to redirect the reader to 1:14 and 6:17-29, where he narrates John's arrest and execution.

In Mark 1:14, the narrator informs the reader that Jesus' ministry began after John was arrested (*paradidōmi*). Mark uses *paradidōmi* to connect the arrest of John to the arrest of Jesus (14:10, 11, 18, 21, 41). John is not only the forerunner to Jesus' ministry; he also foreshadows Jesus' death. Two of the three passion predictions in Mark's Gospel use *paradidōmi*—Mark 9:31 and 10:33.

For my purpose, the most important connection between the death of John and the death of Jesus is that both die as a result of their ministry, and in both cases, Mark exposes human culpability. Mark states explicitly that John was arrested on account of Herodias, Herod's brother's wife, whom he had married (6:17). John's prophetic ministry led him to speak out against the immorality of Herod's actions. Herodias, angered by John's condemnation of her marriage to Herod, persuades Herod to arrest him and her daughter to request his execution (6:24-25).

The occurrence of *paschō* in 5:26 and 9:12 is similar to the 8:31 reference in four important ways. First, each time *paschō* is employed, it is always preceded by *polla*. Mark maintains a consistent form for its use. Second, *paschō* is always in the aorist tense. Unlike the present tense that expresses continuous action, the aorist tense expresses action that is "simply brought to pass."[46] The tense of *paschō* coincides with our definition of pain as temporary. Third, *paschō* always refers to recognized agony that comes as a result of life-affirming ministry behavior. Finally, *paschō* is the result of human, not divine, action. In other words, people cause the agony. Thus, Mark's use of *paschō* corresponds to our womanist understanding of pain.

Furthermore, Mark's use of *paschō* reinforces our interpretation of *dei* as an expression of inevitability. Each instance of pain in Mark's Gospel is the result of human action, not divine necessity. The woman with the issue of blood experiences pain at the hands of her physicians. John experiences pain because of the request of Herodias and her daughter, and Herod's acquiescence to their request. And when we read Mark 8:31 through our womanist lens and in light of these co-texts, we see that Jesus will also experience pain because of human beings who plot to kill him and will reject and execute him, not God.

The final infinitive in the original similarity chain (*pathein, apodokimasthēnai, apoktanthēnai,* and *anastēnai*) is *anastēnai*. Several commentators point out that Mark's word choice here is somewhat odd. First, Mark uses *anistēmi* in the active voice[47] and switches to the passive form of *egeirō* (raise) in the passion narrative (14:28; 15:29; 16:6). Second, both Matthew and Luke deviate from Mark and use the passive form of *egeirō* rather than the active voice of *anastēnai* in their passion predictions.[48] Moreover, C. S. Mann and W. J. Bennett acknowledge that the verbal form of *anistēmi* in the Septuagint is future middle.[49] Bennett explores the possibility of *anistēmi* reflecting an earlier tradition.[50] Ultimately, he concludes, "The question as to why Mark chose 'to rise' or whether he transmitted unchanged an old form of the tradition is, as yet, impossible to determine."[51] The final semantic relation sheds some light on Mark's word choice. I will highlight this relation by way of review.

Our original similarity chain—*pathein, apodokimasthēnai, apoktanthēnai,* and *anastēnai*—shows an interesting structure. The chain is bracketed by two aorist active infinitives (*pathein* and *anastēnai*) with two aorist passive infinitives in the interior (*apodokimasthēnai* and *apoktanthēnai*). The two aorist passive infinitives were shown to be co-hyponyms and therefore subclasses of *pathein*. They describe the social and physical forms of Jesus' pain: rejection and death. The co-extension relationship among *pathein, apodokimasthēnai,* and *apoktanthēnai* also shows that all of the items are not only experiences that are inevitable but also, according to ancient Mediterranean standards, experiences of shame. Furthermore, the relationship of co-extension combined with the identification of the elders, chief priests, and scribes as the ones who reject Jesus suggests that they will also be the ones responsible for his death. Therefore, the similarity chain that includes *pathein, apodokimasthenai,* and *apoktanthenai* reveals that all of these experiences are a result of moral evil.

In similar fashion, the two aorist active infinitives are related. *Pathein* and *anastēnai* are co-extensions in that they share the same general class, inevitability. Upon closer inspection, we also see that *pathein* and *anastēnai* are antonyms. *Pathein* refers to the passion of Jesus, whereas *anastēnai* signals the antithesis of his rejection and death, namely, the resurrection. As noted above, *pathein* relates an experience of shame. Since *anastēnai* refers to an experience that is the functional opposite of *pathein*, I contend that the meaning potential also points us to *pathein*'s opposite cultural value: honor.

Read within this context, Mark's semantic choices are not odd at all. It seems that Mark has put both infinitives in the active voice to signal a semantic relationship between the words. Specifically, the narrator has aligned the verbal form of *anistēmi* with that of *pathein* to signal antonymy. In this way, Mark is able to communicate the passion in terms of shame and Jesus' resurrection in terms of honor. The narrator begins a subversion of the honor/shame codes that he will play out in full in 8:38. Most important, our sociolinguistic analysis through a womanist lens reveals that the similarity chain—*pathein, apodokimasthēnai, apoktanthēnai,* and *anastēnai*—enables Mark to communicate both moral evil and divine agency, apart from his use of *dei*.

In chapter 1, I critiqued several authors, namely, Robert Meye, Morna Hooker, and Werner Kelber, for performing an inconsistent reading of the text. The inconsistency I referred to was their assertion that Jesus' death was both divinely necessitated and the result of human action. I argued that this reading presents a theological and narrative contradiction by putting the religious leaders who plotted to kill Jesus and opposed his ministry on the side of God.

Instead, Mark consistently shows Jesus to be God's beloved Son who steadfastly does the will of God. The religious rulers are consistently depicted as those who neither recognize the work of God nor participate in it. Therefore, if Jesus' passion is the will of God brought about by the religious rulers, those who kill Jesus are on the side of God. This reading was insufficient from a womanist point of view because it placed God on the side of the status quo upheld by the religious and political leaders against the life-affirming ministry of Jesus.

The reason Meye, Hooker, and Kelber reach the conclusions that they do is because they do not interpret *dei* as a neutral term according to its most general definition. This becomes problematic because those who are responsible for Jesus' rejection and the One responsible for Jesus' resurrection are different. The infinitives themselves present at least two different agencies as the forces behind *dei* that are borne out in the co-text and context.

Mann insists that although *anistēmi* is in the active voice, neither a Jew nor a Jewish-Christian would "regard the 'raising' as being self-induced."[52] Even if one does not agree with Mann's interpretation of *anastēnai*, the fact remains that if Jesus' resurrection is self-induced, the force behind *anastēnai* is still different than the force(s) behind *pathein*, *apodokimasthēnai*, and *apoktanthēnai*. At the very least, the reference to Jesus' rejection at the hands of the elders, chief priests, and scribes points to a minimum of two forces behind the infinitives in Mark 8:31. When *dei* is understood as divine necessity, it accurately represents the force behind *anastēnai* only. My reading of the text suggests that if *dei* is understood in its most general form—as that which "in a *given moment* seems to be necessary or inevitable to a man [*sic*] or group of men [*sic*]" (emphasis added),[53] each of the infinitives in our similarity chain can individually represent the force behind *dei* and still occupy the same general field of meaning: inevitability. Furthermore, this reading does not place the religious and political leaders who seek to destroy Jesus on the side of God.

To restate it, Mark portrays Jesus' ministry as that which represents the will of God. For this reason, Jesus' ministry and Jesus himself
are cast in an honorable light. Jesus' agony, rejection, and execution are
the inevitable results of his ministry due to the reaction of the religious
leaders. The opposition of the religious and political leaders represents
moral evil. Their actions are, therefore, shameful. Jesus' resurrection by
God is also the inevitable result of his ministry due to God's vindication of both him and his work. It confirms that Jesus' ministry represents the will of God and the honor status Mark conveys.

The following translation displays (and summarizes) the meaning
potential exposed in Mark 8:31:

> So (in response to what Peter said in Mark 8:29) Jesus began to
> teach them (something new) that it is inevitable for the Son of
> Man to experience great pain (that is, named, recognized agony;
> a temporary condition that comes as a result of life-giving and/or
> life-sustaining behavior), to be rejected by the elders and the chief
> priests and the scribes (whose actions represent moral evil), to be
> killed (as a result of the moral evil of those who reject him), and,
> after three days, to rise.

This series of events—ministry, pain characterized by rejection and
even death, and divine vindication—is not something that is unique to
Jesus. It is a chain of events that all who follow him must be prepared
to endure. We shall see in Mark 8:34-37 that Jesus models his call to
discipleship on this first passion prediction.

Mark 8:34-37

The connection between Mark 8:31-33 and the material in this section can be summarized as follows: "Thus the first lesson in the harsh
nature of discipleship (8:34ff) is taught in conjunction with the first
passion prediction (8:31-33) where the grim fate of Christ is paired
immediately with the high cost of discipleship."[54]

In the previous section, I argued that the experiences depicted in
Jesus' passion prediction[55] (1) are the inevitable result of Jesus' ministry, not divine necessity, and (2) should be understood as expressing
an immediate context of pain, not suffering. Jesus' call to discipleship
also involves this same context of situation. There are two events that

take place in the verses: (1) Jesus issues an open invitation to discipleship, and (2) he issues commands that coincide with the consequences of accepting this call. Mark situates both of these events in a context of pain.

The first thing that is apparent in this section is the inclusive nature of Jesus' call to discipleship. Jesus calls "the crowd" (*ho ochlos*). The teaching that is to ensue will not be the special possession of the Twelve. It will be open to all who meet the standards Jesus sets for discipleship.

Jesus' inclusion of the crowd "indicates that the conditions of discipleship are the same for everyone."[56] The openness of the call is further emphasized by the phrase *ei tis* ("if any," 8:34). The indefinite pronoun *tis* sets no boundaries for discipleship except the forthcoming commands. Elizabeth Struthers Malbon reminds us that this is not the first time Jesus' teaching has been directed to others besides the Twelve.[57] These accounts provide the co-text for Mark 8:34.

In chapter 4, Mark records another teaching segment introduced by the same formulaic expression that opened Mark 8:31, "And he began to teach" (*ērxato didaskein*; 4:1). Similarly, the audience for this teaching is "the crowd." The content of Jesus' teaching includes several parables. Jesus concludes the first parable (the parable of the sower) with "Let anyone with ears to hear listen!" (4:9).

Whereas a "very large crowd" was present when Jesus told the first parable, the next teaching session has as its audience a smaller group. Mark narrates Jesus explaining the previous parable to "those who were with him along with the disciples" (4:10, my translation). Jesus then proceeds to tell a series of parables to this reconstituted audience. The first parable told in this more intimate setting concludes with "Let anyone with ears to hear listen!" (4:23). Although this group is smaller than the crowd that constituted the audience of the first parable, it still confirms that more than the Twelve were the recipients of Jesus' teaching and private instruction. To these is given the mystery of the kingdom of God (4:11). Jesus requires of his audience no special status, not even membership among the Twelve. He only requires "ears to hear."

The work of Robert Meye helps to illumine the significance of Jesus' teaching ministry. Meye's writing emphasizes what he refers to as the "didactic motif" in Mark's Gospel.[58] Although Meye contends that Mark limits the company of disciples to the Twelve, he does insist that

Jesus' teaching ministry is expressly for training his disciples. Meye claims that the Twelve are the only ones to receive the "mystery of kingdom" (4:11) because they are the only ones called to "be with" Jesus (3:3). Therefore, the Twelve are the only ones who can become fishers of people. As fishers of people, the Twelve actualize their calling as disciples by following Jesus and engaging in ministry that is similar to his.[59] Meye does not state that others cannot follow Jesus. Others can follow Jesus, but they cannot be his disciples and therefore cannot be fishers of people. In this way, he also limits who can participate in the work of Jesus. I will argue shortly that this is not a limitation that Mark's Gospel supports.

As demonstrated above, Mark identifies "those around [Jesus] along with his disciples" as the audience for Jesus' explanation of the parable of the sower. These are also the ones who receive the mystery of kingdom. Consequently, more than the Twelve obtain the vital information that Meye insists enables the Twelve to become fishers of people. Those who follow may not be a part of the Twelve or privy to the entire ministry of Jesus. However, neither are all members of the Twelve.[60] Jesus does not exclude those among the Twelve whom he does not call to "be with" him at the same level Peter, James, and John are, nor does he exclude the crowd. Malbon observes, "It would appear that following, while central to discipleship, is not limited to 'disciples.' The category of 'followers' overlaps with the categories of 'disciples' and 'the crowd.'"[61] Both the disciples and the crowd form a "composite portrait of the followers of Jesus."[62]

The moment Jesus calls the crowd to himself and addresses his invitation to discipleship with *tis* (anyone), he opens up the succeeding portions of this verse and this field to anyone who desires to follow him. Discipleship, then, is not limited to a particular number of people but includes all who desire to follow him in a ministry similar to his. "Disciples, crowds, whoever—everyone is a potential follower."[63] In this way, Mark extends the invitation to follow Jesus to a greater audience—those who hear/read this Gospel.[64] Thus, Mark's Jesus exposes persons other than the Twelve to lessons geared toward preparing them for ministry. In addition, he begins to prepare them for the inevitable consequences that come from following Jesus.

Peter's rebuke of Jesus in Mark 8:32 illuminates the need for Jesus to instruct both his disciples and the crowd about the nature of discipleship in light of his passion prediction. Peter's reaction to Jesus' impending passion revealed that he is ill prepared to face such consequences himself. Therefore, Jesus' teaching reveals that a decision has to be made. Anyone who chooses to be his disciple must make a decision about following him given the consequences. I wish to suggest that this call to discipleship introduces no new requirements. It does, however, present additional information in light of the religious leaders' response to Jesus' ministry. Having disclosed his own fate, Jesus invites his disciples and the crowd to make an informed decision. He does this by issuing commands that coincide with the consequences he listed in verse 34. Before attending to the consequences of discipleship, let us first look at what discipleship is.

Discipleship

In the section on Mark 8:31-33, I identified several forms of ministry in which the narrator shows Jesus engaged. Mark portrays Jesus' involvement in a ministry that includes teaching (4:1-34; 6:2, 34), preaching (1:34), healing (5:23-43; 7:32-37), exorcising (1:23-26; 3:11; 5:1-20; 7:26-30), praying (1:35; 6:46), miracle working (6:30-44; 8:1-10), and forgiving (2:5). Mark then depicts persons other than Jesus participating in the same type of work: teaching (6:30), preaching (1:45; 5:20; 6:12), healing (6:13), and exorcising (6:7; 9:38). The participation of the disciples is implied in the feeding miracle. Jesus commands his disciples to give the people something to eat (6:37). Although Jesus wields the power behind the miracle, they participate in Jesus' ministry to the people by distributing the loaves (6:41).

Prior to 8:31, Mark provides no examples of persons other than Jesus extending forgiveness or praying. However, Mark does later show both prayer and forgiveness to be activities Jesus expects his followers to participate in. Peter, James, and John are commanded to pray in the Garden of Gethsemane. Instead, they fall asleep (14:32-40). Jesus expresses the importance of prayer in Mark 9:29, informing the disciples that some demons can only be exorcised through prayer. By so doing, Jesus links exorcism to prayer. Since Mark records persons other than Jesus exorcising demons and Jesus giving the disciples authority to cast out demons (3:15; 6:7), the narrative expectation is that those who follow Jesus will pray. Moreover, the Gospel writer also connects prayer to forgiveness. Jesus instructs his disciples that when they pray, they are also to forgive others (11:25). In Mark's Gospel, Jesus' ministry is the template for discipleship. Larry Hurtado writes, "In fact, Mark makes Jesus the only adequate model for discipleship."[65]

A quick review of the scholarship in chapter 2 discloses the same consensus. Among the group are scholars who categorize Jesus' ministry according to one of four dominant emphases: teaching (Robert P. Meye), preaching (Sean Fréyne, Mary Ann Tolbert, Brian K. Blount, and Donald H. Juel, who also includes healing), political engagement on behalf of the poor (Ched Myers), and suffering (Theodore Weeden, Augustine Stock, Joel Marcus, Norman Perrin). Their understanding of discipleship emphasizes the same aspects they brought to the fore as characteristic of Jesus' ministry.

The remaining scholars represent a combination of the above categories. They assert that discipleship consists of doing what Jesus does, whether that represents a form of *imitatio Christi* (Morna Hooker) or involves engaging in ministry activities similar to those of Jesus (Ernest Best, Joanna Dewey, Werner Kelber, Robert Tannehill). Even those who insist that one must *be with* Jesus in order to be a disciple acknowledge that the purpose of *being with* Jesus is to do the work of Jesus.[66]

Relationship between Discipleship and Ministry

What my examination of Mark's Gospel and review of Markan scholars reveal is that Mark establishes a relation of narrative co-classification between Jesus' ministry and discipleship. Co-classification is a relation among semantic items in which each of the items occupies an identical class but is a distinct member of that class.[67] I refer to the relation between Jesus' ministry and discipleship as one of narrative co-classification because Mark does not employ a single word to signify Jesus' ministry. Instead, Mark conveys the multifaceted nature of Jesus' ministry by chronicling what Jesus does. In like fashion, Mark signifies discipleship narratively by relating accounts in which persons other than Jesus perform the same acts of service that Jesus does.

To illustrate my point, I will compare the relation between Jesus' ministry and following Jesus with an example Ruqaiya Hasan gives. Hasan uses the following sentences to explain co-classification: I play the cello. My husband does, too. "Play the cello" is A and "does" is B. Items A and B are part of the same class, cello playing. The primary class is made explicit by item A. We know what "my husband" does because what he does is connected to what "I" do—play the cello. Although "my husband" and "I" do the same thing—"play the cello," our cello-playing activities are two different situational events. When "I" play the cello, it is not my husband playing the cello, and vice versa. However, when either "my husband" plays the cello or "I" play the cello, we are doing the same thing.[68]

"Jesus' ministry" and "following Jesus" function the same way in Mark's Gospel. "Jesus' ministry" is narrative item A and "following Jesus" is narrative item B. Items A and B are part of the same primary class, Jesus' ministry. This primary class is made explicit by the narrative presentation of item A, which I detailed above. We know what "following Jesus" is, because throughout the narrative Mark has consistently connected "following Jesus" to "Jesus' ministry." Although "Jesus' ministry" and "following Jesus" entail participating in the same activities—teaching, preaching, healing, exorcisms, miracle working, prayer, and forgiveness—the performance of these activities represents two different situational events. When Jesus engages in "[his] ministry," it is not the disciple. When the disciple is "following Jesus," it is not Jesus doing the following. However, when either Jesus engages in "[his] ministry" or the disciple "follow[s] Jesus," they are doing the same thing. Mark's narrative presentation of the relationship between Jesus' ministry and discipleship can be expressed by the following sentences that model Hasan's example: Jesus engages in ministry. His disciples do, too.

Is There Agony in This Ministry?

My analysis of Mark 8:31 showed no form of agony (suffering or pain) to be a constitutive part of Jesus' ministry. Prior to 8:31, there is no narrative account that depicts an experience of agony by Jesus. Based on Jesus' ministry, Peter declares Jesus to be the Messiah. The relation of narrative co-classification revealed similarities between Jesus' ministry and his followers' discipleship. When it comes to agony, the point of similarity between Jesus' ministry and his followers' discipleship is that agony is not a constitutive part of either one. Because agony is neither a characteristic of nor a prerequisite for Jesus' ministry and messiahship, it is not a characteristic of or prerequisite for discipleship. Our reading of verse 34 to this point militates against defining discipleship in terms of any form of agony. Although

I have identified pain as a consequence of discipleship, this pain does not characterize discipleship. Pain only characterizes the consequences of discipleship.

An analysis of the verbal forms in verse 34 reinforces this point. Jesus' call to discipleship is framed by the verb *akoloutheō* (follow). This is not surprising given *akoloutheō* has been consistently used in Mark's Gospel to signify discipleship, especially in the initial calls of Simon, Andrew, James, John, and Levi (1:16-20; 2:14). Mark also employs *akoloutheō* when he narrates the exchange between Jesus and the rich man. Jesus commands the rich man to sell all he has and follow (*akoloutheō*) him (10:21). All of these occurrences of *akoloutheō* are in the present tense and therefore signify continuous action.[69]

However, Mark contrasts the command to follow with the commands to deny oneself and take up one's cross by expressing the former command in the present tense and the latter commands in the aorist tense. Both commands, *aparnesasthō* (deny, as in disown, renounce) and *apatō* (take up) are aorist imperatives. These are actions that are "simply brought to pass."[70] Neither denying oneself nor taking up one's cross is grammatically equivalent to following. Following is the only thing Jesus demands a disciple to do continually. Moreover, the command to follow is the only one shown to represent the content of Jesus' ministry. Therefore, discipleship begins and ends with following, that is, following Jesus in a ministry similar to his.

Following Jesus in a ministry similar to his also places the disciple in a similar position as him: "*Akolouthein* also implies participation in the fate of Jesus."[71] Because the consequence of his ministry is pain, manifested specifically in the form of being rejected and killed, Jesus issues the commands to deny oneself and take up one's cross as a means of preparing those who will follow. To support this view, I first explore the meaning potential of these commands. Afterward, I detail the semantic relations that are the basis for the conclusions I reach.

Self-Denial in Mark

Markan scholars generally view self-denial as a call to selfless living.[72] John R. Donahue and Daniel J. Harrington define self-denial as "act[ing] in a selfless way . . . giv[ing] up one's place at the center of things."[73] William Lane expresses the same sentiment: "Jesus stipulates that those who wish to follow him must be prepared to shift the center of gravity in their lives from a concern for self to reckless abandon to God."[74] C. E. B. Cranfield posits "turn[ing] away from the idolatry of self-centeredness."[75] The problem with the above definitions is that they define self-denial based on a modern notion of the self. The Gospel's original audience would have accessed Mark's meaning from their sociocultural context.

Unlike modern Western cultures that define the self in primarily individualistic terms,[76] first-century Mediterranean societies were "based on collectivism."[77] In other words, ancient Mediterranean persons were dyadic rather than individual persons. A person was always "in relation with and connected to at least one other social unit, usually a group."[78]

This group connection was of ultimate importance, for the group always took precedence over the individual.[79] Moreover, the group bestowed honor by acknowledging the worth of the individual. Apart from the group, a dyadic person has no identity. Malina writes, "This is the group-embedded, group-oriented person, collectivistic personality, one who needs another simply to know who he or she is."[80]

The opinions of the group and the society at large, typified by acceptance or rejection, cannot be underestimated: "[Dyadic] persons internalize and make their own what others say, do and think about them because they believe it is necessary for being human to live out the expectations of others."[81] Not to fulfill group or societal expectations is to be dishonored. Within this cultural context, dishonor is tantamount to no longer being human. At the most basic level, an honorable person is one whose claim to human worth and dignity is accepted by another. Therefore, she or he is deemed worthy of societal maintenance and defense.[82]

To "deny oneself" is not a command to be more selfless or to forsake "the idolatry of self-centeredness." The ancient Mediterranean person did not possess a concept of self apart from the group. The group was always more important than the individual. Malina insists that ancient Mediterranean persons "knew other people 'socially' . . . in terms of the groups in which a person was embedded."[83] The central group was the family unit or kinship group.[84] A person's primary allegiance was to this group.

The ancient Mediterranean collectivistic self always had in mind the best interest of and connection to the family. The family's expectations, which were connected to those of the larger society, held "supreme sway over individual life."[85] By living up to the family's expectations and, by extension, the expectations of society, a person helped to maintain the honor status of the entire familial group. Because one's honor status and identity were so deeply enmeshed in the honor status of the family, a person could elevate or lower the group's social standing. In other words, the person represents the family, and the family represents the person, without exception.

The ancient Mediterranean concept of the person as a collectivistic self exposes meaning potential in Mark 3:20-21, 31-35 that helps to illumine the command to "deny oneself" (8:34). In Mark 2:20-21, Jesus' family comes to "restrain him" because people are saying that he is insane. In response to the people's claims, Jesus' entire family turns out to handle the situation. When the family arrives at the house where Jesus is staying, the crowd reports to him that his "mother and brothers and sisters" are outside (2:32). Read from an honor/shame perspective, Jesus' alleged insanity is a direct reflection of his family unit. For this reason, the whole family responds to a potential crisis of honor.

Jesus, however, does not acquiesce to the wishes of his family. Instead, he redefines his family based on obedience to God rather than blood or marriage ties (2:35). Since Mark has consistently shown Jesus to be one who does God's will, those who follow him are also those who do the will of God and are the family of Jesus.

Jesus' definition of family is a reorientation of his followers' primary loyalty and collectivistic self. Blood relations are no longer to hold supreme sway over their lives. The new family composed of those who do the will of God form the new court of public opinion. Moreover, Mark's use of geographic space reveals the reorientation of group loyalty. In this pericope, the biological family of Jesus remains outside of the house while Jesus and his followers who compose his new family remain inside.

Read within this context, the command to deny oneself is a command to relinquish one's primary group orientation and accept Jesus and his followers as one's new group. It is to "say 'no' to the collectivistic self"[86] that has identified itself with its kinship group and given that group its primary loyalty. Self-denial calls one to a new understanding of the collectivistic self, one that is solely identified with Jesus and his gospel. When persons deny themselves, they look to Jesus to accept and approve their claim to worth. Jesus becomes the court of public opinion for the disciple. John Christopher Thomas's definition of self-denial comes closest to the meaning potential exposed in this verse: "[Self-denial] consists in making Jesus and his mission the object of life and learning so as to serve a new leader."[87]

The command to change one's primary group orientation fits well within Mark's cultural and narrative context. In 8:31, Jesus foretold his impending fate. This fate included being rejected by the elders, chief priests, and scribes. In language replete with honor/shame overtones, Jesus informed his followers that according to the prevailing standards, he would be shamed. The court of public opinion, namely, the religious rulers, would deem him unworthy of public acceptance and acknowledgment. They would dishonor him by rejecting him. This rejection, which would represent a repudiation of his claim to worth, would also have communal implications. Jesus' rejection is a rejection by his community, a community that would no longer see him as a member. From the perspective of the political and religious leaders, Jesus is the outsider, and they are the insiders. Again, Mark will use geographic space to emphasize this point when Jesus is crucified *outside* the city (15:20).

Jesus' rejection will also affect his followers. Although Jesus' group orientation has changed from blood relations to a new kinship group, his actions are still a reflection of his primary group. All identified with him will be susceptible to this shame. Just as Jesus' followers could acquire honor by being associated with a man of such great power and authority, so also they could be shamed by their connection to one so publicly rejected.

Previously, I demonstrated the relation of co-classification between Jesus' ministry and discipleship. I showed how Mark's narrative portrayed both Jesus' ministry and discipleship as consisting of the same activities. In my analysis of Mark 8:31, pain was shown to be the inevitable consequence of Jesus' ministry. The relation of co-classification reveals that pain will also be the inevitable consequence of discipleship. By viewing the text through a womanist cultural lens, we saw that Jesus' pain has social and physical dimensions. His rejection exemplifies the social dimension of his pain. Likewise, Jesus' command to deny one's self addresses the social dimension of a disciple's pain.

Taking Up the Cross in Mark

The command to take up one's cross addresses the physical dimension of a disciple's pain. The cross, mentioned here (8:34) for the first time, foreshadows death in its "extremist form."[88] It also symbolizes perhaps the most extreme example of dishonor to be found in ancient Mediterranean society. Our context of culture highlighted the public nature of honor and shame. Both required witnesses to be valid. Crucifixion was a public event. It was common practice for the condemned person to be tortured and forced to carry his or her crossbeam to the place of execution.[89] To add insult to injury (literally), the naked victim was displayed publicly in a prominent place such as a crossroads or high ground.[90]

To comprehend the level of shame crucifixion represented, we must appeal to our context of culture. Purity, which is a means value of honor, is primarily about maintaining proper boundaries. In ancient Mediterranean society, a person's clothing functions to uphold boundaries: "Clothing is also such a boundary for the physical body, which is a microcosm of the social system. Nudity means the complete absence of boundaries."[91] A person who has no boundaries is a dishonorable person. Moreover, he or she has offended God because nudity "was unacceptable in God's presence."[92]

Crucifixion was the humiliating triumph of those who had power and authority to condemn a person to this form of execution. Neyrey informs us that when someone exposes another man's penis or buttocks it is a "claim of power and superiority."[93] The one who exposes triumphs over the one who is exposed.[94] In effect, the individual or the institution who has the power and authority to execute another in this fashion repudiates all claims to honor the victim may have. Whatever honor the condemned person once possessed becomes the prize of whoever can accomplish this feat. As the instrument of death for criminals in the Roman Empire, crucifixion was a way for the Roman government to regain the honor impugned by criminals and dissenters against the state. If crucifixion did nothing else, it showed who had the last word.[95]

The humiliating nature of crucifixion leads Gundry to conclude that taking up the cross "means no more than exposing oneself to shame and ridicule by following [Jesus]."[96] Although Gundry's interpretation of cross bearing does much to illumine the honor/shame codes of ancient Mediterranean society and 8:38, which we will discuss shortly, it does not take seriously the primary goal of crucifixion—death.

At this point in the narrative, the reader knows nothing about the way in which Jesus will die. The reader, along with the would-be disciples, only knows that Jesus will experience pain, specifically manifested in the form of rejection and death, and rise again. In a society that is all too familiar with the heinous practice of crucifixion, the cross is not a religious symbol but that "terrible form of capital punishment reserved by imperial Rome for political dissenters."[97] At its most basic level, to "take up [one's] cross" means being prepared to die. In light of our narrative, it means being prepared to die as a consequence of following Jesus.

Death, then, is the general class of meaning to which both *apoktanthēnai* (be killed) in Jesus' passion prediction and *apatō ton stauron autou* (take up one's cross) in Jesus' call to discipleship belong. Just as Mark links the command to deny oneself with Jesus' rejection, he also connects the command to take up the cross with Jesus' prediction of his execution. Whereas *apoktanthēnai* conveys the physical dimension of Jesus' pain, Jesus' command to take up the cross expresses the physical dimension of the disciples' pain.

The Relationship between Denying Oneself and Taking Up the Cross

There remains one more semantic relation to examine— *aparnesasthō eauton* (let him/her deny him-/herself) and *aratō ton stauron autou* (let him/her take up his/her cross). These two phrases share a relation of co-extension, the same general field of meaning. They refer to painful actions that are the inevitable consequences of discipleship. Both commands carry the connotation of shame. Furthermore, both commands are precise enough to express the shame associated with them and to accurately reflect the pain that is a consequence of Jesus' ministry in both its social and physical forms. In short, they are general and expansive enough to provide a context of meaning for a multiplicity of painful experiences that are the result of following Jesus.

I will now summarize this point. Jesus will experience pain that results in his rejection and death. His disciples must be ready to endure the same. The invitation to follow and the commands to deny oneself and take up the cross signal what the disciples can expect.[98] As if self-denial and its corresponding rejection are not enough humiliation, Jesus evokes the language of the cross to express the ultimate consequence of following him. In one word, *stauros* (cross), Jesus communicates the most shameful experience an ancient Mediterranean mind can imagine. The cross, then, is not the mundane inconveniences of life or even the existential suffering indicative of the human condition. It is symbolic of the experience of pain in its most humiliating and excruciating form.[99] The cross is the painful consequence of following Jesus in his messianic undertaking. The cross represents the pain that comes as a result of life-affirming behavior modeled after the ministry of Jesus.

The choice to follow Jesus, in an endeavor that will inevitably require self-denial and cross carrying, necessitates a reversal of the would-be disciples' traditional concepts of honor and shame. Jesus has invited them to participate in a ministry that, according to their societal standards, only brings shame. Therefore, the call to follow Jesus is a call to reorient their perspective and affirm Jesus' honor system.[100] Rather than seeking the honor that the religious rulers and other elite members of society have the power and authority to ascribe, they must seek the only true honor—that which God bestows through Jesus.

Finally, the paradoxical nature of discipleship is further emphasized in 8:35–37. This paradox also finds its basis in Mark 8:31. In verse 31, Jesus informs his disciples that he will be rejected and killed on account of his ministry. However, he will also rise. By losing his life, he will gain it. Likewise, those who endure unto death the painful consequences of discipleship will gain their lives (8:35). By enduring the shame of the world for the sake of the gospel, they will acquire honor in the sight of God. Those who succumb to the honor standards of the world and, therefore, forsake the gospel will ultimately lose their lives. In striving for the honor of humans, they will become dishonorable in the eyes of God.

Mark 8:38

The honor/shame issues implicit in Mark 8:31, 34 reach full expression in Mark 8:38. The events of Jesus' passion that are narrated in verse 31 characterize a shameful demise. His rejection by the religious rulers signifies the revocation of his honor. Moreover, it intimates that the court of public opinion will turn on Jesus. The change in the public's perception will result in the downfall of Jesus. The repudiation of his honor will be so extreme that they will attempt to destroy Jesus socially and physically. I say *attempt* because Mark includes the inevitability of Jesus' rising after three days as part of the prediction. The religious leaders will do what is in their power to do; however, Jesus' resurrection prediction suggests that their plan will be foiled. If rejection and death are certain, so, too, is resurrection.

Jesus' call to discipleship follows the same pattern as his passion prediction. It is therefore cast in the same honor/shame tones. Mark correlates the self-denial of the disciple with the rejection of Jesus. In this way, Mark conveys the social dimensions of the pain that is a consequence of following Jesus. Likewise, the narrator links the cross bearing of the disciple with the execution of Jesus and relates physical pain as a possible result of discipleship. Therefore, self-denial and cross bearing communicate the element of shame present in Jesus' prediction of his rejection and execution. The consequences of discipleship, though shameful according to the world's standards, do not nullify the honor that comes from God. Should the disciple lose his or her life for the sake of ministry, she or he will gain it. In this way, Mark uses the resurrection of Jesus as proof that the disciple, too, will be vindicated by God. Thus, following Jesus results in the sharing of his shame *and* his honor.

In Mark 8:38, the narrator forgoes subtlety and states in explicit terms the new honor/shame code that underpins Jesus' call to discipleship.[101] For the first time, being ashamed (*epaischynomai*) of Jesus becomes an unmistakable issue: "The verb *epaischynomai* in the New Testament denotes identification with someone or something which, according to the prevailing social dynamics, would result in a loss of status."[102]

It is here that Gundry's understanding of cross bearing as enduring shame for the sake of the gospel is helpful. In verse 38, Jesus cautions the would-be disciples against allowing the existing honor/shame code and its consequent social ordering to prevent them from following him. Neither the fact that Jesus will be a rejected, executed Messiah nor the disciple's resulting self-denial and cross bearing should cause the disciple to refuse identification with Jesus and his gospel. Things are not what they seem. Although Jesus will die a shameful death, he is really the honorable one. "This generation," in its pretense of honor, is actually shameful. Jesus' resurrection will reveal how shameful their actions really are.

Whereas Mark depicts the religious leaders in exclusively shameful terms, he depicts Jesus in exclusively honorable terms. Jesus is shown to be honorable in three ways. First, he will come back. Second, he will come in the "glory of his Father." Finally, he will come with the holy angels. Let us take each in turn.

In 8:31, Mark is very specific in noting that Jesus' death is not final. He will come back. Jesus will rise "after three days" (*meta treis hemēras*). In Mark 8:38, however, the time of Jesus' return is imprecise. Mark emphasizes this through his use of the subjunctive—*hotan elthē* (when he comes). In effect, Mark connects 8:31 and 8:38 to establish a relation of co-extension between *anastēnai* (to rise) and *hotan elthē* (when he comes). Although *anastēnai* and *hotan elthē* do not recount the same event, these semantic items share the same general field of meaning. Both refer to the post-resurrection appearances of Jesus. Moreover, the description of Jesus' return in unambiguous terms of honor serves to reinforce the honor ascribed to Jesus by means of the resurrection. In short, Jesus' exhortation reminds the would-be disciples that neither pain nor shame will have the last word.

Jesus will come again, not with the honor that humans can bestow, but "in the glory of his Father." He will come with honor that belongs to God alone. Most important is the fact that Jesus' honor is ascribed, not acquired. Ancient Mediterranean society allowed a man to attain honor passively (ascribed honor) or actively (acquired honor).[103] Ascribed honor is the result of one's birth. Because honor is a group value, males born into an honorable group inherit the group's honor status. In similar manner, an honorable person can ascribe honor to another if the person ascribing honor also has the authority to force acknowledgment of the honor bestowed.[104]

Although Jesus has demonstrated excellence in responding to the challenges of the religious rulers, his honor is not the result of mastering the honor/shame repartee. It is not something he has acquired throughout his ministry. According to his words here, there has never been a time in which Jesus was not honorable. He is the "beloved son" (1:11; 9:7) who shares in the honor (*doxa*) of "his Father."

Through the use of personal pronouns, Mark discloses the reciprocal nature of Jesus and the Father's relationship. The narrator thereby certifies that Jesus' relationship with the Father is not one-sided. Jesus suffers from no delusions of grandeur, nor has he overstepped proper boundaries in calling God his Father. Mark emphasizes God's favor of Jesus and acceptance of him as God's Son first. Mark 8:38 is actually the first time the narrator relates Jesus calling God "Father." Before the narrator ever recounts Jesus calling God "Father," the narrator records God referring to Jesus as the "beloved Son." Moreover, Jesus' impending passion, as shameful as it will be according to the prevailing social norms, will not nullify Jesus' status as the "beloved Son." In the pericope that follows, God will reaffirm Jesus' identity as the "beloved Son," in spite of the passion Jesus has just described (9:7). Jesus is therefore a person of ascribed honor with the corresponding means values of power and authority. That is why he has authority to forgive sins (2:10) and is the Lord of the Sabbath (2:28); his honor comes from God.

The first-century Mediterranean social world recognized no higher being than God. Their world "consisted of a set of ranks that embraced all persons, in fact all reality, reaching up to the cosmos with God on the top."[105] God therefore represented the pinnacle of the cosmological order. For this reason, David DeSilva speaks of God as both benefactor and patron. Everyone is indebted to God because God is both the creator and sustainer of life.[106]

Mark shows Jesus to be so closely related to God that he actually serves as an honor broker. In ancient societies, if a patron could not bequest the needed items to his or her client, he or she provided the client a means of access to another patron who could meet the need.[107] In this verse Jesus communicates his role as broker in the honor/shame exchange: "Those who are ashamed of me and of my words in this adulterous and sinful generation, of them the Son of Man will also be ashamed" (8:38). By faithfully following Jesus in a ministry like his, regardless of the consequences, a disciple can gain access to honor that comes from God. Jesus' mediation of this exchange is acceptable to God: "God's raising of Jesus from the dead demonstrates God's vindication of Jesus and the ascription of paramount honor to him. It equally underscores God's approval of Jesus' standards for what is honorable and what is shameful."[108] In order for individuals to access the honor of God, they must not be ashamed of Jesus or his words.[109] In this way, their honor status will no longer be a matter of public opinion. God becomes the court of opinion.

Finally, Jesus' presence among the holy angels seals his honor status. In the cosmological order, archangels then angels were ranked below God. Humans occupied the "social rung" beneath the angels.[110] The presence of the "holy angel" accentuates the level of honor Jesus will enjoy. The society of Jesus' day believed angels to be messengers of God.[111] They dwelled in the midst of holiness and therefore respected the boundaries between clean and unclean. That they will accompany Jesus means that Jesus also possesses the means value of purity. However, the presence of Jesus among angels will not be a new phenomenon. Mark has already shown Jesus and angels together during the course of his ministry. After spending forty days in the wilderness, the angels come and wait upon him (1:13). Jesus' honor status, then, is a present reality that will be publicly displayed at an undisclosed future time (13:32).

In a very simple phrase, "in the glory of his Father with the holy angels" (8:38), Jesus informs the people that he has the highest honor rating among mortals. Moreover, the reference to the Father's glory and to the accompanying train of angels serves to set Jesus' entire ministry in doxological perspective.

In spite of the shame that is a consequence of following Jesus in a ministry like his, the final message of this teaching unit is one of honor. Discipleship rather than the culturally defined values of wealth, purity, and humility becomes a means value for honor. Jesus invites those around him to join him in ministry and share in the honor that comes from God. The invitation is not to suffer or to experience pain. The invitation is to follow.

Conclusion

When we read Mark 8:31-38 through our womanist lens, we can see that Jesus' experience of pain, characterized by rejection and execution, and his resurrection will be the inevitable result of his ministry. Jesus' passion is the result of the moral evil of those who oppose him. His resurrection is a divine counteraction that justifies his life and ministry.

From an honor/shame perspective, the narrator is connecting doing the will of God as exemplified by Jesus' ministry with the cultural value of honor and connecting the opposition to Jesus' ministry (the will of God) to the cultural value of shame. In other words, there is meaning potential in Mark's story of Jesus that depicts Jesus' ministry as honorable and therefore shows him to be an honorable man. The meaning potential shows the opposition of the religious and political leaders to be the reason for Jesus' agony and death and therefore shows this opposition to be shameful.

The resurrection of Jesus confirms that Jesus' ministry does indeed represent God's will and is honorable despite the attempts of his enemies to shame him. In this way, Mark communicates to the reader that to follow Jesus is honorable and to reject him is shameful. However, there are consequences for following Jesus. Mark depicts these consequences as pain, not suffering, and honor.

∞ The Tenor of Discourse

Already, we have seen the sociolinguistic connections in the narrative that argue for the inevitability of Jesus' agony, which we have identified as pain, and pain and honor as the consequences of following him. We have also seen how Jesus' passion prediction and call to discipleship subvert the honor/shame codes of ancient society by presenting discipleship as a means value for honor. Paradoxically, Jesus, bound for the cross, is presented as an honorable man.

An examination of the tenor, that is, the roles and relationships of the characters in our field, will further clarify these findings. From a very early stage in the narrative, Mark shows the scribes, Pharisees, and Herodians to be in conflict with Jesus because of his ministry. Mark then creates a similarity chain that links the Pharisees, Herodians, and scribes to the chief priests and elders. In this way, Mark weaves the groups that oppose Jesus into a single characterization and shows why Jesus will endure the pain of the cross: he will be rejected and killed because of the moral evil of the religious and political leaders. His death will be the inevitable consequence of the religious and political leaders' opposition to his ministry, not a reflection of God's will. Because his agony is temporary (he will rise after three days), named, recognized, and comes as a result of life-giving and/or life-sustaining ministry, Jesus' agony is pain, not suffering.

Furthermore, Mark emphasizes the evil and shameful nature of the leaders' actions by connecting these characters to Satan. In effect, the narrator depicts the honor/shame conflict between Jesus and the religious and political leaders as reflective of a greater battle between

God and Satan. And in this battle, Jesus will be the casualty of war.[112] The disciples, represented by Peter, the crowd, and, by extension, the reader, must decide which side of the battle to join. They must choose recognizing that the pain and honor that result from Jesus' ministry will be the same consequences that result from their discipleship.

Mark 8:31 depicts Jesus in his role as teacher. This verse also lists three other characters:[113] the elders, chief priests, and scribes. Of the three groups referenced here, the scribes are the only ones we see prior to this verse. We shall see that Mark uses the scribes and Pharisees as the lynchpins that connect the Herodians, chief priests, and elders to his chain of oppositional characters.

The narrator mentions the scribes early in the Gospel (1:22). But Mark does not introduce them as characters until the following chapter (2:6). The first reference to the scribes foreshadows conflict with Jesus. Mark recounts Jesus' first act of public ministry as one that calls into question the honor of the scribes. The narrator informs us that Jesus "entered the synagogue and taught" (1:21). Ched Myers explains the significance of his actions: "Jesus has penetrated symbolic space acknowledged to be the domain of the scribes."[114] In Mark's Gospel, the scribes are depicted as the official teachers of the community.[115] Questions regarding the interpretation of Scripture center on what the scribes teach (9:11; 12:35). Yet the people extol Jesus' teaching as "one having authority, and not as the scribes" (1:22).

Jesus not only teaches but also exorcises a demon (1:25-26). In honor/shame terms, the exorcism first confirms Jesus' power. Those who witnessed the event connect his teaching to the exorcism. Jesus' words actually *do* something; they are a performative utterance.[116] The onlookers respond, "What is this? A new teaching—with authority!" (1:27). The narrator frames the exorcism with Jesus' teaching, "suggesting that the exorcism has everything to do with the struggle between the authority of Jesus and that of the scribes."[117] Thus, Mark shows that Jesus possesses two important means values for the acquisition of honor—power and authority.

Power and authority are distinct yet related means values. Power is the "ability to exercise control over the behavior of others."[118] Authority is the "socially recognized and approved ability to control the behavior of others."[119] The difference between power and authority is that authority is socially recognized and approved. In other words, other people must acknowledge one's authority. Power is self-evident and needs no such approval or recognition. In the Gospel accounts, Jesus' ministry, specifically his exorcisms, exemplifies power. In this instance, however, the people also ascribe to Jesus authority. His power is recognized and approved by the onlookers. Within this cultural context, Jesus has acquired honor but at the expense of the scribes.

Myers exposes another aspect of the conflict between Jesus and the scribes. He points out that Jesus' teaching is met with "stiff opposition,"[120] the presence of a man with an unclean spirit. Specifically, he points out the puzzling nature of the demon's challenge: *ti ēmin kai soi* (1:24). The unclean spirit refers to himself in the first person plural: "What do you have to do with *us*?" The spirit continues: *elthes apolēsai emas* (Have you come to destroy us?). Myers therefore wonders to whom "us" refers. He concludes, "It can only be the group already identified in the conflict theme—the scribal aristocracy whose space (social role and power) Jesus is threatening."[121]

Myers's explanation is especially compelling when we compare this passage to Mark 5:1-20. From the outset of this story, it appears that the man is tormented by only one unclean spirit (5:2). Even Jesus addresses the spirit in the singular: *exelthē to pneuma to akatharton ek tou anthrōpou* ("Come out of the man, you unclean spirit!" 5:8). In spite of Jesus' command, the unclean spirit remains. When asked its name, the unclean spirit refers to itself using both singular and plural pronouns: "My name is Legion; for we are many" (5:9). The unclean spirit's name is also the name of a division of Roman soldiers. Jesus has once again invaded the social space of another group. This time it is the space of the Roman military that occupies Palestine. Although Mark does not list the Romans in Jesus' passion prediction, he will later show Rome's participation in the crucifixion of Jesus. From the beginning of his Gospel, Mark links Jesus' opponents to the unclean spirits and shows that Jesus' ministry endangers the positions of both.

It is, therefore, not surprising that throughout the rest of the Gospel, whenever the scribes are present, they are always depicted as opposing Jesus.[122] Because Mark shows the scribes to be unfailingly opposed to Jesus and his ministry since its inception, he leads the reader to expect the same from the elders and chief priests. This expectation is reinforced by the narrative when Jesus foretells his rejection by the elders, chief priests, and scribes.

On four other occasions, Mark specifically conjoins the elders, chief priests, and scribes as opponents of Jesus (11:27; 14:43, 53; 15:1). In Mark 12:1-11, the parable of the tenants, the narrator makes reference to the elders, chief priests, and scribes by relating the hearers' reaction: "When they realized that he had told this parable against them, they wanted to arrest him, but they feared the crowd. So they left him and went away" (12:12). The "they" in this passage are the elders, chief priests, and scribes. Each interaction takes place in Jerusalem. Jesus' presence in Jerusalem and in the temple suggests that he has once again penetrated a symbolic space. This time, it is the territory reserved for the chief priests and the elders.

Jesus' presence is consistently met with opposition from these religious leaders. They want to know "by what authority" he drives out the money changers, buyers, and sellers from the temple (11:28). Jesus' parable of the tenants is met with their desire to arrest him (12:12). Their desire becomes a reality when they send out a crowd with clubs and swords to seize Jesus from the Garden of Gethsemane (14:43), bring him to where they have assembled (14:53), and then take him to Pilate (15:1).

In addition to connecting the elders, chief priests, and scribes, Mark also links the chief priests and scribes without the elders. In his third passion prediction, Jesus informs his disciples that he will be betrayed into the hands of the scribes and chief priests (10:33). Moreover, the narrator reports two occasions in which the scribes and chief priests are looking for a way to kill him (11:18; 14:1).

The narrator also depicts the chief priests acting alone. They are perhaps the most antagonistic group of all toward Jesus. They are the ones to whom Judas goes when he betrays Jesus (14:10). They are the ones who hand Jesus over to Pilate (15:1) and "accuse him of many things" (15:3). They are the ones who get the crowd to agitate for Barabbas's release rather than Jesus' (15:11). And Mark informs the readers/hearers that the chief priests do these things "out of jealousy" (15:10).

Mark shows that the elders, chief priests, and scribes have only one character trait—opposition to Jesus. They therefore form a similarity chain characterized by a relation of co-extension. Specifically, the elders, chief priests, and scribes are synonymous narrative terms. This is not to say that they are identical to each other but that "so far as one kind of meaning goes, they 'mean the same.'"[123] The same meaning these groups convey is deadly opposition to Jesus.

At this point in the narrative (8:31), Jesus' ministry has yet to trouble his social superiors, the chief priests and elders, in Jerusalem. The fact that some scribes came down from Jerusalem to accuse him of having a demon (3:22) intimates the growing concern in Jerusalem. Although the scribes are the only persons listed with whom Jesus has direct contact prior to 8:31, his passion prediction suggests that he will soon attain a social level worthy of the direct consideration of the chief priests and elders.[124] In 8:31, Jesus is still in the northern region of Palestine away from Jerusalem and its temple elites. Here Jesus remains primarily the problem of the local scribes,[125] Pharisees, and Herodians.

Mark introduces two other groups that oppose Jesus before 8:31—the Pharisees and the Herodians. The Pharisees are the first to materialize. Like the scribes, they are mentioned by the narrator before they appear on the narrative scene as characters. Mark immediately casts the Pharisees in a negative light by tying them to the scribes. In Mark 2:16, the "scribes of the Pharisees" question Jesus' table fellowship with sinners. Later in the narrative, the Pharisees appear with the scribes again (7:1, 5). This time the dispute involves observing the traditions of the elders.

The opposition to Jesus of the Pharisees and scribes is not surprising. Anthony Saldarini notes that in Mark's Gospel, "the scribes are the officially recognized and authoritative teachers in the community and the Pharisees are a group with a specific interpretation of certain laws and practices."[126] Mark portrays the Pharisees and scribes as interpreters of the Torah with authority to regulate behavior based on those interpretations. Jesus' actions assume the same, if not a greater, degree of interpretive authority. In light of his increased following, Jesus threatens the system that maintains the social standing of the scribes and Pharisees.

The Pharisees are mentioned for the second time in Mark 2:18. Again they are absent. Here Mark highlights a difference between the fasting practices of the Pharisees and his disciples. The people ask Jesus why his disciples do not fast like the Pharisees or John's disciples (2:18). Before Mark allows the Pharisees to appear on the narrative set, he already casts them as Jesus' opponents and informs his readers/hearers that Jesus and the Pharisees hold contradictory views.[127]

Jesus' first interaction with the Pharisees is detailed in Mark 2:24. Here the Pharisees question Jesus for allowing his disciples to pluck heads of grain on the Sabbath: "Why are [your disciples] doing what is not lawful on the sabbath?" Their question is actually an accusation. In short, they accuse Jesus of allowing his disciples to break Sabbath law. Even though Mark has prepared the reader for possible conflict between Jesus and the Pharisees, the antagonism of the Pharisees rises quickly. In the following episode, the narrator informs us that the Pharisees along with the Herodians plot to destroy Jesus (3:6). Unlike the Pharisees, who are mentioned within the narrative before they appear, the Herodians seem to come out of nowhere. They emerge for the first time in 3:6 and will not appear again until they are commissioned to go with the Pharisees to test Jesus (12:13). On each occasion, they are with the Pharisees. The Herodians, however, are not religious leaders. Their group name signals their political affiliation. More than likely, the Herodians were servants, slaves, officials, or courtiers of Herod. "Herodians" could also more generally designate Herod's supporters.[128] Mark uses the connection between the Pharisees and the Herodians to show the religious and political hostility toward Jesus. John P. Meier explains that "the union of the Pharisees and the Herodians brackets the public ministry, foreshadowing early on in Galilee the deadly opposition and political forces that would finally bear fruit in Jerusalem."[129]

At this point we have seen how Mark connects the scribes to the Pharisees and connects the Pharisees to the Herodians. Our context of culture allows us to connect all three groups and identify a common interest. The Herodians, scribes, and Pharisees were all retainers. In other words, their social and economic positions were dependent upon the governing class including the chief priests and elders.

The connections of the scribes, the Pharisees, and the Herodians to those who were socially higher enabled them to "enjoy a standard of living above that of the lower levels of society."[130] Consequently, the interests of the governing class became the interests of the retainer class.[131] Moreover, our context of culture reveals that the interest of the retainer class was actually the interest of Rome. Given Rome's policy of aligning the interests of the aristocracy with their own and holding them accountable for revenue and social order,[132] the retainer class would have been essential in helping the aristocracy keep the common people in line. This is precisely why the members of the elders and chief priests send the Pharisees and Herodians to test Jesus (12:13)— the Pharisees and Herodians are Jesus' social equals[133] but with the agenda of the chief priests and elders, his social superiors.

Moreover, it is not surprising that the scribes along with the Pharisees and Herodians are the only adversaries of Jesus the narrator has presented before 8:31. Each of them occupied a social rank slightly higher than the peasant class.[134] Jesus' growing popularity among the masses would affect their honor rating and therefore their social status before it endangered that of the chief priests and elders.

From their initial appearances on the narrative set, Jesus and the religious leaders are clearly differentiated. Throughout the Gospel, the religious leaders and the Herodians maintain an adversarial stance toward Jesus. They form an alliance that unites religious and political forces against Jesus. Mark therefore uses these groups to form a similarity chain—they are all opponents of Jesus. This similarity chain reinforces our translation of *dei* as inevitability by clearly showing five groups with political, religious, social, and economic power working together on a single agenda—the destruction of Jesus. Jesus' pain is initiated and brought to pass by human beings who seek to kill him and thereby stop his ministry.

Individually and collectively, the religious and political leaders serve to contrast and therefore illumine the honorable character of Jesus.[135] Mark does this by placing them in a relation of co-extension. The basic commonality between Jesus and the religious leaders is that they all are supposed to represent and do the work of God. However, Mark depicts Jesus as the only representative of God. Consequently, the "narrator consistently maintains a favorable point of view toward Jesus."[136] Jesus' norms and values are what the narrator wants the reader to adopt. Therefore, this similarity chain between Jesus and the religious leaders is characterized by antonymy; Jesus and the religious leadership are opposites. And their human conflict reveals a greater cosmic battle, a battle that has "the kingdoms of God and Satan locked in immortal combat."[137]

In Mark 8:33, Jesus makes reference to both God and Satan, thereby drawing clearly the lines of demarcation. Throughout the Gospel, the narrator has shown Jesus to be approved by God and the representative of God. As noted before, Mark's narrator begins the Gospel by identifying Jesus as the Christ, Son of God. The narrator verifies this claim during Jesus' baptism by recording the voice from heaven extolling Jesus as "my son, the Beloved; in you I am well pleased" (1:11, my translation). The narrator shows that Jesus has the authority of God to forgive sins and to proclaim the good news of God (1:14) and the kingdom of God (1:15). When Jesus performs a miracle, the crowd associates his power with and gives glory to God (2:12). Consequently, the "things of God" that Peter resists are the things of Jesus, namely, the ministry that will result in his passion and resurrection. In short, Peter has allied himself with Satan, who is God's, and therefore Jesus', adversary.

As consistently as the narrator has shown Jesus to be the representative of God, he has also shown Satan to be God's opponent. Although Satan is mentioned only four times apart from 8:33, every reference depicts opposition. Immediately following Jesus' baptism, Satan spends forty days tempting Jesus in the wilderness (1:13). The demons that torment humans and are cast out by Jesus operate under the lordship of Satan (3:23-26). In the parable of the sower, Jesus is the one who sows the gospel, and Satan is the one who "immediately comes and takes away the word" (4:15). Peter's rebuke of Jesus is similar to Satan's role in the parable. Should Jesus forgo his ministry and heed Peter's rebuke (8:23), the word would be taken away.

Peter's actions in 8:32 reveal the complexity of Mark's depiction. The first time the reader encounters Peter, his obedience to Jesus is evident (1:16). Since his initial call, Peter is always among the disciples closest to Jesus. Not only is he the first of the twelve Jesus appoints to be with him, proclaim the Word, and exorcise demons (3:14-16); he is also among the three disciples Jesus takes with him to raise Jairus's daughter (5:37). Most important, Peter is the first human being in the narrative to confess Jesus as the Christ (8:29). Yet Peter is also the first person to reject Jesus' teaching.

The variety of traits and the complexity of his characterization suggest that Peter also functions as a type. He represents a larger group, namely, the disciples and the crowd. Peter's rebuke gives voice to the silent doubts of the crowd (readers). Like Peter, the disciples and the crowd must make a decision between embracing the things of God (which Mark's narrator has shown to be exemplified in the ministry of Jesus) and playing the adversary by thinking the things of humans. To follow Jesus in a ministry that inevitably leads to denying oneself and taking up the cross is embracing the things of God. To reject doing things Jesus' way is to oppose him and align oneself with those who think the things of humans.

It is interesting to note that Jesus' rebuke of Peter conjoins Satan and the thoughts of humans. Blount observes that the only place the perceptions of human beings are linked with Satan is Mark 3:22-30.[138] In this passage, the scribes come from Jerusalem and accuse Jesus of having a demon. By thinking solely within the confines of their social, political, religious, and economic boundaries, they have confused the work of the Holy Spirit with that of Satan. They mistakenly think they represent God and subsequently position themselves as Jesus' adversaries. According to the narrative point of view, the scribes have alienated themselves from God and have aligned themselves with Satan.

The scribes and Pharisees form the link that connects all of Jesus' enemies. The narrator connects the scribes to the elders (seven times), the chief priests (nine times), and Satan (two times). Mark 3:6 links the Pharisees and Herodians. And on three occasions, the scribes and Pharisees appear together (2:16; 7:1, 5). All six characters are consistent in their opposition to Jesus. By connecting the six groups together and consistently showing the conflict between these characters and Jesus, the narrator effectively presents the scribes, chief priests, elders, Pharisees, Herodians, and Satan as God's opponents. Because these characters are cast as rivals of Jesus, the beloved Son of God, their actions are shown to be contrary to the will of God. They represent the antithesis of the divine intent, not its fulfillment.

Of all the characters in our field, only the disciples (Peter included) and the crowd demonstrate the capacity to deviate from their original course of action. Just as Jesus will not veer from his mission, neither will the religious rulers. Jesus and the religious authorities represent opposite sides of the conflict. The disciples and the crowd must choose which side they will join. In essence, they must choose to either maintain their current notions of honor and shame or reorient their perspective. To continue to uphold the societal barriers that exist, the corresponding social structure, and the moral code that supports them is to align oneself with Satan against the rule of God.

The only honorable choice the disciples and the crowd are given is to follow Jesus. In this way, Mark extends the honor/shame discourse from the human realm to the divine. In other words, the societal barriers, social structures, and moral code that attempt to shame Jesus and his followers are shown to be not only dishonorable but also satanic. Likewise, Mark depicts the choice to follow Jesus as not only honorable but godly. Discipleship, then, enables one to access honor, making honor another consequence of following Jesus.

The final "character" in this pericope is the crowd. Before turning to the crowd, I will first explore what Mark calls "this generation" (8:38) in order to situate the crowd within its context. Tolbert notes that Mark uses the phrase "this generation" four times (8:12, 38; 9:19; 13:30).[139] She claims that Jesus' reference to "this generation" is consistently negative, "always referring to the present authorities and groups opposing Jesus' word and way."[140] Therefore, "this generation" refers to "unbelieving, evil and destructive people."[141] Whereas Mark's usage of "generation" always carries a negative connotation, it does not always refer to those who intentionally oppose Jesus or are destructive. I concede to Tolbert's interpretation in every instance except Mark 9:19.

Mark 9:14-29 commences with Jesus returning from the Mount of Olives only to find a great crowd surrounding his disciples and some scribes arguing with them (9:14). Once "the whole crowd" recognizes Jesus, they all rush to him (9:15). "[Jesus] ask[s] them, 'What are you arguing about with them?'"(9:16).

It is unclear to whom Jesus is speaking. Is he addressing the scribes about their argument with the disciples or his disciples about the argument with the scribes? Moreover, the narrator has told us that "the whole crowd" came to Jesus. Neither a scribe nor a disciple answers Jesus' question, but someone from the crowd (9:17). The man from the crowd explains that he has brought his son to Jesus' disciples to cast out a demon, and they could not do it. Jesus begins his response with "You faithless generation" (9:19). Jesus addresses no one in particular but the audience in general, an audience composed of scribes, disciples, and the crowd.

The inclusion of the disciples in this designation is highlighted in Jesus' conversation with the boy's father. Jesus tells the father, "All things can be done for the one who believes" (9:23). Although the father responds with a mixture of belief and unbelief, his son is delivered from the demon (9:24-25). The fact that Jesus' disciples could not exorcise the demon demonstrates that their faith is not as strong as the father's wavering faith. When the disciples question Jesus about their inability to cast out the demon, Jesus responds, "This kind can come out only through prayer" (9:29). Jesus links prayer and faith in Mark 11:24. He instructs his disciples, "Whatever you ask for in prayer, believe that you have received it." The disciples' inability to cast out the demon suggests that they are both prayerless and faithless.

Tolbert, then, is correct in describing "this generation" as unbelieving. However, she overstates the case. Although Mark shows the disciples to be faithless and therefore a part of "this generation," they are neither evil nor destructive as Tolbert claims. In this passage, they do not oppose Jesus' word or way. On the contrary, Mark portrays them trying (unsuccessfully) to follow in the ministry of Jesus by exorcising a demon. What the disciples' inclusion in "this generation" shows is just how easy it is to adopt "this generation's" characteristics. Although "this generation" is never referred to positively, it is not a static entity. It is characterized by its blatant rejection of Jesus as well as fallibility in its attempts to follow Jesus. Therefore, Jesus' ministry and his followers' discipleship among "this generation" can be expected to be met with anything from outright hostility to the inability to consistently follow.

Mark 8:38 contains the most negative characterization of "this generation" in the Gospel. Here "this generation" is personified by the elders, chief priests, and scribes in verse 31. Mark links the elders, chief priests, and scribes to "this generation" by connecting them to the theme of shame. First, Mark identifies the elders, chief priests, and scribes as the persons who shame Jesus. Next, he details the shameful consequences of following Jesus. Then Mark opens verse 38 with the words of Jesus, "Whoever is ashamed of me and my words." Shame, then, is reinforced as the primary obstacle to discipleship. The only persons who are acknowledged for shaming anyone are the religious leaders mentioned in verse 31. Because Mark has linked the consequences of Jesus' ministry to the consequences of discipleship, the religious leaders pose the same threat to Jesus' followers as they pose to Jesus: pain in both its social (rejection) and physical (death) forms.

Moreover, Jesus' scathing critique of "this generation" impugns any notion of honor the religious leaders think they have. First of all, this generation is "adulterous." Jesus lists adultery among things that defile a person (7:22) and behaviors the law prohibits (10:19). In the Old Testament, adultery "refers to the faulted Covenant relationship between God and his [sic] people."[142] As members of the religious elite, this description is particularly damning. Their status as ones who represent God is undermined.

This is not the first time that Jesus speaks to the disparity between the religious leaders' role as representatives of God and their ungodly actions. In chapter 7, Jesus charges the scribes and Pharisees with misinterpreting the law. He provides two examples to substantiate his claim—ritual hand washing (7:1-8, 14-23) and Corban (7:9-13). Jesus asserts that the tradition of hand washing is misguided because a person is not defiled by what goes in but by what comes out of them (7:15). He accuses the Pharisees and scribes of "abandoning the commandment of God [to] keep the tradition of people" (7:8, my translation). Their traditions are human in that they do not uphold what God intends through the law. Next, he insists that the scribes and Pharisees have misinterpreted the law by allowing persons to offer a gift (Corban) to the temple instead of using it to support their parents. This interpretation contradicts the command to honor father and mother and is a worse offense than speaking evil to one's parents, which is punishable by death (7:10).

The traditions involving hand washing and Corban are not the only points of contention. Jesus claims that the scribes and Pharisees "do many things like this" (7:13). By passing down these traditions from one generation to the next, the scribes and Pharisees "nullify (akyroō) the word of God" (7:13, my translation). Akyroō is a legal term used to describe a contract or law that has no force behind it and is, therefore, invalid.[143] According to Jesus, the scribes and Pharisees have made Torah invalid with their misinterpretations. In other words, they have not maintained a proper covenant relationship with God because what they teach and practice does not uphold the law but empties the law of its power. By so doing, the have defaulted on their covenant relationship with God and are adulterers. Although the Pharisees are not listed with scribes, chief priests, and elders in Mark 8:31, the narrator depicts them as having the same shameful characteristics. They, too, are shown to be adulterers and are therefore a part of "this generation."

Not only is "this generation" adulterous; it is sinful. The description of "this generation" as sinful also substantiates the correlation between "this generation" and the religious leaders. Just before Jesus is arrested, he informs his disciples that he will be betrayed into the hands of sinners. At his arrest, the narrator specifically notes that there was a crowd sent to get Jesus from the elders, chief priests, and scribes (14:41, 43). Not only are the religious leaders identified as sinners, but the crowds also. Under the direction of the religious leaders, the crowds become complicit in the sin of the elders, chief priests, and scribes. They are guilty of moral evil that will be the impetus behind Jesus' passion. By labeling them "sinners," Mark informs his readers that those involved in Jesus' rejection and death are neither representatives nor doers of God's will. In this way, he communicates to the readers/hearers that all who form the court of public opinion that rejects Jesus are sinful, shameful, and influenced by Satan. To follow them is to share in their shame. To follow Jesus is to partake in his honor.

The only act or behavior Jesus labels specifically as sin is blasphemy against the Holy Spirit (3:28). The persons in danger of committing this sin are the scribes.

> "Truly I tell you, people will be forgiven for their sins and whatever blasphemies they utter; but whoever blasphemes against the Holy Spirit can never have forgiveness, but is guilty of an eternal sin"—for [the scribes] had said, "He has an unclean spirit."

The scribes credit the prince of demons for the power of God. A comparison of the Matthean and Lukan parallels reveals an interesting deviation from the Markan text. Both Matthew and Luke state that the Spirit descended *ep' auton* ("on him," Matt 3:16, Luke 3:22). Mark, however, records the Spirit descending *eis auton* (literally, "into him," 1:10, my translation; I've translated *eis* according to its most common definition, while the NRSV does not). In this way, Mark clues the reader in to the real source of Jesus' power and therefore militates against the scribes' accusation that Jesus has a demon (3:22). Whereas an unclean spirit speaks on behalf of the scribes (1:24), God is the only person in Mark's narrative to speak on behalf of Jesus (1:11; 9:7).

By attributing Jesus' power to exorcise demons to Beelzebul, the scribes come dangerously close to blaspheming against the Holy Spirit. The participation of the religious leaders in the rejection and death of Jesus suggests that, at best, their relationship with God is so broken that they no longer recognize the workings of the Divine. At worst, they have committed an unpardonable sin because they refused to accept one whom they knew was from God. In either case, Jesus describes the religious leaders in undeniably (and perhaps irrevocably) shameful terms. Unfortunately, it will be a description that their actions will confirm.

We now turn to the crowd, the final group among "this generation." Mark provides us with two very different views of the crowd. According to Jesus, the crowd is pitiable. Mark shows the crowd as whole and individual members in it to be in need of healing (5:27; 10:46); food (6:37; 8:1); and instruction (2:13; 4:1; 6:34). On two occasions, Mark informs the reader that the motivating factor behind Jesus' feeding miracles is his compassion for the crowds (6:34; 8:1-2). Jesus has compassion for them because they are like "sheep without a shepherd" (6:34).

The religious and political leaders' estimation is vastly different. They fear the crowd. The chief priests want to kill Jesus but are afraid of him "because the whole crowd was spellbound by his teaching" (11:18). The scribes, chief priests, and elders are afraid to respond to Jesus' question about the origin of John the Baptist because "they were afraid of the crowd" (11:32) and do not arrest him because "they feared the crowd" (12:12). Even Pilate is afraid of the crowd. In order to "satisfy the crowd," he releases Barabbas, not Jesus (15:15).

Although the crowd is socially lower than their religious and political leadership, they have power. They have the "ability to exercise control over the behavior of others." What the crowd thinks matters. This is precisely why the chief priests incite the crowds to demand Barabbas's release and Jesus' execution (15:11). Unfortunately, within the narrative boundaries of Mark's Gospel, the crowd does not actualize this position. Waetjen writes, "Although they are profoundly alienated from their political and religious leaders, they are economically dependent on the charity of the temple institution."[144] For this reason, they concede to the instructions of the chief priests. Rather than attaining honor through Jesus, they share in the sin and shame of their religious and political rulers. The crowd that once pressed upon Jesus (3:10; 5:24) as eager recipients of his ministry reject him in the end. They, too, become a part of the similarity chain characterized by opposition when they demand Barabbas's release (15:11) and Jesus' crucifixion (15:13).

Conclusion

I noted earlier that Robert Meye, Werner Kelber, and Morna Hooker attribute Jesus' death to both the will of God and the sin of the religious leaders. However, my analysis of the roles and relationships of the characters through our womanist lens shows a clear demarcation between the will of God and the actions of the religious and political leaders. In Mark's Gospel, the divine intent is revealed by the ministry of Jesus. The actions of the religious and political leaders function to stop Jesus' ministry and therefore are a hindrance to the divine purpose.

Read from a womanist perspective, the tenor of discourse exposes the moral evil at work in the rejection and death of Jesus. Not only does Mark show the religious and political leaders to be Jesus' adversaries; he also shows the demonic nature of their opposition by linking them to Satan. The similarity chain that Mark creates includes the Pharisees, Herodians, scribes, chief priests, elders, Satan, and, eventually, the crowds. It is characterized by opposition to Jesus' ministry. This similarity chain supports our rendering of *dei* as inevitability. Jesus will endure pain as a consequence of his ministry due to the moral evil of his enemies.

In our field of discourse, we saw that Mark establishes a relationship of co-classification between Jesus' ministry and his followers' discipleship. In other words, Jesus' followers are to participate in a ministry similar to his. Because there are similarities between what Jesus does and what the disciples will do, there will be similarities in the consequences they face. Our tenor of discourse reveals that the chain of opposition that confronts Jesus is an indication of antagonism his followers will face. Just as pain is the inevitable consequence of Jesus' ministry, it is also an inevitable consequence of discipleship.

Pain, however, is not the only consequence of discipleship. The choice to follow Jesus is honorable and therefore results in the disciple's acquisition of honor. Thus, Mark's presentation of Jesus' ministry and his followers' discipleship reveals both problems and potential. There is the problem of experiencing pain and the potential of gaining honor.

∞ The Mode of Discourse

Sociolinguistics defines text as functional language. Language is meant to do something. The mode of discourse explores the performative function of Mark's text. The key questions we ask in this section are "What part is the language of the text playing?" and "What are the participants expecting the language to do?"[145]

Our field and tenor of discourse exposed meaning potential that enabled me to conclude that agony is a consequence of, not a requirement for, discipleship. The particular type of agony that proceeds from discipleship is pain. However, pain in not the only consequence of following Jesus. Honor is another.

Because Mark identifies pain as one of the consequences of discipleship, the most important function of his language is to persuade his readers/hearers to follow Jesus in a ministry similar to his. Mark does this by first showing his readers/hearers that the essential point of similarity between Jesus and his disciples is ministry, not pain. Next, he convinces his readers/hearers that only Jesus' honor is unimpeachable. By following Jesus, they, too, share in the honor that comes from God. Given the cultural significance of honor in first-century Mediterranean society, Mark uses honor to motivate his readers/hearers to follow Jesus despite the pain.

Although the teaching of Jesus is directed to the disciples and the crowd, the narrator is also addressing the hearers/readers of the Gospel. Consequently, Mark is trying to accomplish the same function with the readers/hearers of the Gospel that Jesus is trying to accomplish among his disciples and the crowds. In order to persuade his readers/hearers to follow Jesus, Mark presents 8:34 as an open call to discipleship. In three successive moves, the narrator broadens the audience of this invitation. In 8:31, Jesus begins to teach "them." Mark 8:28 makes explicit the first audience for Jesus' passion prediction; "they" are the disciples. Jesus expands this group in verse 34 by calling the crowd to him. The identification of the audience immediately melds into *whoever* (8:34, 35, 38). As Malbon observes, "The Markan extension of both the invitation and the demand of followership from the disciples to the crowd sets up its further extension—to the hearers/readers."[146] Jesus gives no criteria for following him except the individual's desire. Whoever wants (th*eilē*) to follow Jesus can. Therefore, Mark's language functions not simply as an open call to discipleship, but its radical inclusivity enables it to function as a universal call to discipleship. Consequently, Mark 8:31-38 exemplifies the womanist affirmation of Jesus as universal.

The language of the Gospel urges the reader to follow Jesus in a ministry similar to his because Jesus is an honorable man. He is therefore trustworthy enough to model godly behavior. The description of "this generation" serves to highlight Jesus' character. This generation is sinful and adulterous. It lacks fidelity, specifically fidelity to God. It embodies the shame that Jesus' language militates against. This generation proves that it is ashamed of Jesus and his words by its rejection of both. Although this generation's notions of honor and shame are sanctioned by the society at large, its standards do not coincide with God's standards.

In essence, Jesus commands his would-be disciples to abandon their present collectivistic understanding for a new one. Obedience to this command will require his followers to adopt a radically different assessment of who and what have honor or shame.[147] Jesus insists that to uphold the society's prevailing notions of honor and shame is to seek honor from those who have none to give. Should this generation choose to reject Jesus based on society's estimation of his worth, it is employing a false standard. Mark has presented Jesus as the only one whose honor is unimpeachable. Therefore, only Jesus, not the religious and political leaders who oppose him, is worthy of being followed.

It is important at this point to recall that Mark establishes a relation of co-classification between Jesus' ministry and discipleship. Discipleship, then, is predicated upon Jesus' ministry. Because pain is neither a characteristic nor component of Jesus' ministry, pain is not a necessary part of discipleship. Jesus' life-affirming ministry is the necessary point of identification for discipleship. There is no discipleship without following Jesus in his ministry. In other words, agony is not the standard by which one measures his or her discipleship; following Jesus in ministry is.

Judith Perkins observes that "Christian texts of the late first and second centuries almost without exception assiduously project the message that to be a Christian is to suffer and die."[148]

Mark, however, is an exception to this. According to my reading of Mark's Gospel, Jesus is not inviting people to experience pain. Jesus is inviting people to follow him. Ministry is to be their primary point of identification with Jesus, not pain.

Because pain is one of the results of following Jesus, Mark uses Jesus' passion prediction and call to discipleship to distinguish the call to discipleship (ministry) from the consequences of discipleship (pain). Mark devotes the material prior to 8:31 to narrating Jesus' ministry. In this way, the narrator presents Jesus' ministry as the model for discipleship. The primary connection Mark makes between ministry and agony prior to 8:31 is to show that Jesus' ministry is characterized by eradicating the agony of others.

In Mark 3:6, the narrator reveals a second relation between ministry and agony. Agony is a consequence of Jesus' ministry. Mark shows that the Pharisees' and Herodians' plot to destroy Jesus is a direct counteraction to his ministry, which saves life rather than destroys it. Through these narrative connections, Mark shows Jesus' passion to be the inevitable consequence of his ministry.

> "Even Jesus himself was not persecuted and brought to the cross as a result of pure arbitrariness, mere misunderstanding, or unfortunate accident; instead, his sufferings resulted almost logically and inevitably out of the very center of his message and his life."[149]

Our field and tenor of discourse confirm this by showing Jesus to be in conflict with the religious and political rulers. The conflict with the religious and political leaders is intense enough for Jesus not only to foretell his death but also to forewarn his would-be disciples about what they will experience. If those who are with Jesus truly desire to follow him, they must be prepared to deny themselves. In other words, they must be prepared to deny their claims to worth based on their initial group membership. They must choose association with Jesus as their primary group, even at the risk of being rejected and therefore shamed. Although Jesus' messianic role is characterized by an ethic of nonviolence, his death is inevitable. By commanding his would-be disciples to take up the cross, Jesus "warn[s] the disciples that association even with a pacific Messiah is bound to invite the same punishment."[150]

However, my investigation reveals that pain is not the only consequence of following Jesus. Honor is a consequence also. Whereas Jesus' passion prediction in 8:31 discloses the pain that will come as a result of pursuing his life-affirming ministry, the inevitability of his resurrection discloses honor as the result of his ministry. Jesus' ministry is divinely sanctioned and shown to be honorable in the sight of God by means of the resurrection. By connecting discipleship to the ministry of Jesus, Mark grants discipleship the same sanction and honor. Following Jesus in a ministry modeled after his will inevitably result in pain, but it will also inevitably result in honor that comes from God. Because honor is a claim to worth that is accepted, discipleship is shown to validate one's worth and personhood, not agony. In this way, Mark encourages his readers/hearers to identify with Jesus in ministry despite the pain.

∞ Cross as Consequence

I began this investigation with two questions: (1) What is the relationship between the agony that the cross symbolizes and discipleship in Mark's Gospel? (2) Is the agony of the cross suffering or pain? My examination reveals that Jesus' passion is the inevitable consequence of his ministry. In Mark 8:31, Jesus foretells the inevitability of his pain, that is, the named, recognized agony that comes as a temporary result of life-affirming ministry. He informs his disciples that his pain will be both socially and physically shameful. Our womanist lens reveals that Jesus' pain will be the result of moral evil. Specifically, it will be a result of socially constructed evil at the hands of particular social groups.

Our tenor of discourse exposes the collusion of the religious and political leaders. Mark shows these groups to act with such cruel singularity that they actually appear to be individual characters. These human beings, not God, will cause Jesus' pain. Moreover, the narrator links these oppositional characters to Satan. Their actions are therefore portrayed as sinful, shameful, and satanic.

In Mark 8:34, Jesus issues a universal call to discipleship. Jesus invites all who desire to follow him. Because discipleship is predicated upon Jesus' ministry, this causal relationship between Jesus' ministry and pain is mirrored in the life of the disciple. Consequently, he informs his would-be disciples that following him will result in self-denial and cross bearing.

Both self-denial and cross bearing are the painful consequences of following Jesus. To deny oneself is to face the socially shameful consequences of following Jesus. It is to so identify with Jesus that he becomes the disciple's court of reputation, the only one necessary for approving his or her claim to worth. The person whose claim to worth is validated by Jesus need not aspire to embody the cultural values of the dominant society that seeks to define him or her. Therefore, self-denial brings with it the risk of societal rejection and alienation.

To "take up the cross" is to face the physically painful consequences of following Jesus. Contra Delores Williams, "rearing children alone, struggling on welfare, suffering through poverty, experiencing inadequate healthcare, domestic violence and various forms of sexism and racism"[151] do not qualify as cross bearing unless these circumstances are the results of following Jesus. My investigation of Mark 8:31-38 militates against using the cross as an unqualified symbol of agony. Mark shows the agony of the cross to be pain. Moreover, his narrative presentation demonstrates that agony can exist apart from the cross. Mark has shown this agony in the lives of people who receive the ministry of Jesus. However, only pain is connected to the cross.

Jesus' call to discipleship exposes Jesus' principal intention—to partner with his followers in ministry, not pain. Mark's depiction of Jesus' ministry confirms this. He shows Jesus' ministry to be primarily characterized by the alleviation and eradication of agony—whether that agony is the named, recognized experience of pain or the unmetabolized, unscrutinized agony of suffering. To this end, Jesus heals the sick, restores withered limbs, opens blind eyes, feeds the hungry, and exorcises demons.

Mark extends this ministerial emphasis to the followers of Jesus by establishing a relation of co-classification between Jesus' ministry and discipleship. As demonstrated above, Mark has shown Jesus' ministry and discipleship to consist of the same general category of actions and behaviors. The narrator recounts specific instances when someone other than Jesus engages in preaching, teaching, healing, miracle working, and exorcism. Although there is no record of anyone other than Jesus praying or extending forgiveness to another, Mark details episodes where Jesus commends these activities to those who follow him. All of the ministry activities that Mark shows Jesus and therefore his followers performing alleviate agony, both pain and suffering. Because Jesus is the beloved Son who is well-pleasing to God, his ministry reveals the divine intent. Jesus' ministry portrays the divine will to be the alleviation of agony.

Within this narrative framework there is no such understanding of divinely necessitated suffering. Thus, our womanist cultural lens has enabled us to expose meaning potential in this text that affirms agony is not the will of God. Given the centrality of Mark 8:31-38 for interpreting Jesus' death and developing an understanding of Christian discipleship, I assert that the concept of divinely willed suffering needs to be challenged beyond the scope of Mark's Gospel.

Finally, Mark shows pain to be only one possible consequence of discipleship. Honor is another (8:38). However, Mark's narrative presentation makes it abundantly clear that honor proceeds from discipleship, not from pain. In other words, the disciple does not access honor from God by sharing in Jesus' pain, but by sharing in Jesus' ministry. Ministry becomes the primary point of identification between Jesus and his followers and the only condition of discipleship. Because both pain and honor are the consequences of discipleship, Mark uses honor as a motivating factor to convince the reader/hearer to follow Jesus despite its painful consequences.

Mark's Gospel ends with the readers/hearers being the only persons left to make a decision about discipleship. The narrator has demarcated our options in order to distinguish clearly between that which is godly, and therefore honorable, and that which is shameful, and therefore satanic. We are left with a choice to follow or forsake Jesus in his ministry. What the reader/hearer decides will determine whether or not she or he is a part of Jesus' family or "this generation."

chapter six

Discerning the Call

De nigger woman is de mule uh de world

so fur as Ah can see. Ah been prayin' fuh it

to be different wid you. Lawd, Lawd, Lawd!

—Zora Neale Hurston, *Their Eyes Were Watching God*[1]

A womanist reading of Mark 8:31-38 causes suffering to lose its sacred standing. Agony is shown to be not God's will but a manifestation of moral evil. Where is God in the midst of human suffering? Why does God allow people to experience agony? The reality is that we may never know. However, the meaning potential in Mark's Gospel allows us to affirm that God is not the one who purposed Jesus' pain, nor the one who wills our agony. Like Donald Juel, who advises the readers of Mark's Gospel not to look to God for the "necessity" of Jesus' death but to look "below,"[2] a womanist reading of this biblical text reminds us to look "below" for the causes of our own agony.

We must look "below" or we will miss the dynamic interaction between God's will and human freedom. This freedom is characterized by the choice to follow God's way as exemplified by Jesus and the choice to oppose it.

Because we are free to act contrary to God's purposes means we cannot assume that God sanctions everything God allows. For this reason, it is essential for us to distinguish between the call of discipleship and its consequences. Otherwise, we may mistakenly believe we have been called to the consequences of discipleship and not the conditions for discipleship.

The call of discipleship is the invitation to follow Jesus. The condition for discipleship is to engage in a ministry similar to his. We are called to engage in life-affirming, God glorifying, agony-eradicating ministry. We are called to partner with Jesus in service, not pain. Pain is a consequence of discipleship. It is not a lifestyle, a life sentence, or a life goal. Pain only signals the level of opposition to ministry. It is not the measure of discipleship; ministry is.

A womanist reading of Mark 8:31-38 demonstrates that both the call and consequences of discipleship are a part of the Gospel story. For this reason, it is important that we include both the call and the consequences in our discussion of discipleship. This was my problem with the field education pastor's decision to remove the "cross" and "blood" songs from the hymnal and liturgy. She removed the consequences and left her parishioners with an incomplete message about discipleship.

The death of Jesus in ancient history and the death of Martin Luther King Jr. in modern history show that engaging in life-affirming, God-glorifying, agony-eradicating ministry is a dangerous endeavor. To ignore their pain is to ignore their profound commitment to the gospel; a commitment that inevitably resulted in their deaths. It is precisely because of the ministry they performed and their refusal to stop that their court of public opinion esteems them as honorable. They attained honor as a result of their ministries, not because of their pain.

Likewise, African American women can achieve honor through discipleship. According to the meaning potential accessed in Mark's Gospel, Jesus calls us to a reorientation of our collectivistic selves so that the dominant society that esteems whiteness, maleness, and wealth as honorable no longer functions as our court of opinion. It also militates against the "ghetto" subculture that esteems the acquisition of money without moral accountability, violence against one's own people, and being a "baby's mama" as honorable.

In light of this, we must also reconsider the traditional understanding of Jesus as the divine cosufferer. Our womanist reading of

Mark's Gospel reveals that Jesus suffered *as a result* of his ministry that challenged the status quo, not because his suffering was the will of God. Ministry is to be our primary point of connection with Jesus. Since pain is one of the consequences of discipleship, only the agony that we endure as a result of life-affirming, God-glorifying, agony-eradicating ministry is analogous to what Jesus experienced and can be identified as a *cross*.

Jesus, then, is not our cosufferer. Although the Gospel narrative recounts his presence among those in agony and depicts his compassion for them, his ministry is characterized not just by empathizing with them but also by alleviating their agony. Because Mark depicts Jesus' ministry, and by extension discipleship, as one that alleviates agony, we have a divine imperative to challenge the individuals and structures that promote our own. In other words, Jesus' presence among us empowers us to fight on because our existential contexts of suffering due to racist, classist, and sexist oppression are not divinely preordained. We should not passively accept

domestic violence and domestic jobs;
dropouts and drive-bys;
the corporate glass ceiling and election vote stealing;
high incarceration but low graduation rates;
inadequate healthcare and inferior housing;
stereotypes that depict us as caricatures rather than complete persons.

These are not crosses for us to bear. They are challenges that we must overcome. And the call, the challenge, is not suffering with Jesus; it is ministering like Jesus.

AB	Anchor Bible
ABD	*Anchor Bible Dictionary*. Edited by D. N. Freedman. 6 vols. New York, 1992
ACNT	Augsburg Commentaries on the New Testament
AmAn	*American Anthropologist*
BSac	*Bibliotheca sacra*
BTB	*Biblical Theology Bulletin*
CBQ	*Catholic Biblical Quarterly*
CGTC	Cambridge Greek Testament Commentary
CurTM	*Currents in Theology and Mission*
ExpTim	*Expository Times*
IBT	Interpreting Biblical Texts Series
Int	*Interpretation*
JBL	*Journal of Biblical Literature*
JETS	*Journal of the Evangelical Theological Society*
JFSR	*Journal of Feminist Studies in Religion*
JITC	*Journal of the Interdenominational Theological Center*
JRT	*Journal of Religious Thought*
JSJ	*Journal for the Study of Judaism in the Persian, Hellenistic, and Roman Periods*
JSNT	*Journal for the Study of the New Testament*
NICNT	New International Commentary on the New Testament
NovT	*Novum Testamentum*
NTS	*New Testament Studies*
R&T	*Religion and Theology*
RevExp	*Review and Expositor*

RTR	*Reformed Theological Review*
SJT	*Scottish Journal of Theology*
SP	Sacra pagina
TDNT	*Theological Dictionary of the New Testament.* Edited by G. Kittel and G. Friedrich. Translated by G. W. Bromiley. 10 vols. Grand Rapids, 1964–1976
TJT	*Toronto Journal of Theology*
WBC	Word Biblical Commentary

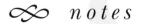 *notes*

Introduction: Discipleship and Suffering

1. Delores S. Williams, *Sisters in the Wilderness: The Challenge of Womanist God-Talk* (Maryknoll, N.Y.: Orbis, 1993), ix.

2. I describe the pastor in terms of her race, political, and theological perspectives in order to describe her sociocultural context. My aim is to show how her sociocultural context affects her theological views. Her views are no more representative of all white people or feminists than my work represents the views of all African Americans or womanists.

3. God's will is defined as "the considered and deliberate divine purpose, intention, or determination." See Terence E. Fretheim, "Will of God in the OT," *ABD* 6:915.

4. Anthony B. Pinn, *Why, Lord? Suffering and Evil in Black Theodicy* (New York: Continuum, 1995), 17.

5. Karen Baker-Fletcher and Garth Kasimu Baker-Fletcher, *My Sister, My Brother: Womanist and Xodus God-Talk* (Maryknoll, N.Y.: Orbis, 1997), 78.

6. Jacquelyn Grant, *White Women's Christ and Black Women's Jesus: Feminist Christology and Womanist Response* (Atlanta: Scholars, 1989), 212.

7. John Oatman Jr. "There's Not a Friend (No, Not One)," in *African Methodist Episcopal Church Bicentennial Hymnal* (Nashville: AMEC, 1984), 381.

8. JoAnne Marie Terrell, *Power in the Blood? The Cross in the African American Experience* (Maryknoll, N.Y.: Orbis, 1998), 17. See also James H. Cone, *The Spirituals and the Blues: An Interpretation* (Maryknoll, N.Y.: Orbis, 1992), 47.

9. "Were You There?" is featured in James Weldon Johnson and John Rosamond Johnson, *American Negro Spirituals* (New York: Viking, 1926), 115.

10. Grant, *White Women's Christ*, 212.

11. Cone, *Spirituals*, 50.

12. Ibid., 49.

13. Baker-Fletcher and Kasimu Baker-Fletcher, *My Sister, My Brother*, 78.

14. With respect to the brutality that female slaves endured, Angela Davis writes, "Slave women were inherently vulnerable to all forms of sexual coercion. If the most violent punishments of men consisted in floggings and mutilations, women were flogged and mutilated as well as raped. Rape, in fact, was an uncamouflaged expression

of the slaveholder's economic mastery and the overseer's control over Black women as workers." Angela Davis, *Women, Race and Class* (New York: Vintage, 1983), 7.

15. See Carter G. Woodson, *The Mis-education of the Negro* (Trenton, N.J.: Africa World, 1990).

16. Mrs. Till stated, "After the body arrived I knew I had to look and see and make sure it was Emmett. That was when I decided that I wanted the whole world to see what I had seen. There was no way I could describe what was in that box. No way. And I just wanted the world to see." Ernest Withers, *Complete Photo Story of Till Murder Case* (Memphis: Wither's Photographers,1955).

17. Audre Lorde, *Sister Outsider* (Berkeley: Crossing, 1984), 171.

18. Frank J. Matera, *What Are They Saying about Mark?* (Mahwah, N.J.: Paulist, 1987), 17.

19. M. A. K. Halliday and Ruqaiya Hasan, *Language, Context, and Text: Aspects of Language in a Social-Semiotic Perspective* (Geelong, Aust.: Deakin University Press, 1985), 10.

Chapter 1: The View through a Womanist Cultural Lens

1. Stephanie Mitchem, *Introducing Womanist Theology* (Maryknoll, N.Y.: Orbis, 2002), 49.

2. Ibid.

3. Alice Walker, *In Search of Our Mothers' Gardens: Womanist Prose* (San Diego and New York: Harcourt Brace, 1983), xi–xii.

4. For a discussion on the appropriateness of using Walker's definition for specifically Christian theological endeavors, see Cheryl J. Sanders et al., "Roundtable: Christian Ethics and Theology in Womanist Perspective," *JFSR* 5 (1989): 83–112.

5. Sanders, "Roundtable," 85. She writes, "The fact is that womanist is essentially a secular category whose theological and ecclesial significations are rather tenuous. Theological content too easily gets 'read into' the womanist concept, whose central emphasis remains the self-assertion and struggle of black women for freedom, with or without the aid of God or Jesus or anybody else" (86).

6. Rufus Burrows Jr., "Toward Womanist Theology and Ethics," *JFSR* 15 (1999): 83.

7. Jacquelyn Grant, *White Women's Christ and Black Women's Jesus: Feminist Christology and Womanist Response* (Atlanta: Scholars, 1989), 205.

8. Grant, *White Women's Christ*; Delores S. Williams, *Sisters in the Wilderness: The Challenge of Womanist God-Talk* (Maryknoll, N.Y.: Orbis, 1993); Emilie M. Townes, ed., *A Troubling in My Soul: Womanist Perspectives on Evil and Suffering* (Maryknoll, N.Y.: Orbis, 1993).

9. Karen Baker-Fletcher, "'Soprano Obligato': The Voices of Black Women and American Conflict in the Thought of Anna Julia Cooper," in Townes, *A Troubling in My Soul*, 172–88.

10. Clarice J. Martin, "Biblical Theology and Black Women's Spiritual Autobiography: 'The Miry Bog, the Desolate Pit, a New Song in My Mouth,'" in Townes, *A Troubling in My Soul*, 13–36.

11. Emilie M. Townes, *Womanist Justice, Womanist Hope*, ed. Susan Thistlethwaite (Atlanta: Scholars, 1993).

12. Delores S. Williams, "Womanist Theology," in *Women's Visions: Theological Reflection, Celebration, Action*, ed. Ofelia Ortega (Geneva: World Council of Churches [WCC], 1995), 117.

13. Ibid., 118.

14. Ibid., 117.

15. Kelly Delaine Brown, "God Is as Christ Does: Toward a Womanist Theology," *JRT* 46 (1989): 12.

16. A. Elaine Crawford, "Womanist Christology: Where Have We Come From and Where Are We Going?" *RevExp* 95 (1998): 371.

17. Delores S. Williams, "The Color of Feminism, or Speaking the Black Woman's Tongue," *JRT* 43 (1986): 50.

18. "The power of the fathers: a familial-social, ideological, political system in which men—by force, direct pressure or through ritual, tradition, law, and language, customs, etiquette, education, and division of labor, determine what part women shall or shall not play, and in which every female is everywhere subsumed under the male." Adrienne Rich, *Of Woman Born: Motherhood as Experience and Institution* (New York: Norton, 1976), 40.

19. Williams, "Womanist Theology," 115.

20. Williams, "Color of Feminism," 52.

21. Crawford, "Womanist Christology," 370.

22. M. Shawn Copeland, "Wading through Many Sorrows: Toward a Theology of Suffering in Womanist Perspective," in Townes, *A Troubling in My Soul*, 111.

23. Williams, "Womanist Theology," 115.

24. Stephanie Mitchem, *Introducing Womanist Theology* (Maryknoll, N.Y.: Orbis, 2002), 60.

25. Grant, *White Women's Christ*, 209.

26. Brown, "God Is," 8.

27. Renita J. Weems, "Reading *Her Way* through the Struggle: African American Women and the Bible," in *Stony the Road We Trod: African American Biblical Interpretation*, ed. Cain Hope Felder (Minneapolis: Fortress Press, 1991), 70.

28. Crawford, "Womanist Christology," 375.

29. Williams, "Womanist Theology," 115.

30. Ibid., 121.

31. Mark Lewis Taylor, *Remembering Esperanza: A Cultural-Political Theology for North American Praxis* (Minneapolis: Fortress Press, 1990, 2004), 122.

32. Katie Geneva Cannon, *Katie's Canon: Womanism and the Soul of the Black Community* (New York: Continuum, 1995), 156.

33. Ibid., 157.

34. Ibid., 160.

35. Ibid., 115.

36. Brown, "God Is," 8.

37. Weems, "Reading *Her Way*," 57.

38. Ibid., 63.

39. Weems writes, "It is certainly true that [the Bible] has been able to arrest African American female readers and persuade them to make their behavior conform according to its teachings." "Reading *Her Way*," 63.

40. Ibid.

41. Crawford, "Womanist Christology," 367.

42. Mitchem, *Womanist Theology*, ix.

43. Ibid., 46

44. Ibid.

45. Brown, "God Is," 15.

46. Ibid., 16.

47. Ibid.

48. Crawford, "Womanist Christology," 368.

49. Ibid., 375.

50. "Nobody Knows de Trouble I Seen," in James Weldon Johnson and John Rosamond Johnson, *American Negro Spirituals* (New York: Viking, 1926), 140.

51. James H. Cone, *The Spirituals and the Blues: An Interpretation* (Maryknoll, N.Y.: Orbis, 1992), 50.

52. Brown, "God Is," 16.

53. Crawford, "Womanist Christology," 370.

54. Ibid.

55. Brown, "God Is," 14.

56. Ibid.

57. Ibid., 14–15.

58. Brown, "God Is," 14.

59. Grant, *White Women's Christ*, 212.

60. Terrell, *Power in the Blood?* 124.

61. Brown, "God Is," 16.

62. Williams, *Sisters*, 164.

63. Ibid.

64. Ibid., 165.

65. Karen Baker-Fletcher and Garth Kasimu Baker-Fletcher, *My Sister, My Brother: Womanist and Xodus God-Talk* (Maryknoll, N.Y.: Orbis, 1997), 78.

66. Ibid.

67. Ibid., 75.

68. Ibid.

69. Ibid., 80.

70. Ibid., 77.

71. Ibid., 46.

72. Williams, *Sisters*, 167.

73. Baker-Fletcher and Kasimu Baker-Fletcher, *My Sister, My Brother*, 79.

74. Delores S. Williams, "Black Women's Surrogacy Experience and the Christian Notion of Redemption," in *After Patriarchy: Feminist Transformations of World Religions*, ed. Paula Cooey (Maryknoll, N.Y.: Orbis, 1991), 1.

75. Williams, *Sisters*, 60.

76. Ibid., 61–62.

77. Ibid.

78. Ibid., 2.

79. Williams, "Black Women's Surrogacy," 4.

80. Emilie M. Townes, "Living in the New Jerusalem: The Rhetoric and Movement of Liberation in the House of Evil," in Townes, *A Troubling in My Soul*, 78.

81. Ibid.

82. Williams, *Sisters*, 160.

83. Crawford writes, "[The] cross does not sacralize abuse but is an example of it." "Womanist Christology," 379.

84. Baker-Fletcher and Kasimu Baker-Fletcher, *My Sister, My Brother*, 80.

85. Copeland, "Wading through Many Sorrows," 120.

86. Williams, *Sisters*, 165.

87. Ibid., 166.

88. Ibid., 169.

89. Delores S. Williams, "A Crucifixion Double-Cross?" *The Other Side* (1993): 26.

90. JoAnne Marie Terrell, *Power in the Blood? The Cross in the African American Experience* (Maryknoll, N.Y.: Orbis, 1998), 100, 110.

91. Williams, *Sisters*, 167.

92. Ibid., 166.

93. Ibid., 167.

94. Terrell, *Power in the Blood?* 124.

95. Ibid., 122.

96. Ibid., 125.

97. Copeland, "Wading through Many Sorrows," 111.

98. Ibid., 109.

99. Ibid.

100. Jamie T. Phelps, "Joy Came in the Morning: Risking Death for Resurrection; Confronting the Evil of Social Sin and Socially Sinful Structures," in Townes, *A Troubling in My Soul*, 49.

101. Ibid.

102. Ibid., 48.

103. Ibid.

104. Audre Lorde, *Sister Outsider* (Berkeley: Crossing, 1984), 171.

105. Townes, "Living in the New Jerusalem," 84.

106. Ibid., 85.

107. Ibid.

108. Lorde, *Sister Outsider*, 171.

109. Townes, "Living in the New Jerusalem," 85.

110. Ibid.

111. Ibid., 84.

112. Ibid.

113. Ibid., 85.

114. Ibid., 84.

115. Ibid.

116. Ibid., 85.

117. Ibid., 124.

118. Ibid.

119. Terrell, *Power in the Blood?* 125.

120. Ibid.

121. James H. Cone, *God of the Oppressed*, rev. ed. (Maryknoll, N.Y.: Orbis, 2000), 163.

122. Ibid., 178.

123. Ibid., 163.

124. Theophus H. Smith, *Conjuring Culture: Biblical Formations of Black America*, ed. Howard S. Stout (Oxford: Oxford University Press, 1994), 169.

125. Copeland, "Wading through Many Sorrows," 109.

126. Terrell, *Power in the Blood?* 78.

127. Phelps, "Joy Came," 49.

128. Jacquelyn Grant, "The Sin of Servanthood and the Deliverance of Discipleship," in Townes, *A Troubling in My Soul*, 214.

129. Ibid., 204.

130. Ibid., 214.

131. Ibid., 214–15.

132. Ibid., 210.

133. Ibid., 215.

134. Ibid., 216.

135. Ibid.

136. Ibid.

137. Ibid.

138. Ibid., 118.

139. Copeland, "Wading through Many Sorrows," 109.

140. Terence E. Fretheim, "Will of God in the OT," *ABD* 6:915.

141. Daniel L. Migliore, *Faith Seeking Understanding: An Introduction to Christian Theology* (Grand Rapids: Eerdmans, 1991), 101.

142. Ibid.

143. Ibid.

144. Stanley Grenz, David Guretzki, and Cherith Fee Nordling, *Pocket Dictionary of Theological Terms* (Downers Grove, Ill.: InterVarsity, 1999), 48.

145. Phelps, "Joy Came," 48-49.

146. This is not to say that evil lies outside the power of God. My point is that what God allows (what happens) and what God intends are not always the same. For example, the existence of human suffering does not mean God wills human beings to suffer. I contend that this is an important distinction for African American women to make so that they do not sacralize their suffering. This distinction also motivates one to look not only to God but also to human beings for the cause(s) of human suffering.

Chapter 2: Perspectives on Discipleship and Suffering in Mark

1. Pheme Perkins, review of *Then the Whisper Put on Flesh: New Testament Ethics in an African American Context*, *Theology Today* 59, no. 3 (2003): 83.

2. Frank J. Matera, *What Are They Saying about Mark?* (Mahwah, N.J.: Paulist, 1987), 17.

3. Robert P. Meye, *Jesus and the Twelve: Discipleship and Revelation in Mark's Gospel* (Grand Rapids: Eerdmans, 1968), 13.

4. Ibid., 60.

5. Ibid.

6. Ibid., 210.

7. Ibid., 103.

8. Ibid., 123.

9. Ibid., 121.

10. Ibid., 125.

11. Ibid., 103.

12. Ibid.

13. Ibid., 108.

14. Ibid. As noted above, Meye has already acknowledged that others participated in the ministry of the word in the form of preaching. In Mark 9:38, Mark
mentions an unknown exorcist who casts out demons in Jesus' name and is not
one of the Twelve. Yet Meye refuses to identify these individuals as disciples.

15. Ibid., 47.

16. Ibid., 48.

17. Ibid., 232.

18. Ibid.

19. Theodore J. Weeden, "The Heresy That Necessitated Mark's Gospel," in *The
Interpretation of Mark*, ed. William Telford (Philadelphia: Fortress Press, 1985), 64.

20. Ibid.

21. Ibid.

22. Ibid., 64–65.

23. Ibid., 65.

24. Ibid.

25. Ibid.

26. Ibid., 67.

27. Ibid., 72.

28. Ibid., 68.

29. Joanna Dewey, *Disciples of the Way: Mark on Discipleship* (Women's Division
Board of Global Ministries, the United Methodist Church, 1976), 48.

30. Ibid., 49.

31. Ibid., 52.

32. Ibid.

33. Ibid., 55.

34. Ibid., 56.

35. Ibid., 60.

36. Ibid., 74.

37. Ibid., 91.

38. Ibid.

39. Ibid.

40. Ernest Best, *Following Jesus: Discipleship in the Gospel of Mark* (Edinburgh:
T&T Clark, 1981), 12.

41. Ibid.

42. Ibid.

43. Ibid., 13.

44. Ibid., 22.

45. Ibid., 199.

46. Ibid., 83.

47. Ibid., 86.

48. Ernest Best, *Disciples and Discipleship: Studies in the Gospel according to Mark* (Edinburgh: T&T Clark, 1986), 3.

49. Best, *Following Jesus*, 249.

50. Ibid., 13.

51. Ernest Best, *Mark: The Gospel as Story* (Edinburgh: T&T Clark, 1983), 86.

52. Ibid.

53. Best, *Disciples*, 7.

54. Best, *Mark*, 68.

55. Ibid., 92.

56. Ibid.

57. Werner Kelber, *Mark's Story of Jesus* (Philadelphia: Fortress Press, 1979). Robert C. Tannehill, "The Disciples in Mark: The Function of a Narrative Role," in Telford, *Interpretation of Mark*.

58. Augustine Stock, *Call to Discipleship: A Literary Study of Mark's Gospel* (Wilmington, Del.: Michael Glazier, 1982), 140.

59. Ibid., 146.

60. Ibid., 140.

61. Ibid., 145.

62. Ibid., 142.

63. Ibid., 146.

64. Ibid., 141.

65. Ibid., 144.

66. Ibid., 140.

67. Ibid., 188.

68. Ibid., 187.

69. Ibid.

70. Morna Hooker, *The Message of Mark* (London: Epworth, 1983), 105.

71. Ibid.

72. Ibid.

73. Ibid., 110–11.

74. Ibid., 114.

75. Ibid., 114–15.

76. Ibid., 115.

77. Morna Hooker, *The Gospel according to Saint Mark*, ed. Henry Chadwick (Peabody, Mass.: Hendrickson, 1999), 249.

78. Morna Hooker, *Not Ashamed of the Gospel: New Testament Interpretations of the Death of Jesus* (Carlisle, UK: Paternoster, 1994), 48.

79. Ibid., 53.

80. Ibid., 54.

81. Hooker, *Message of Mark*, 115.

82. Ibid.

83. Jack Dean Kingsbury, *Conflict in Mark: Jesus, Authorities, Disciples* (Minneapolis: Fortress Press, 1989), 91.

84. Ibid., 90.

85. Ibid., 103.

86. Ibid., 104.
87. Ibid., 91.
88. Ibid., 56.
89. Ibid., 105.
90. Ibid., 44.
91. Ibid., 103.
92. Ibid., 116.
93. Ibid., 57.
94. Ibid., 85.
95. Ibid.
96. Tannehill, "The Disciples in Mark," 134.
97. Ibid., 136.
98. Ibid., 141.
99. Ibid., 136.
100. Ibid.
101. Ibid.
102. Ibid., 149.
103. Ibid., 148.
104. Ibid.
105. Ibid., 143.
106. Ibid., 148.
107. Ibid.
108. Kelber, *Mark's Story of Jesus*, 52.
109. Ibid.
110. Ibid., 19.
111. Ibid., 24.
112. Ibid., 46.
113. Ibid., 86.
114. Ibid.
115. Ibid., 51.
116. Ibid.
117. Ibid., 52.
118. Ibid., 86.
119. Sean Fréyne, *The Twelve: Disciples and Apostles* (London: Sheed & Ward, 1968), 114.
120. Ibid.
121. Ibid., 144.
122. Ibid., 118.
123. Ibid., 120.
124. Ibid.
125. Ibid., 148.
126. Ibid., 149.
127. Ibid.
128. Ibid., 140.
129. Ibid., 149.
130. Ibid., 143.
131. Ibid., 145.

132. Ibid., 132.

133. Ibid., 134.

134. Ibid., 135.

135. Ibid., 138.

136. "'Awake, O sword, against my shepherd, against the man who is my associate,' says the LORD of hosts. Strike the shepherd, that the sheep may be scattered; I will turn my hand against the little ones" (Zech 13:7).

137. Fréyne, *The Twelve*, 136.

138. Norman Perrin, *A Modern Pilgrimage in New Testament Christology* (Philadelphia: Fortress Press, 1974), 84.

139. Ibid., 85–86.

140. Ibid., 100.

141. Ibid., 81.

142. Ibid.

143. Ibid., 84.

144. Ibid., 89.

145. Ibid., 91.

146. Ibid.

147. Ibid.

148. Ibid., 84.

149. Ibid.

150. Ibid., 93.

151. Joel Marcus, *The Way of the Lord: Christological Exegesis of the Old Testament in the Gospel of Mark* (Louisville, Ky.: Westminster John Knox, 1992), 40.

152. Ibid, 40–41.

153. Ibid., 7.

154. Ibid., 40.

155. Ibid., 145.

156. Ibid., 194.

157. Ibid., 177.

158. Ibid., 42.

159. Ibid., 195.

160. Ched Myers, *Binding the Strong Man: A Political Reading of Mark's Story of Jesus* (Maryknoll, N.Y.: Orbis, 1988), 5.

161. Ibid., xxviii.

162. Ibid., 137.

163. Ibid.

164. Ibid.

165. Ibid., 244.

166. Ibid.

167. Ibid., 242.

168. Ibid., 246.

169. Ibid.

170. Ibid., 8.

171. Ibid.

172. Ibid., 416.

173. Mary Ann Tolbert, *Sowing the Gospel: Mark's World in Literary Perspective* (Minneapolis: Fortress Press, 1989), 3.

174. Ibid., 136.

175. Ibid., 138.

176. Ibid., 240.

177. Ibid., 236. It is important to note that here again Jesus' actions assume that repentance can occur. Yet based on Tolbert's interpretation of the parable of the sower, it is inconsistent that path, rocky, or thorny soil can be anything other than what it is. Therefore, repentance is impossible.

178. Mark 12:8.

179. Tolbert, *Sowing the Gospel*, 262.

180. Ibid.

181. Ibid.

182. Ibid., 163.

183. Ibid.

184. Tolbert notes that Mark consistently uses the phrase "this generation" to "portray the unbelieving, evil and destructive people of the world (e.g. 8:38; 9:19)." *Sowing the Gospel*, 182.

185. Elizabeth Struthers Malbon, "Fallible Followers: Women and Men in the Gospel of Mark," *Semeia* 28 (1983): 29. According to Malbon, there is no restriction on who can become a disciple; discipleship is open to everyone. See Malbon, "Disciples/Crowds/Whoever: Marcan Characters and Readers," *NovT* 28 (1986): 104. Tolbert is not so inclusive. Only those who are "good soil" are able to be disciples because only "good soil" can yield the fruit characteristic of true discipleship. The word reveals rather than transforms the nature of the individual. The people in Mark's Gospel are either good soil or bad. Therefore, Jesus' preaching can only reveal which type they are. It is their response to the Gospel that lets the reader know to which category they belong. Tolbert, *Sowing the Gospel*, 162–63, 299.

186. Ibid., 266.

187. Ibid., 202.

188. Donald H. Juel, *The Gospel of Mark*, IBT (Nashville: Abingdon, 1999), 129.

189. Donald H. Juel, *Mark*, ACNT (Minneapolis: Augsburg Books, 1990), 43.

190. Ibid., 149.

191. Juel writes, "The reasons for Jesus' death arise from his conflict with those in charge of human affairs, the religious and political authorities." *Gospel of Mark*, 163.

192. Ibid.

193. Ibid.

194. Ibid., 165.

195. Juel, *Mark*, 123.

196. Brian K. Blount, *Go Preach! Mark's Kingdom Message and the Black Church Today* (Maryknoll, N.Y.: Orbis, 1998), 7–8.

197. Ibid., 8.

198. Ibid., 83.

199. Ibid., 10.

200. Ibid., 174.

201. Best, *Following Jesus*, 96.

202. Blount, *Go Preach!* 83.

203. Ibid., 9.

204. Ibid.

205. Ibid., 129.

206. Ibid., 132.

207. Ibid., 9.

208. Delores S. Williams, *Sisters in the Wilderness: The Challenge of Womanist God-Talk* (Maryknoll, N.Y.: Orbis, 1993), 169.

209. Although it is beyond the purview of this book, the review of Markan scholarship suggests that womanist theology and biblical scholarship would benefit from a womanist interpretation of Mark 10:45. I believe that situating this text within the context of African American women's experience of surrogacy and classical atonement theories that assert Jesus died in the place of humans would also yield new possibilities for understanding this passage in a way that does not sacralize black women's surrogacy.

∞ Chapter 3: A Model for Womanist Reading

1. Mieke Bal, *Narratology: Introduction to the Theory of Narrative*, 3rd ed. (Toronto: University of Toronto Press, 1997), 11.

2. R. A. Hudson, *Sociolinguistics* (Cambridge: Cambridge University Press, 1980), 1.

3. M. A. K. Halliday and Ruqaiya Hasan, *Language, Context, and Text: Aspects of Language in a Social-Semiotic Perspective* (Geelong, Aust.: Deakin University Press, 1985), 5.

4. Ibid., 46.

5. Ibid.

6. Ibid.

7. Ibid., 12.

8. Ibid., 10.

9. Brian K. Blount, *Cultural Interpretation: Reorienting New Testament Criticism* (Minneapolis: Fortress Press, 1995), 3.

10. Ibid.

11. Ibid., 17.

12. Ibid.

13. Ibid.

14. Enrique Dussel, *Philosophy of Liberation*, trans. Aquila Martinez and Christine Morkovsky (Maryknoll, N.Y.: Orbis, 1985), 2.

15. M. A. K. Halliday, *Explorations in the Function of Language* (New York: Elsevier North-Holland, 1973), 14.

16. Ibid.

17. Ibid.

18. Halliday defines a grammar as the "linguistic device for hooking up together the selections in meaning which are derived from the various functions of language, and realizing them in a unified structural form." *Explorations*, 34.

19. Ibid., 28.

20. Ibid., 28–34.

21. Ibid., 58.

22. Ibid.

23. Ibid., 29.

24. Blount, *Cultural Interpretation*, 11.

25. Halliday, *Explorations*, 58.

26. Ibid.

27. Halliday and Hasan, *Language, Context, and Text*, 10.

28. Ibid., 85.

29. Halliday, *Explorations*, 64.

30. Ibid.

31. Blount, *Cultural Interpretation*, 11.

32. Ibid., 17.

33. Ibid.

34. Ibid., 11.

35. Ibid.

36. Ibid.

37. Ibid., 92.

38. Ibid., 94.

39. Ibid.

40. Ibid., 94.

41. Rudolph Bultmann, "Is Exegesis without Presuppositions Possible?" in *New Testament Theology and Mythology and Other Basic Writings*, ed. Schubert M. Ogden (Philadelphia: Fortress Press, 1989), 149.

42. Ibid.

43. Blount, *Cultural Interpretation*, 92–94.

44. Ibid., 92.

45. Ibid.

46. Bultmann, "Is Exegesis without Presuppositions Possible?" 145.

47. Bal, *Narratology*, 5.

48. Mark Allen Powell, *What Is Narrative Criticism?* Guides to Biblical Scholarship, ed. Dan O. Via (Minneapolis: Fortress Press, 1990), 23.

49. Robert Scholes and Robert Kellogg, *The Nature of Narrative* (London: Oxford University Press, 1966), 4.

50. Robert M. Fowler, *Let the Reader Understand: Reader-Response Criticism and the Gospel of Mark* (Harrisburg, Pa.: Trinity, 1991), 9.

51. Mary Ann Tolbert, *Sowing the Gospel: Mark's World in Literary Perspective* (Minneapolis: Fortress Press, 1989), 31.

52. Robert W. Funk, *The Poetics of Biblical Narrative* (Sonoma, Calif.: Polebridge, 1988), 16.

53. Seymour Chatman, *Story and Discourse: Narrative Structure in Fiction and Film* (Ithaca, N.Y.: Cornell University Press, 1978), 21.

54. Ibid., 46.

55. Powell, *What Is Narrative Criticism?* 40.

56. Chatman, *Story and Discourse*, 47.

57. Ibid., 45.

58. Elisabeth Struthers Malbon, "Narrative Criticism: How Does the Story Mean?" in *Mark and Method: New Approaches in Biblical Studies*, ed. Janice Capel Anderson and Stephen Moore (Minneapolis: Fortress Press, 1992), 28.

59. Powell, *What Is Narrative Criticism?* 42.

60. Malbon, "Narrative Criticism," 12.

61. Tolbert, *Sowing the Gospel*, 31.

62. New Criticism took the opposite approach of traditional criticism to interpretation by focusing on the text rather than the author. New Critics rejected the emphasis on authorial intent and deemed the text self-sufficient. Background information on the author or even knowledge of who wrote a particular text was unnecessary. The text could be read and understood as it was. These developments meant that the text could be more than a window through which one could view the *Sitz im Lebem* of an "ancient" people. Literary principles could be employed to explore the text in its final form. Moreover, the lack of authorial identity would not preclude interpretation. Tremper Longman III, *Literary Approaches to Biblical Interpretation*, ed. Moises Silva (Grand Rapids: Academie Books, 1987), 26.

63. Malbon, "Narrative Criticism," 28.

64. Halliday and Hasan, *Language, Context, and Text*, 48.

65. Ibid., 73.

66. Ibid.

67. Ibid.

68. Ibid., 74.

69. Dr. Seuss, *Green Eggs and Ham* (New York: Random House), 12.

70. Ibid., 48.

71. Ibid.

72. Longman, *Literary Approaches*, 67.

73. Powell, *What Is Narrative Criticism?* 9.

74. Tolbert, *Sowing the Gospel,* 52.

75. Bal, *Narratology*, 11.

76. Koala Jones-Warsaw, "Toward a Womanist Hermeneutic: A Reading of Judges 19–21," *JITC* 22 (1994): 30.

77. Elisabeth Schüssler Fiorenza, *Bread Not Stone: The Challenge of Feminist Biblical Interpretation* (Boston: Beacon, 1984), 15–18.

78. Alice Walker, *In Search of Our Mothers' Gardens: Womanist Prose* (San Diego and New York: Harcourt Brace, 1983), xi.

79. Ibid., 375.

∞ Chapter 4: Establishing Mark's Social Context

1. Halvor Moxnes, "Honor, Shame, and the Outside World in Paul's Letter to the Romans," in *Social World of Formative Christianity and Judaism*, ed. Jacob Neusner et al (Philadelphia: Fortress Press, 1989), 207.

2. See, for example, C. E. B. Cranfield, *The Gospel according to Saint Mark*, CGTC (Cambridge: Cambridge University Press, 1959); Vincent Taylor, *The Gospel according to St. Mark* (London: MacMillan, 1966).

3. See, for example, Willi Marxsen, *Mark the Evangelist* (Nashville: Abingdon, 1969); Ched Myers, *Binding the Strong Man: A Political Reading of Mark's Story of Jesus* (Maryknoll, N.Y.: Orbis, 1988).

4. See, for example, Howard Clark Kee, *Community of the New Age: Studies in Mark's Gospel* (London: SCM, 1977); Joel Marcus, "The Jewish War and the *Sitz im Leben* of Mark," *JBL* 111 (1992): 441–62.

5. Donald H. Juel, *Mark*, ACNT (Minneapolis: Augsburg Books, 1990), 20.

6. Mary Douglas, *Natural Symbols: Explorations in Cosmology* (New York: Routledge, 1973, 2000), 16.

7. Herman C. Waetjen, *A Reordering of Power: A Socio-political Reading of Mark's Gospel* (Minneapolis: Fortress Press, 1989), 13.

8. Juel, *Mark*, 18.

9. Werner H. Kelber, *The Kingdom in Mark: A New Place and Time* (Philadelphia: Fortress Press, 1974), 129.

10. Marcus, "Jewish War," 461 n. 97.

11. Waetjen, *A Reordering of Power*, 14.

12. C. Clifton Black, "Was Mark a Roman Gospel?" *ExpTim* 105 (1993): 36.

13. Marcus, "Jewish War," 451.

14. Marcus, "Jewish War," 460–61.

15. Mary Ann Tolbert, *Sowing the Gospel: Mark's World in Literary Perspective* (Minneapolis: Fortress Press, 1989), 36.

16. Ibid.

17. Daniel J. Harrington, *The Gospel of Matthew*, SP1 (Collegeville, Minn.: Liturgical, 1991), 1.

18. Brian K. Blount observes that "Jesus [*sic*] story represents an inclusion of Gentiles in the cause of God's kingdom intervention." *Go Preach! Mark's Kingdom Message and the Black Church Today* (Maryknoll, N.Y.: Orbis, 1998), 63.

19. Blount, *Go Preach!* 259–60.

20. John R. Donahue and Daniel J. Harrington, *The Gospel of Mark*, SP 2 (Collegeville, Minn.: Liturgical, 2002), 239.

21. Ibid.

22. Ched Myers, *Binding the Strong Man: A Political Reading of Mark's Story of Jesus* (Maryknoll, N.Y.: Orbis, 1988), 205.

23. Joel Marcus asserts that Galilee's significance for Mark is not because his community resides there. Instead, Galilee is historically and theologically important to Mark because Jesus actually ministered there and Galilee is a place "from in which, and from which, the Marcan Jesus can plausibly interact with Gentiles, since it is contiguous to Gentile regions." "Jewish War," 461.

24. Kelber, *Kingdom*, 130.

25. G. Stemberger, "Galilee—Land of Salvation?" appendix 4 in W. D. Davies, *The Gospel and the Land: Early Christianity and Jewish Territorial Doctrine* (Berkeley: University of California Press, 1974), 415–21.

26. Marcus, "Jewish War," 461 n. 93.

27. Kee, *Community of the New Age*, 103.

28. Marcus, "Jewish War," 446 n. 29.

29. Ibid., 445–46.

30. Josephus, *Against Apion* 1.13 (Thackeray, LCL).

31. Josephus, *War* 2.478 (Thackeray, LCL).

32. Ibid., 2.18.1–2, cited by Marcus, "Jewish War," 452.

33. U. Rappaport, "Jewish-Pagan Relations and the Revolt against Rome in 66–70 C.E.," *Jerusalem Cathedra I* (1981): 81–95.

34. Marcus, "Jewish War," 461.

35. Waetjen identifies Mark's original audience as "village folk residing in the rural territory that, as the Latinisms suggest, was occupied by Roman legions and exploited by Roman business entrepreneurs and traders." *A Reordering of Power*, 13.

36. Tolbert, *Sowing the Gospel*, 125.

37. Waetjen, *A Reordering of Power*, 13.

38. Kee, *Community of the New Age*, 100.

39. Marcus, "Jewish War," 460.

40. Ibid., 460 n. 90.

41. Marcus, "Jewish War," 448.

42. Richard A. Horsley, "Popular Messianic Movements around the Time of Jesus," *CBQ* 46 (1984): 482.

43. Ibid., 482.

44. Adela Yarbro Collins, *The Beginning of the Gospel: Probings of Mark in Context* (Minneapolis: Fortress Press, 1992), 86.

45. Blount, *Go Preach!* 56.

46. Marcus, "Jewish War," 447–78.

47. See Juel, *Mark*, 179–80.

48. Marcus, "Jewish War," 454.

49. Cheryl Townsend Gilkes, "The 'Loves' and 'Troubles' of African American Women's Bodies: The Womanist Challenge to Cultural Humiliation and Social Ambivalence," in *A Troubling in My Soul: Womanist Perspectives on Evil and Suffering*, ed. Emilie M. Townes (Maryknoll, N.Y.: Orbis, 1993), 242.

50. bell hooks, *Ain't I A Woman: Black Women and Feminism* (Boston: South End, 1981), 33.

51. Angela Davis writes that one of the essential tools of white racism is defining African Americans as "servants." *Women, Race, and Class* (New York: Vintage, 1983), 94.

52. Jacquelyn Grant, "The Sin of Servanthood and the Deliverance of Discipleship," in Townes, *A Troubling in My Soul*, 214–15.

53. Bruce J. Malina, *The New Testament World: Insights from Cultural Anthropology*, 3rd ed. (Louisville, Ky.: Westminster John Knox, 2001), xiii.

54. Ibid., 27–57. See also Anthony J. Saldarini, *Pharisees, Scribes and Sadducees in Palestinian Society* (Grand Rapids: Eerdmans, 1998), 54. David A. DeSilva, *Honor, Patronage, Kinship and Purity: Unlocking New Testament Culture* (Downers Grove, Ill.: InterVarsity, 2000), 23.

55. Bruce J. Malina and Richard L. Rohrbaugh, *Social-Science Commentary on the Synoptic Gospels*, 2nd ed. (Minneapolis: Fortress Press, 2003), 5.

56. Ibid.

57. Ibid., 3.

58. Ibid.

59. Ibid., 3–4.

60. Ibid., 4.

61. John J. Pilch and Bruce Malina, eds. *Biblical Social Values and Their Meaning: A Handbook* (Peabody, Mass.: Hendrickson, 1993), xxxviii.

62. Malina and Rohrbaugh, *Social-Science Commentary*, 4.

63. See Christopher Rowland and Mark Corner's discussion of Boff's model in *Liberating Exegesis: The Challenge of Liberation Theology to Biblical Studies* (Louisville, Ky.: Westminster John Knox, 1989), 43–44.

64. Blount, *Go Preach!* 201.

65. Joseph Plevnik, "Honor/Shame," in Pilch and Malina, *Biblical Social Values*, 95.

66. Malina, *New Testament World*, 29.

67. Bruce J. Malina, "Authoritarianism," in Pilch and Malina, *Biblical Social Values*, 11.

68. Malina, *New Testament World*, 29.

69. Ibid., 29.

70. Ibid., 31.

71. Plevnik, "Honor/Shame," 95.

72. Malina, *New Testament World*, 31.

73. Plevnik, "Honor/Shame," 96.

74. Ibid.

75. Ibid.

76. John S. Kloppenburg, "Alms, Debt, and Divorce: Jesus' Ethic in Their Mediterranean Context," *TJT* 6 (1990): 185.

77. Blount, *Go Preach!* 216.

78. Ibid.

79. Ibid., 233.

80. Ibid., 53.

81. Ibid., 60–61.

82. Ibid. See also Saldarini, *Pharisees, Scribes and Sadducees*, 40–44.

83. Waetjen, *A Reordering of Power*, 10.

84. John Barclay, *Early Christian Thought in Its Jewish Context* (New York: Cambridge University Press, 1996), 12.

85. Saldarini, *Pharisees, Scribes and Sadducees*, 40.

86. Myers, *Binding the Strong Man*, 52.

87. Ibid., 51.

88. Ibid.

89. Kloppenburg, "Alms, Debt, and Divorce," 188–89.

90. Richard A. Horsley, *Sociology and the Jesus Movement* (New York: Crossroads, 1989), 89.

91. Ibid., 27.

92. Richard A. Horsley, "High Priests and the Politics of Roman Palestine," *Journal for the Study of Judaism* 17 (1986): 28.

93. Saldarini, *Pharisees, Scribes and Sadducees*, 40–41.

94. Ibid.

95. Ibid., 41.

96. Waetjen, *A Reordering of Power*, 9.

97. Richard A. Horsley, "Ancient Jewish Banditry and the Revolt against Rome, A.D. 66–70," *CBQ* 43 (1981): 417.

98. Barclay, *Early Christian Thought*, 13.

99. Horsley writes, "Social banditry arises in traditional agrarian societies where peasants are exploited by landowners and governments, especially in situations where peasants are economically vulnerable and administration is insufficient." "Ancient Jewish Banditry," 412.

100. Ibid., 413.

101. Ibid.

102. Saldarini, *Pharisees, Scribes and Sadducees*, 55.

103. Means values "facilitate the realization of core and secondary values." Pilch and Malina, *Biblical Social Values*, xvii.

104. Waetjen, *A Reordering of Power*, 5.

105. Bruce J. Malina, "Wealth and Poverty in the New Testament and Its World," *Int* 41 (1987): 366.

106. Ibid., 355.

107. Ibid., 366.

108. Ibid.

109. Bruce J. Malina, "Humility," in Pilch and Malina, *Biblical Social Values*, 107.

110. George Foster, "Peasant Society and the Image of the Limited Good," *AmAn* 67 (1965): 296, quoted in Kloppenburg, "Alms, Debt, and Divorce," 188.

111. Waetjen, *A Reordering of Power*, 5.

112. John P. Meier, "The Historical Jesus and the Historical Herodians," *JBL* 119 (2000): 742.

113. Saldarini, *Pharisees, Scribes, and Sadducees*, 74.

114. Josephus, *Ant.* 1.3 (Thackeray, LCL).

115. Saldarini, *Pharisees, Scribes, and Sadducees*, 74.

116. Anthony Saldarini, "Scribes," *ABD* 5:1015.

117. Saldarini, *Pharisees, Scribes and Sadducees*, 274.

118. Ibid.

119. Ibid., 276.

120. Saldarini also affirms that the Gospels' portrayals of the scribes are "very probable." It is not unreasonable for them to have served as officials in Jerusalem and copyists in the villages of Galilee. For the most part, scribes "fulfilled a number of roles" and stood for a "plethora of Jewish community officials." Saldarini, "Scribes," *ABD* 5:1015.

121. John G. Gager, *Kingdom and Community: The Social World of Early Christianity* (Englewood Cliffs, N.Y.: Prentice-Hall, 1975), 24.

122. Blount, *Go Preach!* 61.

123. Ibid.

124. Myers, *Binding the Strong Man*, 39.

125. Delores S. Williams, *Sisters in the Wilderness: The Challenge of Womanist God-Talk* (Maryknoll, N.Y.: Orbis, 1993), 74.

126. U.S. Census Bureau, "Poverty in the United States: 2002," 1.

127. bell hooks, *Ain't I a Woman: Black Women and Feminism* (Boston: South End, 1981), 54.

128. Mark Lewis Taylor, *Remembering Esperanza: A Cultural-Political Theology for North American Praxis* (Minneapolis: Fortress Press, 1990, 2004), 142.

129. Davis, *Women, Race, and Class*, 91.

130. hooks, *Ain't I a Woman*, 85.

131. Sue K. Jewell, *From Mammy to Miss America and Beyond: Cultural Images and the Shaping of US Social Policy* (London: Routledge, 1993), 37–46. Jewell states that the Jezebel image was created to explain why sexual liaisons would occur between white men and black women—the white man was coerced. Jezebel is the amalgamation of seductress/evil nature of all women combined with the savage nature of black women. The result is a mulatto who conforms to the standards of white beauty but has the supposed hypersexuality of an African.

132. Ibid., 35–36.

∞ Chapter 5: Discipleship and the Cross in Mark

1. Mary Ann Tolbert, *Sowing the Gospel: Mark's World in Literary Perspective* (Minneapolis: Fortress Press, 1989).

2. M. A. K. Halliday and Ruqaiya Hasan, *Language, Context, and Text: Aspects of Language in a Social-Semiotic Perspective* (Geelong, Aust.: Deakin University Press, 1985), 12.

3. Robert H. Gundry, *Mark: A Commentary on His Apology for the Cross* (Grand Rapids: Eerdmans, 1993), 104.

4. M. A. K. Halliday asserts that the beginning of a text serves as the context for what will come after it. Therefore, every text is both text and context simultaneously. Halliday and Hasan, *Language, Context, and Text*, 48. Ruqaiya Hasan speaks in terms of context and co-text. The co-text is the "language accompanying the linguistic unit," whereas the context is the "extra-linguistic environment." *Language, Context, and Text*, 75–76. For our purposes, I will use the terminology employed by Hasan in order to distinguish the narrative co-text from its cultural context.

5. Theodore J. Weeden, "The Heresy That Necessitated Mark's Gospel," in *The Interpretation of Mark*, ed. William Telford (Philadelphia: Fortress Press, 1985), 65.

6. William D. Lane, *The Gospel according to Mark*, NICNT (Grand Rapids: Eerdmans, 1974), 292–93.

7. For Weeden, suffering is the only "authentic" characteristic for being the messiah. "The Heresy," 72.

8. Wilbur Jackson Bennett Jr., "The Role of *Dei* in the Marcan Understanding of the Passion" (Ph.D. diss., Drew University, 1968), 4–14.

9. Ibid., 4.

10. Rudolph Otto, *The Kingdom of God and the Son of Man*, trans. Floyd V. Filson and Bertram Lee Woolf (London: Lutterworth Press, 1938).

11. Although Werner Kelber does not refer to Mark 8:31 in his interpretation, his work reflects this assumption when he writes that there is "no success without the suffering that precedes it." Herman C. Waetjen, *A Reordering of Power: A Sociopolitical Reading of Mark's Gospel* (Minneapolis: Fortress Press, 1989), 52.

12. Ethelbert Stauffer, *New Testament Theology*, trans. John Marsh (New York: MacMillan, 1955).

13. H. E. Tödt, *The Son of Man in the Synoptic Tradition*, trans. Dorothea M. Barton (Philadelphia: Westminster, 1965).

14. Terence E. Fretheim, "Will of God in the OT," 6:915.

15. Walter Grundmann, "*Dei*," *TDNT* 2:21.

16. Ibid.

17. Ched Myers, *Binding the Strong Man: A Political Reading of Mark's Story of Jesus* (Maryknoll, N.Y.: Orbis, 1988), 243.

18. Ibid., 244.

19. Ibid.

20. Bennett, "The Role of *Dei*," 19.

21. Halliday and Hasan, *Language, Context, and Text*, 84.

22. Ibid.

23. Ibid.

24. Ibid., 74.

25. Bruce J. Malina, *The New Testament World: Insights from Cultural Anthropology*, 3rd ed. (Louisville, Ky.: Westminster John Knox, 2001), 36.

26. David M. May, "Mark 3:20-35 from the Perspective of Shame/Honor," *BTB* 17 (1987): 84.

27. This type of exchange is a challenge-riposte. David A. DeSilva, *Honor, Patronage, Kinship and Purity: Unlocking New Testament Culture* (Downers Grove, Ill.: InterVarsity, 2000), 29.

28. Malina defines a challenge as a "claim to enter the social space of another." Challenges can be positive or negative. A positive challenge can take the form of gift giving or inviting someone to a party. The intent is to attain some mutual ground with the person approached or to pursue some mutually beneficial end. A negative challenge is an attempt to remove another from his or her place of honor. This can take the form of a physical attack or some form of inappropriate social boundary crossing. Malina, *New Testament World*, 33–36. See also DeSilva, *Honor, Patronage, Kinship and Purity*, 31.

29. DeSilva, *Honor, Patronage, Kinship and Purity*, 31.

30. "The basic notion of all studies of honor and shame is that they represent the value of a person in her or his own eyes but also in the eyes of his or her society." Halvor Moxnes, "Honor and Shame," *BTB* 23 (1993): 208.

31. Bruce J. Malina, "Authoritarianism," in *Biblical Social Values and Their Meaning: A Handbook*, ed. John J. Pilch and Bruce Malina (Peabody, Mass.: Hendrickson, 1993), 11.

32. John J. Pilch, "Power," in Pilch and Malina, 139.

33. Stanley Grenz, David Guretzki, and Cherith Fee Nordling, "Moral Evil," in *Pocket Dictionary of Theological Terms* (Downers Grove, Ill.: InterVarsity, 1999), 48.

34. I shall return to the roles and relationships among the Pharisees, Herodians, and crowds in the tenor of discourse. There I will argue that the crowds form the "court of reputation" for the Pharisees and Herodians.

35. It is important to emphasize that honor is a publicly recognized and accepted claim to worth that is limited in supply. Mark depicts the crowds as an overwhelming multitude that follows Jesus to the point that neither the paralytic (2:4) nor the members of Jesus' family can get through the people to see him (3:32); there is a danger that they might crush him (3:9); the disciples cannot even eat (3:20); he must teach them from a boat rather than the coast where they have gathered (4:1-2); he feeds five thousand men plus women and children (6:44) and four

thousand people on another occasion (8:9). Therefore, the enthusiasm with which the crowd receives the ministry of Jesus means he is a very real threat to the honor of others.

36. H. G. Liddell and R. Scott, "*Apollymi*," in *An Intermediate Greek-English Lexicon*, 7th ed. (Oxford: Oxford University Press, 1995), 101–2.

37. Malina, *New Testament World*, 40.

38. Hasan acknowledges that "general field of meaning" is a vague description for establishing relations of co-extension. The three sense relations of synonymy, antonymy, and hyponymy help to set boundaries for relations of co-extension. Halliday and Hasan, *Language, Context, and Text*, 80.

39. Ibid.

40. Ibid.

41. Michaelis, *TDNT* 5:914.

42. Jamie T. Phelps, "Joy Came in the Morning: Risking Death for Resurrection: Confronting the Evil of Social Sin and Socially Sinful Structures," in *A Troubling in My Soul: Womanist Perspectives on Evil and Suffering*, ed. Emilie M. Townes (Maryknoll, N.Y.: Orbis, 1993), 49.

43. Bennett, "The Role of *Dei*," 21.

44. Contra Michaelis, who claims, "The uniqueness of the passion of Jesus is reflected in the fact that *pathein* occurs only in the sayings of Jesus relating to His own person" (Wilhelm Michaleis, *TDNT* 5:916), Mark 8:31 is not the only occurrence of *pathein* in the Gospel. Mark employs *paschō* three times in the entire Gospel—5:26; 8:31; and 9:12.

45. In chapter 1, I defined agony as "the disturbance of our inner tranquility caused by physical, mental, emotional, social, and spiritual forces that we grasp as jeopardizing our lives, our very existence."

46. Herbert Weir Smyth, *Greek Grammar*, ed. Gordon M. Messing (Cambridge, Mass.: Harvard University Press, 1984), 144.

47. In remaining passion predictions, the narrator uses the middle voice of *anistēmi* (9:31 and 10:34).

48. See Craig A. Evans, *Mark 8:27—16:20*, WBC 34B (Nashville: Thomas Nelson, 2001), 18. Gundry, *Mark*, 430. John R. Donahue and Daniel J. Harrington, *The Gospel of Mark*, SP 2 (Collegeville, Minn.: Liturgical, 2002), 262. C. S. Mann, *Mark: A New Translation with Introduction and Commentary*, AB 27 (New York: Anchor Bible/Doubleday, 1986), 242–43.

49. Mann, *Mark*, 347. Bennett, "The Role of *Dei*," 23–25.

50. Bennett, "The Role of *Dei*," 23–25.

51. Ibid., 25.

52. Mann, *Mark*, 343.

53. Grundmann, "*Dei*," *TDNT* 2:21.

54. Mark McVann, "Reading Mark Ritually: Honor-Shame and the Ritual of Baptism," *Semeia* 67 (1994): 188.

55. Although 8:31 is traditionally referred to as a passion prediction, this designation is not entirely accurate. Our reading shows that among the inevitable events listed is the resurrection. Donahue and Harrington, *Gospel of Mark*, 262.

56. John Christopher Thomas, "Discipleship in Mark's Gospel," in *Faces of Renewal*, ed. Paul Ebert (Peabody, Mass.: Hendrickson, 1988), 72.

57. Elizabeth Struthers Malbon, "Disciples/Crowds/Whoever: Marcan Characters and Readers," *NovT* 28 (1986) 124–25.

58. Robert P. Meye, *Jesus and the Twelve: Discipleship and Revelation in Mark's Gospel* (Grand Rapids: Eerdmans, 1968), 13.

59. Ibid., 108.

60. Mark portrays Peter, James, and John as Jesus' inner circle. On three occasions, Jesus only allows these three to accompany him: at the raising of Jairus's daughter (5:37), when he is transfigured on the Mount of Olives (9:2), and when he prays in Gethsemane (14:33).

61. Malbon, "Disciples/Crowds/Whoever," 109.

62. Elizabeth Struthers Malbon, "Fallible Followers: Women and Men in the Gospel of Mark," *Semeia* 28 (1983): 31

63. Malbon, "Disciples/Crowds/Whoever," 110.

64. Ibid., 104.

65. Larry W. Hurtado, "Following Jesus in the Gospel of Mark—and Beyond," in *Patterns of Discipleship in the New Testament*, ed. Richard N. Longenecker (Grand Rapids: Eerdmans, 1996), 25.

66. Donahue and Harrington conclude, "The two essential elements of the call to discipleship are 'being with' Jesus and doing the things of Jesus." *Gospel of Mark*, 31. Thomas expresses this view succinctly: "[The] disciple's communion with Jesus will result in a sharing in the work of Jesus." "Discipleship in Mark's Gospel," 74.

67. Halliday and Hasan, *Language, Context, and Text*, 74.

68. Ibid.

69. Smyth, *Greek Grammar*, 144.

70. Ibid.

71. "*Akolouthein*," *TDNT* 1:214.

72. It is interesting to note that three of the four scholars whose work I am building upon (Tolbert, Juel, and Blount) do not address this command. Any attention they give to Mark 8:34 focuses on the second command and initial use of cross language.

73. Donahue and Harrington, *Gospel of Mark*, 263.

74. Lane, *Gospel according to Mark*, 307.

75. C. E. B. Cranfield, *The Gospel according to Saint Mark* (Cambridge: Cambridge University Press, 1972), 281.

76. Clifford Geertz comments on the "peculiarity" of the Western view of the self: "The Western conception of the person as a bounded, unique, more or less integrated motivational and cognitive universe, a dynamic center of awareness, emotion, judgment and action organized into a distinctive whole and set contrastively both against other such wholes and against its social and natural background, is, however incorrigible it may seem to us, a rather peculiar idea within the context of the world's cultures." "'From the Native's Point of View': On the Nature of Anthropological Understanding," *Meaning in Anthropology*, ed. K. H. Basso and H. A. Selby (Albuquerque: University of New Mexico Press, 1976), 225.

77. Ibid., 62.

78. Bruce J. Malina, "Dealing with Biblical (Mediterranean) Characters: A Guide for U.S. Consumers," *BTB*, vol. 19, no. 4 (October 1989): 128.

79. Moxnes, "Honor and Shame," 208.

80. Malina, *New Testament World*, 75.

81. Ibid., 62.

82. Joseph Plevnik, "Honor/Shame," in Pilch and Malina, *Biblical Social Values*, 95.

83. Malina, "Dealing with Biblical (Mediterranean) Characters," 127.

84. Ibid., 131.

85. Ibid.

86. Bruce J. Malina, "'Let Him Deny Himself' (Mark 8:34): A Social-Psychological Model of Self-Denial," *BTB* 24 (1994): 185–86.

87. Thomas, "Discipleship in Mark's Gospel," 73.

88. David P. Seccombe writes, "The sufferings and degradation of crucifixion have no parallel in the modern world." "Take Up Your Cross," in *God Who Is Rich in Mercy: Essays Presented to Dr. D. B. Knox*, ed. Peter T. O'Brien and David G. Peterson (Grand Rapids: Baker, 1986), 139.

89. Martin Hengel, *Crucifixion in the Ancient World and the Folly of the Message of the Cross* (Philadelphia: Fortress Press, 1977), 87.

90. Ibid.

91. Jerome H. Neyrey, "Nudity," in Pilch and Malina, *Biblical Social Values*, 123.

92. Ibid., 119.

93. Ibid., 121.

94. Malina, *New Testament World*, 49.

95. "Again and again the literature on crucifixion stresses the themes of the sovereignty of the state, its rule and power." Michael Green, "The Meaning of Cross-Bearing," *BSac* (1983): 125.

96. Gundry, *Mark*, 435.

97. Ched Myers, "Embracing the Way of Jesus," *Sojourners* 16 (1987): 37.

98. Jesus "must prepare them to suffer (in their own time and way) rejection, persecution, and even martyrdom. This martyrdom, he suggests under its extremist form, the cross, understood quite literally." Donald P. Fletcher, "Condemned to Die: The Logion on Cross-Bearing; What Does It Mean?" *Int* 18 (1964): 160–61.

99. Plevnik, "Honor/Shame," 102.

100. C. Clifton Black writes, "Jesus' models of discipleship consistently subvert conventional assumptions about social status." "Was Mark a Roman Gospel?" *ExpTim* 105 (1993): 38.

101. The "exhortation itself [is] cast *explicitly* in honor-shame terms." McVann, "Reading Mark Ritually," 187.

102. Myers, *Binding the Strong Man*, 247.

103. Kloppenberg, "Alms, Debt, and Divorce,"187.

104. Malina, *New Testament World*, 32.

105. Ibid., 104.

106. DeSilva, *Honor, Patronage, Kinship and Purity*, 126.

107. Ibid., 97. DeSilva states that Jesus is "cast more frequently in the New Testament in the role of mediator of God's favor and broker of access to God." Ibid., 133.

108. Plevnik, "Honor/Shame," 103.

109. The temptation to be ashamed of Jesus is the primary obstacle that Peter will have to overcome. In verse 32, Peter rebukes Jesus after Jesus has spoken *ton logon* openly. Peter's rebuke of Jesus suggests that he is already ashamed of Jesus' words. In chapter 15, Mark will also detail Peter's denial of Jesus. Three times, Peter shows himself to be ashamed to associate with Jesus.

110. Malina, *New Testament World*, 104–5.

111. Ibid.

112. Donald H. Juel, *Mark*, ACNT (Minneapolis: Augsburg Books, 1990), 123.

113. Consistently, the narrator presents these groups as a collective unit. In effect, each group functions as a single person. There is only one occasion in which Mark narrates an interaction between Jesus and an individual from among their ranks (12:28). By so doing, Mark contrasts this scribe's openness to Jesus with the rejection of his group.

114. Myers, *Binding the Strong Man*, 142.

115. Waetjen describes the scribes of Jesus' time as the "official interpreters of the law." *A Reordering of Power*, 8. John E. Stambaugh and David L. Balch note that the scribes "taught students." *The New Testament in Its Social Environment* (Philadelphia: Westminster, 1986), 99.

116. Tolbert, *Sowing the Gospel*, 172.

117. Myers, *Binding the Strong Man*, 141–42.

118. Pilch, "Power," 139.

119. Malina, "Authoritarianism," 11.

120. Myers, *Binding the Strong Man*, 142.

121. Ibid.

122. See Mark 2:6, 16; 3:22; 7:1; 9:14.

123. Halliday and Hasan, *Language, Context, and Text*, 80.

124. Mark 11:27 is the first time Jesus encounters the elders, chief priests, and scribes in person. At this point, he is in Jerusalem and has cleansed the temple. His symbolic act attracts the attention of the religious elites. The chief priests and elders must acknowledge him because his actions threaten the temple system and therefore threaten the honor of those who operate it. They must now lend the weight of their social standing to support the fight against Jesus.

125. Anthony J. Saldarini notes that the scribes "could have been low-level officials and judges both in Jerusalem and in the towns and villages of the country." "Scribes," *ABD* 5:1015.

126. Anthony J. Saldarini, *Pharisees, Scribes and Sadducees in Palestinian Society* (Grand Rapids: Eerdmans, 1998), 155.

127. E. P. Sanders argues, "There was no substantial conflict between Jesus and the Pharisees with regard to the Sabbath, food, and purity laws." *Jesus and Judaism* (Philadelphia: Fortress Press, 1985), 265. James G. Dunn questions Sanders's presentation of Jesus and the Pharisees, noting that the similarity Sanders draws between Jesus and the Pharisees actually provides a reason *for* conflict. Dunn insists that similarity between Jesus and the Pharisees would intimidate the Pharisees most. He writes, "A Jesus who was as loyal to the covenant but who had different ideas of what covenant loyalty involved would almost certainly pose a threat to Pharisaic self-understanding and identity." "Pharisees, Sinners and Jesus," in *Social World of*

Formative Christianity and Judaism, ed. Jacob Neusner et al. (Philadelphia: Fortress Press, 1989), 276. Jacob Neusner also presents evidence that suggests a possible conflict between Jesus and the Pharisees over the same issues presented in the Gospel. He contends that the primary marks of the Pharisees were the "observance of ritual purity outside of the Temple" and "keeping the agricultural rules." Each of these emphases "affected table fellowship." According to Neusner, the disputes between Jesus and the Pharisees regarding table fellowship assert that "Christian table fellowship does not depend on the sorts of rules important to the table fellowship of other groups." He also points out that "67% of the legal pericopae that allude to those assumed to be Pharisees deal with dietary laws," namely, ritual purity for meals, agricultural rules, and Sabbath festivals. "Mr. Sanders's Pharisees—and Mine," in *Ancient Judaism: Debates and Disputes* (Atlanta: Scholars, 1993), 190, 196. The emphasis these issues receive in the rabbinic writings along with their congruity with the Gospel's depiction suggests that these issues were indeed a point of conflict. I think Dunn summarizes the situation well: "For behind the particular objections and charges leveled against Jesus was the central fact that Jesus was ignoring and abolishing boundaries which more sectarian attitudes had erected *within* Israel." "Pharisees, Sinners and Jesus," 283.

128. John P. Meier, "The Historical Jesus and the Historical Herodians," *JBL* 119 (2000): 742.

129. Ibid., 744.

130. Waetjen, *A Reordering of Power*, 9.

131. Ibid.

132. Richard A. Horsley, "High Priests and the Politics of Roman Palestine," *Journal for the Study of Judaism* 17 (1986): 27–28.

133. Malina states that in ancient Mediterranean society, only social equals could challenge one another. *New Testament World*, 35.

134. Saldarini, *Pharisees, Scribes and Sadducees*, 9.

135. Joanna Dewey, Donald Michie, and David Rhoads, *Mark as Story: An Introduction to the Narrative as Gospel*, 2nd ed. (Minneapolis: Fortress Press, 1999), 117.

136. Ibid., 105. The narrative point of view refers to "the perspectives present in a narrative." A narrative can have varying perspectives represented by its characters. However, the narrator "controls the overarching point of view of the story." This is the point of view the narrator leads the reader to adopt. Ibid., 116.

137. Brian K. Blount, *Go Preach! Mark's Kingdom Message and the Black Church Today* (Maryknoll, N.Y.: Orbis, 1998), 99.

138. Ibid., 132.

139. Tolbert, *Sowing the Gospel*, 182.

140. Ibid., 268.

141. Ibid., 182.

142. Mann, *Mark*, 350. See, by way of comparison, Hosea 2:2; Isaiah 1:4; and Ezekiel 16:32.

143. Liddell and Scott, "*Apollymi*," 101–2.

144. Waetjen, *A Reordering of Power*, 11.

145. Halliday and Hasan, *Language, Context, and Text*, 12.

146. Malbon, "Discipes/Crowds/Whoever," 124–25.

147. Plevnik, "Honor/Shame," 101–2.
148. Judith Perkins, *Suffering Self* (New York: Routledge, 1994), 24.
149. Dorothee Soelle, *Suffering* (Philadelphia: Fortress Press, 1975), 188.
150. J. Gwyn Griffith, "The Disciple's Cross," *NTS* 16 (1969–1970): 363.
151. Ibid., 169.

∞ Chapter 6: Discerning the Call

1. Zora Neale Hurston, *Their Eyes Were Watching God* (New York: Harper-Collins, 2000), 14

2. Donald H. Juel, *Mark*, ACNT (Minneapolis: Augsburg Books, 1990), 123.

∞ bibliography

Baker-Fletcher, Karen. "'Soprano Obligato': The Voices of Black Women and American Conflict in the Thought of Anna Julia Cooper." Chap. 10 in *A Troubling in My Soul: Womanist Perspectives on Evil and Suffering*. Edited by Emilie M. Townes. Maryknoll, N.Y.: Orbis, 1993.

Baker-Fletcher, Karen, and Garth Kasimu Baker-Fletcher. *My Sister, My Brother: Womanist and Xodus God-Talk*. Maryknoll, N.Y.: Orbis, 1997.

Bal, Mieke. *Narratology*. Toronto: University of Toronto Press, 1985.

Beardslee, William A. *Literary Criticism of the New Testament*. Philadelphia: Fortress Press, 1970.

Belo, Ferdando. *A Materialist Reading of the Gospel of Mark*. Translated by Matthew J. O'Connell. Maryknoll, N.Y.: Orbis, 1981.

Bennett, W. J., Jr. "The Herodians of Mark's Gospel." *NovT* 17 (1975): 9–14.

Best, Ernest. *Disciples and Discipleship: Studies in the Gospel according to Mark*. Edinburgh: T&T Clark, 1986.

———. "Discipleship in Mark: Mark 8:22—10:52." *SJT* 23 (1970): 323–37.

———. *Following Jesus: Discipleship in the Gospel of Mark*. Edinburgh: T&T Clark, 1981.

———. *Mark: The Gospel as Story*. Edinburgh: T&T Clark, 1983.

Black, C. Clifton. *The Disciples according to Mark: Markan Redaction in Current Debate*. Sheffield: Sheffield Academic, 1989.

———. "Was Mark a Roman Gospel?" *ExpTim* 105 (1993): 36–40.

Blassingame, John W. *The Slave Community*. New York and Oxford: Oxford University Press, 1979.

Blount, Brian K. *Cultural Interpretation: Reorienting New Testament Criticism.* Minneapolis: Fortress Press, 1995.

———. *Go Preach! Mark's Kingdom Message and the Black Church Today.* Maryknoll, N.Y.: Orbis, 1998.

———. *Then the Whisper Put on Flesh: New Testament Ethics in an African American Context.* Nashville: Abingdon, 2001.

Bowker, John. *Jesus and the Pharisees.* Cambridge: Cambridge University Press, 1973.

Brown, Kelly Delaine. "God Is as Christ Does." *JRT* 46 (1989): 7–16.

Bultmann, Rudolph. *New Testament Mythology and Other Basic Writings.* Philadelphia: Fortress Press, 1984.

Burrows, Rufus, Jr. "Toward Womanist Theology and Ethics." *JFRS* 15 (1999): 77–95.

Cade, Toni. *The Black Woman: An Anthology.* New York: New American Library, 1970.

Cannon, Katie Geneva. *Black Womanist Ethics.* Atlanta: Scholars, 1998.

———. *Katie's Canon: Womanism and the Soul of the Black Community.* New York: Continuum, 1995.

Collins, Adela Yarbro. *The Beginning of the Gospel: Probings of Mark in Context.* Minneapolis: Fortress Press, 1992.

Cone, James H. *A Black Theology of Liberation.* Maryknoll, N.Y.: Orbis, 1992.

———. *God of the Oppressed.* Maryknoll, N.Y.: Orbis, 2000.

———. *The Spirituals and the Blues.* Maryknoll, N.Y.: Orbis, 1992.

Cooey, Paula M., William R. Eakin, and Jay B. McDaniel. *After Patriarchy: Feminist Transformation of the World Religions.* Maryknoll, N.Y.: Orbis, 1991.

Copeland, M. Shawn. "Wading through Many Sorrows: Toward a Theology of Suffering in Womanist Perspective." Chap. 7 in *A Troubling in My Soul: Womanist Perspectives on Evil and Suffering.* Edited by Emilie M. Townes. Maryknoll, N.Y.: Orbis, 1993.

Cranfield, C. E. B. *The Gospel according to Mark.* Cambridge: Cambridge University Press, 1959.

Crawford, Elaine A. "Womanist Christology: Where Have We Come From and Where Are We Going?" *RevExp* 95 (1998): 367–82.

Davis, Angela Y. *Woman, Race, and Class.* New York: Vintage, 1981.

Derrett, J. Duncan M. "Taking Up the Cross and Turning the Cheek." *SPCK* (1985): 61–78.

DeSilva, David A. *Honor, Patronage, Kinship and Purity: Unlocking New Testament Culture.* Downers Grove, Ill.: InterVarsity, 2000.

Detweiler, Robert. "After the New Criticism: Contemporary Methods of Literary Interpretation." In *Orientation by Disorientation.* Edited by Richard A. Spencer. Pittsburgh: Pickwick, 1981.

Dewey, Joanna. *Disciples on the Way: Mark on Discipleship.* Women's Division Board of Global Ministries, the United Methodist Church, 1976.

———. "Feminist Reading, Gospel Narratives and Critical Theory." *BTB* 22 (1992): 167–73.

Donahue, John R. "A Neglected Fact in the Theology of Mark." *JBL* 101 (1982): 563–94.

———. *The Theology and Setting of Discipleship in the Gospel of Mark.* Milwaukee: Marquette University Press, 1981.

Donahue, John R., and Daniel J. Harrington. *The Gospel of Mark.* SP 2. Collegeville, Minn.: Liturgical, 2002.

Douglas, Kelly Brown. *The Black Christ.* Maryknoll, N.Y.: Orbis, 1994.

Dowd, Sharyn Echols. *Prayer, Power, and the Problem of Suffering.* Atlanta: Scholars, 1988.

Dyson, Michael Eric. *Reflecting Black African American Cultural Criticism.* Minneapolis: University of Minnesota Press, 1993.

Evans, Craig A. *Mark 8:27—16:20.* Word Biblical Commentary 34B. Nashville: Thomas Nelson, 2001.

Fasold, Ralph. *The Sociolinguistic Society.* Oxford: Blackwell, 1984.

Ferguson, Everett. *Backgrounds of Early Christianity.* Grand Rapids: Eerdmans, 1987.

Fiorenza, Elisabeth Schüssler. *Bread Not Stone: The Challenge of Feminist Biblical Interpretation.* Boston: Beacon, 1984.

———. *Jesus and the Politics of Interpretation.* New York: Continuum, 2001.

Fletcher, Donald P. "Condemned to Die: The Logion on Cross-Bearing; What Does it Mean?" *Int* 18 (1964): 156–64.

Fowler, Robert M. *Let the Reader Understand: Reader-Response Criticism and the Gospel of Mark.* Minneapolis: Fortress Press, 1991.

Frei, Hans W. *The Eclipse of the Biblical Narrative: A Study in Eighteenth and Nineteenth Century Hermeneutics*. New Haven: Yale University Press, 1974.

Fretheim, Terence E. "Will of God in the OT." Pages 914–20 in vol. 6 of *Anchor Bible Dictionary*. Edited by D. N. Freedman. 6 vols. New York, 1992.

Fréyne, Sean. *The Twelve: Disciples and Apostles*. London: Sheed & Ward, 1968.

Funk, Robert W. *The Poetics of Biblical Narrative*. Sonoma: Polebridge, 1988.

Gager, John G. *Kingdom and Community: The Social World of Early Christianity*. Englewood Cliffs, N.J.: Prentice-Hall, 1975.

Gerstenberger, Erhard S., and Wolfgang Schrage. *Suffering*. Nashville: Abingdon, 1977.

Gould, Ezra P. *A Critical and Exegetical Commentary of the Gospel according to Mark*. Edinburgh: T&T Clark, 1955.

Grant, Jacquelyn. "The Sin of Servanthood and the Deliverance of Discipleship." Chap. 12 in *A Troubling in My Soul: Womanist Perspectives on Evil and Suffering*. Edited by Emilie M. Townes. Maryknoll, N.Y.: Orbis, 1993.

———. *White Women's Christ and Black Women's Jesus: Feminist Christology and Womanist Response*. Atlanta: Scholars, 1989.

Green, Michael. "The Meaning of Cross-Bearing." *BSac* (1983): 117–33.

Grenz, Stanley, David Guretzki, and Cherith Fee Nordling. *Pocket Dictionary of Theological Terms*. Downers Grove, Ill.: InterVarsity, 1999.

Griffin, Paul R. *Seeds of Racism in the Soul of America*. Cleveland: Pilgrim, 1999.

Griffith, J. Gwyn. "The Disciple's Cross." *NTS* 16 (1969–1970): 358–64.

Gundry, Robert H. *Mark: A Commentary on His Apology for the Cross*. Grand Rapids: Eerdmans, 1993.

Halliday, M. A. K., *Explorations in the Functions of Language*. New York: Elsevier North-Holland, 1973.

Halliday, M. A. K., and Ruqaiya Hasan. *Language, Context, and Text: Aspects of Language in a Social-Semiotic Perspective*. Geelong, Aust.: Deakin University Press, 1985.

Hengel, Martin. *Crucifixion*. Philadelphia: Fortress Press, 1977.

Hinlicky, Paul R. "Conformity to Christ in the Gospel of Mark." *CurTM* 15 (1988): 364–68.

Holmberg, Bengt. *Sociology and the New Testament*. Minneapolis: Fortress Press, 1990.

Hooker, Morna D. *The Gospel according to St. Mark*. Peabody, Mass.: Hendrickson, 1999.

———. *The Message of Mark*. London: Epworth, 1983.

———. *Not Ashamed of the Gospel: New Testament Interpretations of the Death of Jesus*. Carlisle, UK: Paternoster, 1994.

hooks, bell. *Ain't I a Woman: Black Women and Feminism*. Boston: South End, 1981.

Horsley, Richard A. "Ancient Jewish Banditry and the Revolt against Rome, A.D. 66–70." *CBQ* 43 (1981): 409–32.

———. "High Priests and the Politics of Roman Palestine." *JSJ* 17 (1986): 23–55.

———. "Popular Messianic Movements around the Time of Jesus." *CBQ* 46 (1984): 471–95.

———. "Popular Prophetic Movements at the Time of Jesus: Their Principal Features and Social Origins." *JSNT* 26 (1986): 3–27.

———. *Sociology and the Jesus Movement*. New York: Crossroad, 1989.

Hudson, R. A. *Sociolinguistics*. Cambridge: Cambridge University Press, 1980.

Iser, Wolfgang. *The Act of Reading: Theory of Aesthetic Response*. Baltimore: Johns Hopkins University Press, 1978.

Jewell, K. Sue. *From Mammy to Miss America and Beyond: Cultural Images and the Shaping of US Social Policy*. London: Routledge, 1993.

Johnson, James Weldon, and John Rosamond Johnson. "Were You There?" *American Negro Spirituals*. New York: Viking, 1926.

Jones-Warsaw, Koala. "Towards Womanist Hermeneutics: A Reading of Judges 19–21." *JITC* 22 (1994): 18–35.

Juel, Donald H. *The Gospel of Mark*. Nashville: Abingdon, 1999.

———. *Mark*. ACNT. Minneapolis: Augsburg Books, 1990.

———. *A Master of Surprise: Mark Interpreted*. Minneapolis: Fortress Press, 1994.

Kee, Howard Clark. *Community of the New Age: Studies in the Gospel of Mark*. Philadelphia: Westminster, 1977.

Kelber, Werner. *The Kingdom in Mark: A New Time and a New Place.* Philadelphia: Fortress Press, 1974.

———. *Mark's Story of Jesus.* Philadelphia: Fortress Press, 1979.

Kermode, Frank. *The Genesis of Secrecy: On the Interpretation of Narrative.* Cambridge, Mass.: Harvard University Press, 1979.

Kingsbury, Jack Dean. *Christology of Mark's Gospel.* Philadelphia: Fortress Press, 1983.

———. *Conflict in Mark: Jesus, Authorities, Disciples.* Minneapolis: Fortress Press, 1989.

Klijn, A. F. J. "Scribes, Pharisees, High Priests, and Elders in the New Testament." *NovT* 3 (1959): 259–67.

Kloppenburg, John S. "Alms, Debt, and Divorce: Jesus' Ethics in Their Mediterranean Context." *TJT* 6 (1990): 182–200.

Lane, William L. *The Gospel according to Mark.* Grand Rapids: Eerdmans, 1974.

Lightfoot, R. H. *The Gospel Message of Mark.* London: Oxford Press, 1962.

Longman, Tremper. *Literary Approaches to Biblical Interpretation.* Grand Rapids: Zondervan, 1987.

Lorde, Audre. *Sister Outsider.* Berkeley: Crossing, 1984.

Malbon, Elizabeth Struthers. "Disciples/Crowd/Whoever." *NovT* 28 (1986): 104–30.

———. "Fallible Followers." *Semeia* 28 (1983): 29–48.

———. "Narrative Criticism: What Does the Story Mean?" Chap. 2 in *Mark and Method.* Edited by Janice Capel Anderson and Stephen D. Moore. Minneapolis: Fortress Press, 1992.

———. *Narrative Space and Mythic Meaning.* Sheffield: JSOT Press, 1991.

Malherbe, Abraham J. *Social Aspects of Early Christianity.* Philadelphia: Fortress Press, 1983.

Malina, Bruce J. "Dealing with Biblical (Mediterranean) Characters: A Guide for U.S. Consumers." *BTB* 19 (1989): 127–41.

———. "'Let Him Deny Himself' (Mark 8:34): A Social-Psychological Model of Self-Denial." *BTB* 24 (1994): 106–21.

———. *The New Testament World: Insights from Cultural Anthropology.* 3rd ed. Rev. and expanded. Louisville, Ky.: Westminster John Knox, 2001.

————. "The Social Science and Biblical Interpretation." *Int* 36 (1982): 229–42.

————. "Wealth and Poverty in the New Testament and Its World." *Int* 41 (1987): 354–67.

Mann, C. S. *Mark: A New Translation with Introduction and Commentary.* Garden City, N.Y.: Doubleday, 1986.

Marcus, Joel. "The Jewish War and the *Sitz im Leben* of Mark." *JBL* 113 (1992): 441–62.

————. *Mark 1–8.* Anchor Bible 27. Garden City, N.Y.: Doubleday, 1999.

————. *Way of the Lord.* Louisville, Ky.: Westminster John Knox, 1992.

Martin, Clarice. "Biblical Theology and Black Women's Spiritual Autobiography: The Miry Bog, the Desolate Pit, a New Song in My Mouth." Chap. 1 in *A Troubling in My Soul: Womanist Perspectives on Evil and Suffering.* Edited by Emilie M. Townes. Maryknoll, N.Y.: Orbis, 1993.

————. "Womanist Interpretation of the New Testament: The Quest for Holistic and Inclusive Translation and Interpretation." *JFSR* 6 (1990): 41–61.

Marxsen, Willi. *Mark the Evangelist: Studies on the Redaction History of the Gospel.* Nashville: Abingdon, 1969.

Matera, Frank J. *What Are They Saying about Mark?* Mahwah, N.J.: Paulist, 1987.

May, David M. "Mark 3:20-35 from the Perspective of Shame/Honor." *BTB* 27 (1987): 83–87.

McVann, Mark. "Reading Mark Ritually: Honor-Shame and the Ritual of Baptism." *Semeia* 67 (1995): 179–97.

Meier, John P. "The Historical Jesus and the Historical Herodians." *JBL* 119 (2000): 740–46.

Meye, Robert P. *Jesus and the Twelve: Discipleship and Revelation in Mark's Gospel.* Grand Rapids: Eerdmans, 1968.

Migliore, Daniel L. *Faith Seeking Understanding: An Introduction to Christian Theology.* Grand Rapids: Eerdmans, 1991.

Mitchem, Stephanie Y. *Introducing Womanist Theology.* Maryknoll, N.Y.: Orbis, 2002.

Moore, Stephen. *Literary Criticism and the Gospel: The Theoretical Challenge.* New Haven: Yale University Press, 1989.

Moxnes, Halvor. "Honor and Shame." *BTB* 23 (1993): 167–75.

––––––. "Honor, Shame, and the Outside World in Paul's Letter to the Romans." Chap. 9 in *The Social World of Formative Judaism and Christianity*. Edited by Jacob Neusner, Ernest S. Frerichs, Peder Borgen, and Richard Horsley. Philadelphia: Fortress Press, 1989.

Munro, W. "Women's Discipleship in Mark? Mark 8:22—10:52." *SJT* 23 (1970): 323–37.

Myers, Ched. *Binding the Strong Man: A Political Reading of Mark's Story of Jesus*. Maryknoll, N.Y.: Orbis, 1994.

––––––. "Embracing the Way of Jesus." *Sojourners* 16 (1987): 27–30.

––––––. "The Last Days of Jesus, Mark 14:1—16:8: Collapse and Restoration of Discipleship." *Sojourners* 16 (1987), 26–32.

Neusner, Jacob. *Ancient Judaism: Debates and Disputes*. 3rd series. Atlanta: Scholars, 1993.

Nineham, D. E. *St. Mark*. Baltimore: Penguin, 1963.

Noble, Lowell L. *Naked and Not Ashamed*. Jackson, Mich.: Jackson Printing, 1975

Osborne, B. A. E. "Peter: Stumbling-Block and Satan." *NovT* 15 (1973): 187–90.

Perkins, Judith. *The Suffering Self*. New York: Routledge, 1994.

Perrin, Norman. *Modern Pilgrimage in New Testament Christology*. Philadelphia, Fortress Press, 1974.

Petersen, Norman R. "Literary Criticism in Biblical Studies." Pages 25–50 in *Orientation by Disorientation*. Edited by Richard A. Spencer. Pittsburgh: Pickwick, 1980).

Phelps, Jamie T. "Joy Came in the Morning: Risking Death for Resurrection; Confronting the Evil of Social Sin and Socially Sinful Structures." Chap. 3 in *A Troubling in My Soul: Womanist Perspectives on Evil and Suffering*. Edited by Emilie M. Townes. Maryknoll, N.Y.: Orbis, 1993.

Pilch, John J., and Bruce J. Malina. *Biblical Social Values and Their Meaning*. Peabody, Mass.: Hendrickson, 1993.

Pinn, Anthony B. *Why, Lord? Suffering and Evil in Black Theology*. New York: Continuum, 1995.

Powell, Mark Allan. *What Is Narrative Criticism?* Minneapolis: Fortress Press, 1990.

Rabichev, Renata. "The Mediterranean Concepts of Honour and Shame as Seen in the Depiction of the Biblical Women." *R&T* 3 (1996): 51–63.

Rainwater, Lee, ed. *The Moynihan Report and the Politics of Controversy.* Cambridge, Mass.: MIT Press, 1967.

Rhoads, David, et al. *Mark as Story: An Introduction to the Narrative of a Gospel.* Philadelphia: Fortress Press, 1982.

Rich, Adrienne. *Of Woman Born: Motherhood as Experience and Institution.* New York: Norton, 1976.

Robbins, Vernon K. *Jesus the Teacher: A Socio-rhetorical Interpretation of Mark.* Philadelphia: Fortress Press, 1984.

Roberts, Samuel K. *In the Path of Virtue: The African American Moral Tradition.* Cleveland: Pilgrim, 1999.

Robinson, James M. *The Problem of History in Mark and Other Marcan Studies.* Philadelphia: Fortress Press, 1982.

Rowland, Christopher, and Mark Corner. *Liberating Exegesis: The Challenge of Liberation Theology to Biblical Studies.* Louisville, Ky.: Westminster John Knox, 1989.

Ruether, Rosemary Radford. "Crisis in Sex and Race: Black Theology vs. Feminist Theology." *Christianity and Crisis* (1974): 67–73.

Russell, Letty, ed. *Feminist Interpretation of the Bible.* Philadelphia: Westminster, 1985.

Saldarini, Anthony J. *Pharisees, Scribes and Sadducees in Palestinian Society.* Grand Rapids, Mich.: Eerdmans, 1998.

Sanders, Cheryl J., Katie G. Cannon, Emile M. Townes, M. Shawn Copeland, bell hooks, and Cheryl Townsend Gilkes. "Roundtable: Christian Ethics and Theology in Womanist Perspective." *JFSR* 5 (1989): 83–112.

Sanders, E. P. *Jesus and Judaism.* Philadelphia: Fortress Press, 1985.

Schenke, Ludger. *Glory and the Way of the Cross: The Gospel of Mark.* Chicago: Franciscan Herald, 1982.

Scholes, Robert, and Robert Kellogg. *Nature of Narrative.* London: Oxford University Press, 1966.

Schweizer, Eduard. *The Good News according to Mark.* Richmond: John Knox, 1970.

Seccombe, David P. "Take Up Your Cross." In *God Who Is Rich in Mercy: Essays Presented to Dr. D. B. Knox.* Edited by Peter T. O'Brien and David G. Peterson. Grand Rapids: Baker, 1986.

Senior, Donald. *The Passion of Jesus in the Gospel of Mark*. Wilmington, Del.: Michael Glazier, 1984.

Smith, Theophus H. *Conjuring Culture: Biblical Formations of Black America*. Edited by Howard S. Stout. Oxford: Oxford University Press, 1994.

Soelle, Dorothee. *Suffering*. Philadelphia: Fortress Press, 1975.

Stambaugh, John E., and David L. Balch. *The New Testament in Its Social Environment*. Philadelphia: Westminster Press, 1986.

Stock, Augustine. *Call to Discipleship: A Literary Study of Mark's Gospel*. Wilmington, Del.: Michael Glazier, 1982.

———. "Jesus, Hypocrites, and Herodians." *BTB* 26 (1986): 3–7.

Strecker, Georg. "The Passion and Resurrection Predictions in Mark's Gospel." *Int* 22 (1968): 421–42.

Tannehill, Robert. "Disciples in Mark: The Function of a Narrative Role." In *The Interpretation of Mark*. Edited by William Telford. Philadelphia: Fortress Press, 1985.

Taylor, Mark Lewis. *The Executed God: The Way of the Cross in Lockdown America*. Minneapolis: Fortress Press, 2001.

———. *Remembering Esperanza: A Cultural-Political Theology for North American Praxis*. Minneapolis: Fortress Press, 1990, 2004.

Taylor, Vincent. *The Gospel according to Mark: The Greek Text with Introduction, Notes and Indexes*. New York: St. Martin's, 1966.

Terrell, JoAnne Marie. *Power in the Blood? The Cross in the African American Experience*. Maryknoll, N.Y.: Orbis, 1998.

Theissen, Gerd. *Sociology of Early Palestinian Christianity*. Philadelphia: Fortress Press, 1978.

Thomas, John Christopher. "Discipleship in Mark's Gospel." In *Faxes of Renewal*. Edited by Paul Elbert. Peabody, Mass.: Hendrikson, 1988.

Thomas, Kathy. "Creating a Womanist Theology: Why Feminist Theology Is Not Enough for the African American Woman." *A.M.E. Zion Quarterly Review* (1989): 26–34.

Tolbert, Mary Ann. *Sowing the Gospel: Mark's World in Literary-Historical Perspective*. Minneapolis: Fortress Press, 1989.

Tolmie, D. F. *Narratology and Biblical Narratives*. San Francisco: International Scholar, 1999.

Townes, Emilie M. *Embracing the Spirit: Womanist Perspectives on Hope, Salvation, and Transformation*. Maryknoll, N.Y.: Orbis, 1997.

———. *Womanist Justice, Womanist Hope*. Atlanta: Scholars, 1993.

———. "Living in the New Jerusalem: The Rhetoric and Movement of Liberation in the House of Evil." Chap. 5 in *A Troubling in My Soul: Womanist Perspectives on Evil and Suffering*. Edited by Emilie M. Townes. Maryknoll, N.Y.: Orbis, 1993.

Waetjen, Herman C. *A Reordering of Power: A Socio-political Reading of Mark's Gospel*. Minneapolis: Fortress Press, 1989.

Walker, Alice. *In Search of Our Mothers' Gardens*. San Diego: Harcourt Brace, 1983.

Weeden, Theodore. "The Heresy That Necessitated Mark's Gospel." In *Interpretation of Mark*. Edited by William Telford. Philadelphia: Fortress Press, 1985.

———. *Traditions in Conflict*. Philadelphia: Fortress Press, 1971.

Weems, Renita J. "Reading Her Way through the Struggle: African American Woman and the Bible." In *Stony the Road We Trod: African American Biblical Interpretation*. Edited by Cain Hope Felder. Minneapolis: Fortress Press, 1991.

Wilder, Amos N. *The Bible and the Literary Critic*. Minneapolis: Fortress Press, 1991.

Williams, Delores S. "The Color of Feminism or Speaking the Black Woman's Tongue." *JRT* 43 (1986): 42–58.

———. "A Crucifixion Double-Cross?" *The Other Side* (1993): 25–27.

———. *Sisters in the Wilderness: The Challenge of Womanist God-Talk*. Maryknoll, N.Y.: Orbis, 1993.

———. "Womanist Theology." In *Women's Visions: Theological Reflection, Celebration, Action*. Geneva: WCC, 1995.

Williams, Joel F. "Discipleship and Minor Characters in Mark's Gospel." *BSac* 153 (1996): 332–43.

Williamson, Lamar. *Mark*. Atlanta: John Knox, 1983.

Withers, Ernest. *Complete Photo Story of Till Murder Case*. Memphis: Wither's Photographers, 1955.

Woodson, Carter G. *The Mis-education of the Negro*. Trenton: Africa World, 1990.

index